# A Sinner and A Saint

## The Lonely Road Home

An Autobiography
Part 1

To cousin Lesley
Love, Don

Don Bast

ISBN:1505568439
ISBN-13:978-1505568431

# DEDICATION

This is dedicated, first and foremost, to my wife of 44 years, Marja-Liisa. I am so thankful we didn't give up along the way. It has taken us such a long time to learn to love and to enjoy life together to the full.
Secondly I dedicate this writing to my children, Ben, Caroleen, and Star; you have brought me joy unspeakable. Looking back I wish I would not have been so busy trying to make a better life for us all. Instead, I should have spent more time with you, enjoying the good life we already had together. "Too late smart and too soon old". I can now see, how I could have done better in the role of a husband and parent. I trust that within these pages you will gain a better understanding of what I have been doing all these years and why; I pray that by you knowing it will help.
Thirdly, this writing is dedicated to my grandchildren Mahlon Jr., Reann, Jorja, Cale and Kianna. I am so thankful for you and proud to be your Papa. Distance and time often keeps us apart, but you are continually in my thoughts and prayers. I have no idea how many more days are allotted me on this old earth but my goal is to enjoy the time we are together today and tomorrow more fully than I did yesterday. Watching you growing up is a thing of pure delight. The 5 of you make life worth living.
Lastly, this is also dedicated to each person mentioned in the book. You have had an impact on my life and I thank you for being there and for just being you. Hopefully there is something in my life story that will be meaningful and helpful to all.

# CONTENTS

# INTRODUCTION

## Looking Back

As long as I can remember numbers have fascinated me in a way that is not "normal" or at least extremely uncommon. More than one person has informed me that I have "an obsession". I can't help it; I need to know how things add up; how they relate to each other; what do you get if you multiply or divide them. I find significance in people's ages and birth dates. I notice house numbers; license plate numbers and I keep an eye on my car's odometer reading. Mathematics was the one subject I did well at in school. Along with being good with numbers comes the need for order. Being an organized, systems type person comes naturally, although, it has also been pointed out to me that I am a little too obsessed with order, to the point I have "a disorder".

Although, I admit I carry things to the extreme, I have found there are advantages to having a system. Besides, I find purpose and satisfaction in being methodical, efficient and thorough in the most monotonous tasks. As soon as my feet hit the floor in the morning, my routine begins; I do the same tasks, in the same order, as I did the day before. The problem is, if necessity distracts me, I easily get thrown off and end up forgetting to do something. Allow me to give a couple examples. A few minutes ago I took a break from writing, went down two flights of stairs to feed my wood stove, which is our main source of heat and it is December. This means a trip to the basement every couple hours. I have been heating with wood most of my adult life and because of years of experience and my obsessive nature I was able to quickly find 3 ideal pieces of wood to throw in.

I must mention I have 4 face cords of dry firewood neatly piled 6 feet away from the stove with a partition in the middle of the pile. I burn the wood on the left side first so any snow or surface moisture on the right side, dries thoroughly. When the left side is empty I restock it from the wood crib, nearby outside. In a short time I can throw in enough wood, through the window, beside the pile, to fill the empty side. This will dry for a week or two, while I use the wood on the other side, so on and so on.

During the day I use up medium size pieces, the least uniform in length and shape, the ugly pieces. Big uniform pieces are saved for stacking the stove before climbing into bed at night. In order for the fire to burn for 8+ hours and keep the house reasonably warm and also provide me with a layer of hot coals in the morning the wood must be placed tightly together and fill the stove. Most of the wood I burn I cut myself. I split a good supply of square “night blocks”. The vents are set to provide the right amount of air for the long cold night ahead. In the morning, a few small pieces are strategically placed and with a few ugly ones on top with plenty of space between. The goal is to get the stack temperature high enough to burn the creosote in the stovepipe and chimney created from the slow burn mode all night and then to maintain an efficient burn range to keep the system as clean as possible. The advantage of this seemingly obsessive behavior is first of all, safety. Besides it saves time and money. This is my 7$^{th}$ winter here and I have not needed to clean the stovepipe or chimney. For the most part, day in and day out, through the cold winter my wife and I enjoy a comfortable room temperature. She gives little thought to the fact; a thermostat does not control the room temperature. Nor does she worry about having an obsessive husband, not for this reason, at least. By the way, the heat that comes from wood is superior to all others. Also, coffee brewed on a wood stove or home cooked meals taste better and wood provides a good back up if the power is off for any length of time.

Bear with me as I provide one more example; this one is not quite as practical and maybe a little more extreme but again with good reasons in mind. Don't knock it until you have tried it. When I eat a meal I eat the particular foods on my plate in the same order over and over. This does cause a problem if I run out of one food before the others, which is easily rectified.

Let me explain my reasoning. If I have a traditional dinner of vegetables, potatoes and meat, for example, I start with a bite of veggies, then potatoes and meat last. If I am enjoying a glass of wine with the meal I then have a sip after the meat. I do this partially because I like to save the best for last and therefore start with the food I generally enjoy the least.

There is another reason. I start with the food that has the most moisture and work my way to the driest food and often the saltiest before I have a sip of wine. Have you noticed wine tastes better with nuts or chips, something crunchy, dry and salty? This is really not a bother at all. Since I have been feeding myself for well over 60 years, I seldom think about why I eat the food in this order.  I am naturally drawn to the right item, at the right time, for my full eating pleasure. I have also noticed I am enjoying food more all the time, the older I get, and more thankful for this simple but necessary part of life.

## The Number 7

With a sense of joy and honor I announce I was born on the 7th day, 7th month, 1950. In the Old Testament of the Bible every 50 years was a year of jubilee; 49 years of debt was cancelled and all started with a new slate. 50 is also special because it follows 49, (7 x 7). My wife Marja was born in 1949.

As you probably realize, number 7 is referred to as "lucky 7". This may be so, but more importantly, most Bible scholars recognize 7 as the great number of spiritual perfection. *The Words of Jehovah are pure words, like silver refined in an earthen furnace purified* ***seven times*** (Psalms 12:6). So for these reasons and more I find pleasure in the number 7; crazy aye?

It is not surprising therefore, that with little difficulty; I am able to divide the first 36 ½ years of my life into 5 segments each lasting a little more than 7 years. This is the time of my life documented in this writing. At this point in the writing I decided it was too much for one volume and decided this was a good place to end "Part 1". Over the years I have written copious notes and finally finished typing them this fall. When I downloaded them into the book template there was over 1200 pages. In "Part 2" I will continue with a 6th chapter, which covers approximately 6 years. 6 is the number of man. A 7th distinct period began on the day I finally realized the grace of God in truth, which lasted about 5 years; 5 is the number of grace. Finally I can identify two more segments both about 7 – 7 ½ years in duration, which brings me up to the winter of 2012 / 2013 when I formally started this writing. A crisis or crossroads and a dramatic change separate each period. I use these turning points in my life as chapter breaks in my story.

I grew up on the front pew of a Mennonite Mission Church in Northern Ontario, Canada. The 1st chapter, "The Early Years" begins with a little family history before my birth in 1950. It ends in 1957, when, at the age of 7, I had a dramatic conversion experience, which left a profound imprint that still remains to this day. The 2nd chapter, "Age of Innocence" covers the period of my life from 1957 - 1964. It closes, when at the age of 14, I was baptized and became a member of the church. I then entered my "Age of Accountability", the 3rd chapter, of my life, from 1965 – 1972. At the age of 21 the Lord stopped me in my tracks, on the road I had been traveling, the road to destruction. Little did I know, at the time, I was jumping from the frying pan into the fire. The 4th chapter from 1972 - 1979 is called "The Cult Years". At the age of 29 the Lord once again, came to my rescue, this time from religious bondage. During this period I ventured back into a church setting, a Pentecostal church. I immediately became very involved. This 5th chapter from late 1979 - 1986 is called, "Working for the Lord". At the age of 36 I came out of "Christendom" for the third time. I walked away from organized religion and turned a new page in my life-long pursuit to know God.

## Number 7 in the Bible

"In Hebrew, seven is (shevah). It is from the root (savah), to be full or satisfied, having enough of. Hence the meaning of the word "seven" is dominated by this root. On the seventh day God rested from the work of Creation; it was full and complete, and good and perfect. Nothing could be added to it or taken from it without marring it. Hence the word (Shavath), to cease, desist, rest and Shabbath, Sabbath or day of rest. This root runs through various languages; e.g., Sanscript, saptan; Zend. hapta; Greek, (hepta); Latin, septem. All these preserve the "t", which in the Semitic and Teutonic languages is dropped out; e.g. Gothic, sibun; German, sieben; English, seven. It is seven, therefore, that stamps with perfection and completeness that in connection with which it is used. In the creative works of God, seven completes the colours of the spectrum and rainbow, and satisfies in music the notes of the scale. In each of these the eighth is only a repetition of the first." (Number in Scriptures, E.W.Bullinger, pp. 167,168)

In the proper context, it is a true that numbers don't lie. However, it is not too difficult for someone adept with numbers to manipulate them in a way to impress those who may not be as gifted in this area. If you happen to be one of the few that considers math to be your forte, you may already be suspicious that I have been working the numbers in my favor, for the purpose of impressing or tricking readers. If this is your view, possibly this book is not for you. Having said that far be it from me to discourage anyone from reading my writings. I simply address the matter in case this is what you have been thinking.

I trust an explanation will be helpful. With my love for numbers comes an ability to recognize order and to arrange things in a fashion that is meaningful to me. It is not my goal to convince you that the "Supreme Deity" decided ahead of time that my life would be divided into specific and definable segments but rather that you would rejoice with me, in the possibility, there is a Creator of heaven and earth, Who is operating all according to His wisdom and purpose from the beginning of time to the end. If this is true, it follows that we all may find order and meaning in every chapter of our lives, if we look for it.

## We are His Workmanship

It has been said, "Hindsight is 20-20". As I look back on my life and reminisce I am amazed at God's handiwork. It brings me great joy to be able gather together the copious pieces of information that I have collected over the years. I have few ambitions left in life, however, as long I live, I want to share the marvelous works and words of God wherever, whenever, however and with whomever, I am able, especially with my family. I can clearly see the Creator's involvement in my personal life as well as in the universe, as a whole. Like the number 7, my life has been full; I am satisfied and frankly many days I feel like I have had enough already. But, before I exit, my desire is to share the things of consequence I have seen, heard and experienced, the good and the bad, over these brief but full years, with the hope that they will be a blessing to those I love.

A few days ago, I was sharing candidly with my good friend, Rick Ahola, who is less than a year older than me. He had recently been diagnosed with terminal cancer. We agreed that life has been good and although, we have no fear of dying, we have a common, strong desire to be with our children and to see our grandchildren grow up into the beautiful persons God has purposed for them to be. If this is not to be, I want to at least, leave my story, especially for them.

PS. Rick died on May 23, 2012. He was 63 years old.

## Numbers are Important to God

Before I go on, I should clarify; I am in no way suggesting that being born on July 7th, 1950 makes me more special than anyone else born on any other day. However, I do suspect there may be a strong connection with the fact my birthday is 7-7-50 and with my fascination with numbers. I am not sure if I continually see things that are connected because I love numbers or that I love numbers because I see the connections. I don't think it matters. Either way, bear with me a little longer. My wife Marja was born on October 10$^{th}$, 1949, (10-10-49). 10 x 10 = 100, which is half of 50, the year I was born. 7 x 7 is 49 the year Marja was born. To top it off we were married on the 10th day of the 7th month, which is the Day of Atonement on the Jewish calendar. Our wedding day was also 3 days after my 21$^{st}$

birthday; 3 x 7 is 21. I could go on and on but will spare those who are easily bored with such matters. I will mention one more interesting statistic. When I was 7 years old my father began building our 2nd home at 49 Moxam Drive. This is where I lived until I was married and was my parent's address for 53 years, from 1958 to 2011.

I feel better, about my obsession, knowing that numbers are important to God, also. Let us consider a few facts about the sheer vastness and greatness of the universe in which we have been placed. So amazing is it the Bible says, *"From the very creation of the world, God's invisible perfections - namely **His eternal power** and divine nature - have been rendered intelligible and **clearly visible by His works"*** (Romans 1:19,20).

The details regarding the arrangement of the universe are no doubt unfathomable but even a glimpse of its beauty, order and vastness, will reveal the wisdom and power of a Supreme Deity to any seeker of truth. First, consider a seemingly insignificant detail such as the fact that the *hairs of your head have all been numbered*. Why does our Creator even care how many hairs you and I have. Two short answers are; because *God is love* and He is interested in detail, in the small things.

In contrast consider the vastness of the universe. Our galaxy, the Milky Way, is apparently 100,000 light years in diameter and within its boundaries are some 400,000,000,000 stars. Current estimates claim there are about 120,000,000,000 galaxies. If the average number of stars in each galaxy is the same as the Milky Way the total is close to 48,000,000,000,000,000,000,000, if my math is right. Not that it really matters; I can't even tell you for sure what this number is. I think it may be forty-eight thousand, trillion. If anyone can confirm this I would be delighted to know.

## Numbers Don't Lie

I recently had a tour of the Toyota plant in Kitchener. Each day about 1000 new Corollas roll off the end of line; that translates into 1 every 55 seconds. It took this plant 25 years to get to this level of production and they still look for ways to get better. One might wonder what this has to do with my story. I am attempting to make a point that has profoundly affected my outlook on life. First of all, for Toyota to accomplish such a feat, precise records were kept in each and every department and station, daily and hourly for years. Every worker's production is tracked, logged and records are compared to previous days and months and other workers numbers. In order to improve Toyota depends totally on these facts. If numbers were subjective or ambiguous like words and ideas there would be no definite starting point and no way to set realistic and precise goals. The point I am making is "**numbers don't lie**". 2 + 2 = 4. The answer has always been 4 and it always will be; you can count on it. I realize the equation 2 + 2 = 5 is a lot closer than 2 + 2 = 9 but close doesn't count. To me numbers represent absolute truth.

*The works of God are great, sought out by all desiring them.* Deep down in each of us is an innate desire to know more about creation and our Creator. God Himself did careful calculations when creating this vast universe. When He formed the oceans and lakes He took time to measure the water in the hollow of His hand (Isaiah 40:12,13). We see by the word "measure" that He had a specific number of gallons or what ever measurement He used, in mind. Man can calculate roughly the amount of water in lakes or oceans; God knew exactly what He wanted. If He would not have cared about the amount of water He was creating or if it would not have mattered to the operation of His amazing universe and if it didn't affect mankind, His prize creation, then He would not have bothered to measure.

The prophet Isaiah continues to say that God also regulates the heavens with a span. A span (of a man's hand) is an old unit of measure equal to approximately 9 inches. Our galaxy, the Milky Way, is around 100,000 light years in diameter. He knows how many spans, meters or feet, if you prefer, wide it is because He created it with a specific size in mind. Likewise He *contains, in a peck measure, the soil of all the earth, and weighs, with a balance, the mountains, and the hills with scales?*

Consider, again our galaxy, the Milky Way, which is only the size of a spec of dust compared to the universe, which apparently is expanding. Likewise the earth is as a spec in our galaxy. So also if we continue the analogy we are only as a spec compared to our planet earth but God is so interested in us and concerned about us that He has numbered our hairs. You see the point I am making; God is the God of all; the big and the small. He is also the Father of us all; *the One healing the broken heart and binding up the grievous wounds and* the *One* ***counting the number of stars****, and is* ***calling them all by their names.*** *Great is our Lord and vast in vigor; As to His understanding, there is no enumeration of it* (Psalms 147: 3-5).

I realize this is more incredible than we can fathom. Can you imagine; He calls all the billions of mammoth heavenly bodies of light, by name. He also made us and knows us intimately. If God took such care in planning with such extreme detail, we can be assured He left nothing to chance and there is an explanation for all that happens in life. This knowledge creates in me a great desire to know Him. Regardless of our IQ or our education we can take comfort in knowing there is a Creator, Who has all under control. This is the absolute truth I love.

We seldom know what He is doing; the important thing is we know He is the One doing it. We can't fully grasp His wisdom, power or love. But it gives us joy and confidence meditating on these things. If He can operate a complex, measureless universe in perfect harmony, I'm sure He can take care of us.

I can now see His handiwork in my past experiences; in both the good and the evil; in the happy times and tragedies; at the time I often couldn't but now I can. I experienced a little success over the years and survived several terrible failures. My spirit has soared like an eagle and my soul has wallowed in the depths of despair. Many days I had no desire to face tomorrow. I made some wise decisions along the way and many mistakes; some so stupid I find them almost unbelievable but I am convinced God has been working all these together for my good since the day I was born. I am thrilled to afford you the opportunity to rejoice with me and to mourn with me. If anything of my story delights or encourages you, especially my children and grandchildren, this has been a worthwhile endeavor.

This morning, January 25, 2015, an author was interviewed on CBC radio. He said the prevailing theme in all his fiction novels is, "The use and abuse of power". When I heard this I instantly realized the people and the events, so vividly stamped on my memory are somehow connected to this issue. The abuse of power I witnessed affected me deeply. As wrong as it was, at times I have been guilty of the same. Thank God there is only One in the universe with ultimate power and that He is the very essence of love, itself. I am persuaded He will use His power to the end of time for the good of all created beings.

It has been my desire to live my life as an open book. It has also been my daily obsession, for some time, to present my story of "A Sinner and A Saint" in book form. I have attempted to be as honest as I feel is possible and wise. I trust it will be a blessing to you the reader.

John Steinman 1939 – My Dad's Grandfather

Mahlon 1942 – Grade 9 – front, center

Mahlon – late teens

Mom and Dad's wedding day

Mom and Dad's 1st house - Sept. 1948 – Dec. 1948

Their 2nd home, Old Soo Road –Dec. 1948 - 1958

The Bast Family 1954

Art, winter 1951

Dressed For Church – Sunday Morning

The Boys First Building Project

Don, Fay, Marilyn, Helen and Art

# CHAPTER 1

# The Early Years: 1950 - 1957

## Humble Beginnings

On July 7th 1950 I was born at home, in a quiet Northern Ontario community called Waters Township. Compared to today's standards we were poor but compared to the "Depression Years" of my parent's childhood, we were well off. It is all relative I suppose, although I never gave it a thought in the early years. In fact, I don't remember a lot from this time. However, the people, the places and the events I do recall, have had a profound influence in forming who I am today.

My dad once told me, "If you don't know where you came from how can you know where you are going?" Could he have meant, if you don't know the people you came from, as well as the places? I'm not sure but when the dates of events, such as birthdays, ages or deaths, of my loved ones, are in question, my interest in numbers is keenest. I am not only speaking about relatives; there are other families also that I made a point of getting to know all I could about them, how they are connected by blood, by location and the events that caused our paths to cross. The more I search and discover about my past, the more interested I become in learning more. I write down facts and memorize them so they will remain with me and not be lost. The next few pages are about where, when and how my life started, the way I see it, anyway.

My Parents, Mahlon Carl Bast and Norma Gascho, both come from Amish Mennonite decent. Also, both spent their childhood on family farms, in Perth County, west of Kitchener – Waterloo, Ontario. My Mom was born on August 22, 1928 near Poole. She shares the same birthday as my father-in-law, Elias Laamanen, who was born in 1919, in Finland. My dad was born 2 weeks after Mom on September 5, 1928 near the town of Wellesley.

Neither Mom or Dad had the luxury of a high school education. After grade 8 Mom worked on her parent's farm. Dad did go to grade 9 for a short time. When he arrived at school for grade 8 the teacher advised him there was nothing more she could teach him and sent him directly to Wellesley High School. He was not there long when he got caught smoking behind the school with a few older boys and they were all expelled. He was only 14 years old but was well aware of how to put in a good days work and quickly joined a silo building crew. Thus in 1942 his working careen began and didn't end until 2008, when he retired, shortly before his 80$^{th}$ birthday. Over these 65+ years his jobs and the companies he worked for varied greatly.

Mom and Dad were married on May 25th 1948 at Maple View Mennonite Church near Wellesley. They were 19 years old. Their handwritten wedding invitation announced there would be a reception at the home of the bride's parents. A few weeks later they packed their few belongings and jammed them into their old car. Possessing the same pioneer spirit, that caused their forefathers to migrate from Europe to the land of religious freedom, they headed north to start a new life together. This same trait was obviously passed on to all their 4 children and particularly evident in yours truly. To move 300 miles north, at 19 years old, away from the security of family, the tight Mennonite community and way of life, was huge. They were about to enter a strange new world, and there they would stay for the balance of their long lives.

At this time Hwy 69 was not completed all the way from Sudbury to Parry Sound. To get to Sudbury from the south one had to go via Hwy 11, through downtown North Bay to Hwy 17 west. Dad knew exactly where he was going because he had been there before. He was headed for the "Great White North". The previous year he had spent several months there working for a local sawmill and was somewhat assured a job when he arrived. Now married, and with his wife, he knew wherever he was going she was also going. Their destination was a small bush town 30 miles east of Sudbury called Markstay. Another trip, a story Dad loved telling, gives a picture of what was involved in merely getting there. It was winter and he was with a carload of adventurous, teenage, Mennonite, buddies. The roads and the cars, in 1947, were far inferior to what they are today. On that cold road trip, they not only drove through blizzards but also ran out of gas and had 12 flat tires. The heater in the old car didn't work, which was a mere inconvenience for boys who had grown up riding horse and buggy.

## Men of The Cloth

It was here; in the back woods of Northern Ontario they joined Art and Marie Gingrich who had started a mission church here in 1936. In 1941 Art built a rustic but solid log house on Nepawassi Lake Road south of Markstay; a place I remember fondly. The Ginrich's continued there as missionaries until 1960 and then moved into Sudbury so their 7 children could attend high school. In 1969 they moved back to Southern Ontario with their 3 youngest children, still living at home. Thomas Martin with his wife Elvina, both with "Old Order" Mennonite roots, had preceded my parents to Markstay in 1945 along with their two small children, Paul and Erma, to also help in the mission work of the north and lived in a little trailer down the road. The Bast's and the Martin's would soon join their efforts in a work that is ongoing today, with both families still at the forefront.

I did not view Art Gingrich as a "normal Mennonite preacher". This may be one reason why he and Dad were drawn to this unknown wilderness, far removed from the "Religious Setting" they had grown up in. I have a hunch, like their ancestors they were seeking religious freedom, also. It was no picnic though, times were hard, people were poor and winters were long and cold. Art makes reference to temperatures of -64 Fahrenheit in his book "Like a River Flowing". (Organized by Go Promotions, Printed by Kwik Copy, London, ON) There are no rivers flowing at -64F. The Gingrich's like the Bast's did not move north just to escape the old way. They had a vision of something new.

We will never know all the people they blessed or to what extent they impacted lives. George Elssaser, a local 14-year old, Art's first convert, joined the "evangelistic team" providing much of the musical leadership. Unlike most Anabaptists, He was a bubbly, charismatic guy. Until these two men came into my life I had only met stern, Mennonite clergy. At first I had my doubts about them; they seemed so out of place. I watched them closely; I couldn't help it; they had something I admired. George was the only "Christian" I knew, as a young child, that played a guitar. I loved music and his guitar captivated me. As far as I know he spent his entire adult life in "full-time ministry" singing, preaching and working where he felt God wanted him.

When I sang the old hymns I could feel the pleasure of the Lord from head to toe. The louder I sang the better I felt. I was sure I sang louder than anyone else in the church. Until I heard Paul Reimer, my sister's husband, sing I didn't think anyone could sing louder than me. I'm sure no one sings as loud as Paul; well maybe Steve Tyler.

Musical instruments were forbidden in the churches my parents grew up in and still are today in the more conservative groups. Others allow the song leader to a give the starting note with a small round pitch finder. In most of these groups the piano and organ are not missed. After the first note a many voice choir breaks out in beautiful 4-part harmony. The young men are taught early to learn to sing tenor or base depending on their voice range and most girls can sing both soprano and alto.

Five of Art and Marie's seven children were older than me and although I didn't get to know them real well, whenever we were together I kept my eyes open and they left a lasting impression. Their four boys were given good Bible names; Peter, Phillip, John and Michael. The three girls were Sarah (Sally), Mary and Margaret. They seemed happy but not religious. The teenage daughters actually sat on their older brothers knees as we visited in our living room. This was so out of character for Mennonite kids but something about it appealed to me, although I would not dare admit it to anyone or myself until later in life. When I was in my early teens our church youth group went to their house for a Halloween Party. This was also unheard of amongst any "Christian" circles anywhere else in the world, I was sure. It didn't make sense to me but I liked them a lot and didn't try to figure it all out.

A picture of their house was imprinted in my memory. Over 25 years later, when I had the opportunity to design and help build my own house, the design of Gingrich's log home was easily transferred from my memory banks to the drawing board, although, I can't be certain how accurate the memory really is. I remember lots of wood and an open concept. I was more captivated by the atmosphere, the warm, cozy feeling. I loved the smell and the flickering light from the open fireplace. I remember the log walls and wooden ceiling and benches of wood against an outside wall in the living room, where one could sit and look up at the 2nd floor balcony.

In March of 2004 when Art Gingrich died, at the age of 91, I faxed a note to my brother Gerry who had moved to Alberta, about Art's death. It was actually a copy of a short letter my parents had sent to the Gingrich family for the funeral and it was titled "Passing of your Father".

I never thought about it; I was just forwarding my parent's note to my brother about the death of a family friend. I can understand how Gerry was a little taken aback when he first looked at the fax titled, "The Passing of Your Father". He quickly wrote back, "Thanks for the note. However, please don't ever again send me a letter with the title "Passing of your father".

The note is special and worth sharing.

"To Art and Marie Gingrich family: It is with deep sadness we send these words to you today. Our memories go back 56 years when we first came to Markstay. We were young and needed a mature family to relate to. Your father's (and mother's) doors and arms were always open to everyone. We have many fond memories of their friendship and hospitality. Although, we can't be with you today our thoughts and prayers are. God has blessed us richly by having you as friends. We wish you all God's grace and peace today and always. Love Mahlon, Norma, Art, Don, Marilyn and Gerry.

After George married he moved to Waterloo County, where his wife Ruth Steinman, my dad's first cousin, grew up. I lost track of him until 1994. At my dad's school reunion near Wellesley I met his daughter Janine and her husband Bob Shultz. We have since become good friends. Bob was born in 1956 in the same hospital on the same day as my cousin Larry Metzger.

Men like Art and George were not only strong visionaries with leadership qualities but were unique, happy individuals, also. They were able to express their joy of life and their love for God by just being themselves. I didn't know how that was possible and shoved the reality of it somewhere in the back of mind only to retrieve it at a much later time. I didn't give it much thought until recently but the fact my parents, especially my dad, were attracted to these special people speaks volumes to me, now.

## Waters Mennonite Church

As fond as my parents were of the people in this little community, they didn't stay long. Dad and Thomas decided to move to Water's Township (Walden) 10 miles west of Sudbury, where Thomas had been holding regular house meetings. Here they felt they could be of better service and bought building lots beside one another on what is now called the Old Soo Road.

Dad started building a small story and a half house in September 1948. The main floor was 16' x 20' and the upstairs was about 12' x 12'. When I look at old pictures of our home, I see what would be considered a shack today, not unlike others on our street. It was my home and I never thought of it as anything else. We were too busy and too happy to worry about such things. In November Thomas started building his house with help from men from the south. They had to build on cribbing stilts because the frost was already in the ground.

The Martin and the Gingrich families were similar in some ways. Both families had 7 children, 4 boys and 3 girls, 5 older than me and 2 younger. Marie's first child was a boy; they named him Peter. Elvina's first was also a boy; they named him Paul. Both were born in 1941. Next to Jesus, Peter and Paul are the two most prominent figures in the New Testament of the Bible. After Peter, Phillip, Sarah (Sally), Jonathon (John), Mary, Marg and Michael, were born in that order. After Paul, came Erma, John, Ruth, Mary, David and Ray. Both had boys named John, one born in 1945 and the other in 1947 and each had girls named Mary both born in 1949.

Thomas Martin seemed more like the devout, stern men of the cloth, I was used to. Interestingly, Waters Mennonite church has plugged along now 60+ years since then; pastors and people have come and gone but the work goes on. There are several Basts and Martins still very involved. On the other hand, shortly after Art and Marie left Markstay, the work ceased. Today the only church in Markstay is Pentecostal other than the Catholic Church, which is a landmark in almost all Northern Ontario towns, especially the predominantly French.

My older brother, Arthur John, named after Art Gingrich and grandpa Gascho, was born February 21, 1949, nine months, less 4 days, after my parents were married. Mom and Dad both had brothers named John, also. He was the only one of us four born in a Hospital. Yours truly, Donald Ivan, was born 16½ months later. The spring of 1950 Mom's brother, Ivan Gascho and a friend of the family, Don Forbeck, came north looking for work and adventure. They stayed with my parents for what turned out to be an extended visit. My given names, Donald and Ivan were easy pickings for my parents. I became very fond of both these men at a very young age and even more so as I got older. They were both easy going, likeable men and I am happy to be associated with them in this way and proud to be their namesake, especially now that they are both gone. 60+ years later, it brings a smile to my face, realizing that I have been blessed with some of the same traits I recognized in them.

Marilyn, Grace was born 13 months after me on August 3rd 1951. Although, she has a beautiful name, neither her nor I know who she is named after. If you are old enough to be thinking about Marilyn Bell, you are close but wrong. Although, she has the same given names; Grace is her middle name also; she didn't become famous until 1954 when she became the first person to swim Lake Ontario. Not knowing your namesake seems a small price to pay to actually be named "Grace".

Gerald, Edwin came 15 months after Marilyn. His namesakes are a favorite cousin of Mom, Gerald, "Gerry" Gascho and one of Dad's first bosses, Edwin Shantz, the owner of a silo building company called Shantz Elevator's from Hespler. Gerry Gascho was one of many sons born to grandpa Gascho's brother "Christian". Not sure I would want to grow up in an Amish Mennonite community with a name like "Christian", although it was common. I actually knew a Mennonite boy our age whose name was "Emanuel". He had 18 siblings. As a teen he preferred his nickname "Puss". Can't say I blame him.

In 1953 Mom was pregnant again but miscarried. She was very ill after Gerry's birth and now that she had lost this baby, her doctor strongly advised her to be content with 4 children. This was a relatively small family in 1952, especially in our neighborhood. The Martins had 7 children next door to the east, Moxams on the other side of them had 14 and Youngs our westerly neighbors had 10. Can you imagine 35 kids being born within a few hundred feet of each other? Although, when you have families that large, some of the older ones move out to make room for younger ones. So all 35 were not all living there at the same time but still, what a change from today.

## My Dad

I remember so little about my Dad from the early years. I know he worked hard and long hours. He worked 3 different shifts for INCO at Creighton Mine for 10 of my pre-teen years. He also was involved helping Thomas Martin with church activities. He was a hands-on kind of a guy and took on many of the practical aspects of running a church. Thomas concentrated on spiritual things. He enjoyed fishing with Don Forbeck and the Moxam's when he could get away and did some hunting, also.

A few times I got to tag along on fishing trips and enjoyed hearing the stories retold periodically over the years and often I rehearse them in my own mind. I'm not sure how accurate they are. They change each time but I still enjoy hearing them and telling them. It has been said, no one actually remembers the way things really happened originally; we just remember the last memory about the event. Having said that, I recall on one fishing trip cuddling up beside my brothers, in our sleeping bags close to a fire on a large, flat rock. The rock was also smooth and sloped down to the lake. Unknown to us, during the night, we inched our way down the hill. Dad had to pull us back up the hill, sleeping bag and all to safety and warmth a few times.

Another favorite family story was the night my dad got lost in the bush while out fishing alone. The fish were biting and he was enjoying himself so much that he waited too long before he started the several mile trek back to his car. He got turned around and darkness settled in on him before he could find his way out. He spent a restless night feeding the mosquitoes his blood and trying to get comfortable. On his way back to his car in the morning he was surprised to meet a search and rescue party. He really was not that concerned about the whole ordeal. I can't imagine he didn't realize Mom would be out of her mind with worry. For the Moxam men, who had introduced him to this wilderness, this was a mere inconvenience and probably an exciting challenge. Well maybe a slight test of manhood but surely not anything to fear or despair over.

I can only remember going ice fishing on one occasion with my dad. It was in 1955. Art and I were invited to go along with him and two friends. Ron Witherell was one of the men and I don't remember the other. We all drove together in one car, a station wagon, I believe. Don't know whose; not ours.

We drove to the Lake Penage marina, followed the tracks across the parking lot, onto the ice. The ploughed road continued as if there was no division between land and water. There were other vehicles on the ice, coming and going and I noticed several little fishing huts scattered about with no apparent pattern but strategically placed over a favorite fishing spot, no doubt. I know of one lake just north of Sudbury that is so heavily populated with fish huts each winter they actually put up street signs and the huts have house numbers. All without exception have a hole or two in the floor so that fishing, through the ice, can be done in the comfort of your winter, getaway, fishing hut.

I noticed tracks going off one direction or the other periodically. We followed one set that was heading down the lake in the direction we wanted to go. I can't remember how many miles we had driven, when all of a sudden the ice under the car starting cracking and the breaking. The car stopped rather abruptly and we started sinking. The men quickly opened windows and started climbing out. My dad climbed onto the roof and we didn't need to be told what to do. He held out his hand and I grabbed on. He then pulled me up and threw me towards an outstretched hand of one of the other men kneeling a few feet away, apparently on solid enough ice. Art didn't wait for me, instead he headed for the front driver window and got his foot caught in the steering wheel for a few seconds; like we needed a little more excitement. I was thankful for the thick snow pants I was wearing, that in my mind, helped me float across the water to safety.

Not sure how long we waited until someone came along but I do remember getting a ride back to the marina in a large jeep type vehicle on tracks similar to the commercial trail grooming machines of today. We obviously didn't catch any fish that day but we had a good fish story though, one that would be told many times over. Art was in grade 1 and told the story for the public speaking contest and won first prize.

## Dad's Varied Working Career

Growing up on a farm my dad was a capable tractor and truck driver long before he was old enough to get a license and it was not difficult for him to get a job driving delivery or dump trucks. Voitta Rintala and Oiva Santala, two local Finns, had work for him driving dump trucks. In 1953, at the age of 24 he was finally heavy enough to get on with the International Nickel Company, the largest producer of nickel in the world. In order to work underground for INCO, a man had to weigh at least 140 pounds. Dad was close to the required weight and ate several pounds of bananas and drank a couple quarts of milk before waddling in for his medical and passed. Although the wages and benefits were better than anything he had previously enjoyed, he was only able to tolerate 10 years of mining. It was damp, hard on his back and he knew it was just plain, not good for ones health. He quit working for Inco in May of 1962. This was the year the Mennonite Church sanctuary was built, so he kept busy on the building project. Services were held in the church basement for several years prior. That fall, with the building still under construction, the contractor El Rio Construction went bankrupt. Dad, who was the chairman of the building committee, was hired by the bonding company as the new superintendent to finish the job. We moved upstairs in December of that year.

Quitting Inco at the age of 34, with 5 dependants to support didn't seem like a smart move on his part. However, he lived to the ripe old age of 86 so it appears he made a the right move after all. Most of my friend's fathers worked for INCO, either underground or at the Smelter. Almost without exception they died in their late 60's. Driving by Copper Cliff before the super-stack was erected in 1970, my throat would often burn and my eyes water because of the sulphur in the air. People who lived and worked there may have gotten used to the smell but didn't realize the damage it was doing. It was common for Inco to pay for new paint jobs for vehicles parked near the smelter. This was just a cost of doing business for mining companies.

The rocks for miles around were barren and black from the sulphur fallout. If trees and grass couldn't grow here what do you think it did to the lungs of the residents and the workers. Apparently the US astronauts, in preparation to walk on the moon in 1969, came to Coniston, east of Sudbury, to view the land because it was similar to that which they expected to find on the moon. Not a fact that Sudburians generally boast about.

After Dad left mining he never looked back. In the prime of his life, he eagerly tackled several more challenging careers and business ventures. He partnered with an egg farmer down south, Clayton Steinman, and they went into business selling eggs to the grocery stores across Northern Ontario. He quickly became known as "The Egg Man". Art more than the rest of us got to enjoy trips with him to Sault Ste. Marie on the "egg run" in the big "Semi". Eggs were stored in our basement in the "egg room", where else? They came in boxes of 15 dozen. When the truck arrived from the south my brothers and I had our work cut out for us unloading the truck and stacking boxes of eggs to the ceiling. Like many industries it became increasingly difficult competing with the big companies. Besides, a couple stores suffered financial problems and never paid their large accounts. When the time came for Dad to move on he did.

After the egg business he tried his hand at selling diesel truck engines for "Harper GM Diesel" and then heavy equipment for "Allatt Truck Parts". At one point he and Don Forbeck bought a small apartment building in downtown Sudbury, which brought more grief than profits. He also owned and operated a produce store, "Mel's Green Acers" for several years. He eventually went back driving truck driver like his brother Alvin before him and brother-in-laws Mervin and Johnny. He told me once that driving truck for a living was a cop out; not a job at all; all you do is sit and think all day, enjoying the changing scenery.

In the late 70's Dad began getting restless. He wanted to accomplish more in life than just earning a living. The plight of our Native Indians had concerned him for some time and when the opportunity to get involved arose Dad grabbed it. An Indian elder friend of his, Art Solomon, invited him to travel with him to Ontario Penitentiaries, "crowbar hotels", as they were called. For years Art had been teaching Native Studies courses to Indian inmates but his age and poor heath were starting to slow him down. He needed a helper, preferably an Indian but maybe a Mennonite with the right attitude, training and education would do, which meant a University degree. Dad hadn't been in school since 1942 but in the fall of 1976 at the age of 48 he enrolled in a graduate course at the Mennonite Bible College, part of the University of Manitoba in Winnipeg. At the end of his first school year he moved back home and decided to continue his education at Laurentian University in Sudbury.

Back home he was once again able to join Art on his visits to the prisons on weekends. The spring of 1982 he earned a Bachelor of Arts degree in "Law and Justice" and "Native Studies". His final was an oral exam in Ojibwa. With his degree he was quickly hired by Sudbury University. Unfortunately, not long after, the funding to the Native Studies Department of the University dried up and he no longer had a job. He then discovered that if he had a Master's Degree he might get a job as a professor, teaching correspondent University courses in Native Studies. So, he would have to go back to school again. He enrolled at the University of Waterloo as a full-time student. When his school week ended on Friday afternoons, he drove to Toronto, jumped into a Wilson's truck and spent the weekend hauling a 40' trailer to Thunder Bay and back, grabbing a few hours sleep here and there. On Monday morning he was back in class.

This was quite a feat for an ex- miner, especially at his age, and we could tell this lifestyle was taking its toll on him. His sleep patterns got so messed up that it affected him for years. Also, because of his concentration on his studies he was not really "with it" in other areas. This is the period when we jokingly, called him the absent-minded professor. Somehow he persevered and in June of 1990 at the age of 61 he received a Masters of Theological Degree from Conrad Grebel College a part of the University of Waterloo. His graduate thesis was "The environmental Crisis – A Spiritual Crises". Shortly after he began teaching Native Study correspondent courses through the Sudbury University, a part of Laurentian University. He actually enrolled in a French class because he had students who preferred corresponding in French. He continued teaching and working part-time for the family businesses until the University funding again dried up in the late 90's. He didn't stop working until early August 2008, a month shy of his 80$^{th}$ birthday.

Even at the age of 83 he still often talked about getting his drivers license back and applying for a job at the University because he knew they needed his help. I am sure they did but although he would never admit it, his work days were over and now was the time to relax and catch up on all that missed sleep, which he did.

Over his 66-year working career the only regular "R and R" he enjoyed was gardening and visiting. He never had a hobby or a sport as a diversion from work; as far as I know he never looked for one. He learned early to enjoy work and keeping busy came as natural as breathing. In the spring of 2011 he and Mom, after 53 years at 49 Moxam moved, to the Meadowbrook Retirement Complex. In July 2012 they moved again, this time to Lake Nepawassi into a lakeside apartment that I, for the most part, built for them in Paul and Marilyn's house. Their last move was to Extendicare York Retirement Home in September 2013. Mom died there, on March 17, 2014 and Dad on March 2, 2015. They now rest in peace, waiting the resurrection.

## Life Built on a Solid Foundation

My parents lived in the same neighborhood, one block from the Mennonite Church, for almost 63 years. One might think it is a contradiction to be planted in one place for so long while at the same time jumping from one career or one pursuit to another. There is nothing contrary about this in my mind; it makes perfect sense to me. Their family, their church and their community were their life not their jobs. This is where they decided to put their roots down. Here they lived by faith, discovered who they were and why they had been placed on earth. A job was only necessary to pay the bills while they contended the ideal contest of life set before them.

A solid foundation had been laid deep inside them before they moved north. Once that was established the need to look for security in a job, a retirement package or in a financial plan was never a serious consideration. I am not suggesting there is not a price to pay to enjoy this freedom in life; what I am saying is, no price is too high to find it. I**n God we live and move and are**; not in the clothes we wear, the house we own, the car we drive or the career we choose, but in Him.

My parents had no stocks, bonds, or retirement package other than the Government CP and OAS. They had no savings other than the equity from their house but they were rich in other ways. They have both lived well beyond the fourscore allotted to mankind by reason of their strength; long enough to see their 4 children, 12 grandchildren and 3 step-grandchildren grow into adulthood; not to mention the joy their 15 great grandchildren have afforded them. Besides their immediate family they have many good friends and relatives around the world thinking about them and praying for them. They are rich indeed.

## My Mom

I have fond memories of Mom. She was always there for us, most everyday of our childhood life. She was a stay home mom and she had one responsibility in life, one "raison d'etre" above all else, to be a mom and a homemaker. She made the most of our humble clapboard covered house. She dressed us the best she could, making much of our wardrobe herself and sewing patches on worn through knees. When I look at old pictures of these early days we are usually neat and clean, even in our well worn hand-me-down clothes. On Sunday's we were dressed to the nines, hair combed, wearing a big smile.

Mom taught Sunday school, led women's Bible studies and helped organize other activities. I have her attendance records back as early as 1954 for Summer Vacation Bible School. Vivian Moxam was her assistant; they had almost 40 students who seldom missed any of the 10 days it ran. Most of them were non-church kids from the surrounding community. Drivers made runs for several miles in all directions picking up kids in the hopes that a seed would be planted in the heart of a few. They taught the good news the best they could. The message was simple, "Jesus loves you and died for your sins". Waters was a "Mission Church" and even though the Mennonite style of evangelism is quite passive or a "soft sell", non-the less they viewed Waters Township as their mission field.

I enjoy reading the newsletters Mom sent out at the end of each year to family and friends. Most of them started with her thanking God for His care, guidance and blessings. Her interests and energies were family and church life centered and so were ours. For example, it was a big event, when Art was baptized in June 1963. Our Gascho grandparents came from Millbank and Simon Martin the pastor from Monetville came to officiate. Simon was a big man; quite stern and like most church leaders took his religion seriously. I was polite enough to him but kept my distance. I was convinced these fearless "men of God" had been given the keys of blessing and cursing, heaven and hell.

Mom was also our nurse. Suspiciously, Marilyn and I both contracted chronic eczema at 1-yr old, shortly after our first booster shots. My skin was almost always itchy. When exposed to dust or when I overheated from playing too hard it was burning itchy. My arms and behind my knees were the worst and were often scratched raw, bleeding and weeping. At one point my doctor recommended that I be put into the hospital for 3 weeks so he could tie my arms to the bedposts to give my skin a chance to heal. Mom would never agree to such torture, instead she made long, cotton sleeves with tie strings that could be tightened on top. These we wore to bed. This didn't really hinder scratching much but kept the zinc ointment and the weeping sores from soiling the sheets.

It is impossible to describe the torment of an extreme itch to someone who has not experienced it. I heard a saying, "there's a difference between scratching and tearing". I guess, this can be applied to many different things but directly relates to the way I dealt with my itch. Everyone gets an itchy spot here or there from time to time. They scratch the area for a moment and then forget about it or don't even consciously think about it while scratching. When I scratched I didn't get instant relief and then forget about it, it got worse. In fact, the itch always seemed to be there just under the surface. Any excitement, stress, dust, pollen or heat triggered my scratching and once I started it was difficult to stop. The pain of scratching my skin raw was the only way I knew to get relief.

The cold, dry winters made things worse. I often sought some relief by opening the car window and alternating arms out into the freezing cold to numb the itch or stuck my head out to cool my enflamed face. I lived with a phobia of overheating. I knew once I reached a certain point there was no turning back; I lost it. This memory is stamped in the archives of my mind, an ever-present lurking fear. Once the line is crossed I go out of my mind, into a frantic frenzy. It is like I am demon possessed for a few minutes. I cannot think, relax or exercise any amount of self-control. Applying a wet, cold cloth or ice soon enough may bring me under control. If not, I would literally scratch many parts of my body until the pain took over the itch. Relief is so temporary though. Once the healing starts, the itch increases and the process starts over again; around and around the never ending vicious circle continues.

After many years of experimenting with different salves and creams, paying attention to tell tale signs and avoiding certain situations and circumstances, I can usually keep myself under control. However, in the back of my mind, after all these years the phobia lingers. This "problem" affects almost every aspect of life. For example, although I love the outdoors and have literally spent 1000's of hours "in the bush", often alone, camping overnight in the wild or sleeping in a tent was never really a consideration for me. I know my children would have loved this time of family bonding. It still hurts today, when I think about what we missed because of my ailment.

When I get tired in the evening the irritation of the days sweat and grime demands my attention. I must have my shower and clean thoroughly; then apply cream from head to toe. When I was young we discovered cortisone to be the salve that helped the most. It was applied liberally to all infected areas as per the doctor's instruction. It would be too embarrassing to go through this ordeal at a friend's house; sleeping over seldom happened.

This condition has had other profound effects on my life. The few activities in life that had the power to captivate my interest in such a way that I could actually forget about being itchy, for an hour or two at a time, have become extremely important to me, to the point of being addicting.

I discovered early that I could get totally consumed in playing sports, especially hockey and baseball. I gravitated to these and would play from morning till night if I could. However, I was so competitive that I couldn't help pushing myself to the limit and then overheating was inevitable; It was always a bitter-sweet relationship participating in these activities I loved.

## Helen

Mom found each pregnancy increasingly difficult. After giving birth to her 4th child, Gerry, she was bed ridden. It was at this time Helen Lindhorst came to stay with us, to help for awhile, which turned into years. Mom was too weak to care for her 4 small children, all under 4 years old. Helen was almost 42 years old when she moved in and my parents had just turned 24. She was a hard working, independent, energetic, single woman who never married. Like many Mennonites she was also a seriously religious woman and set in her ways. She easily adapted to taking charge of the household, especially when Dad wasn't home, which was fine with Mom who needed and appreciated her help. When Dad was home Helen had a hard time adjusting and a hard time being quiet about it. She was eager to help in every aspect of our lives and took control whenever and wherever she could. Obviously my dad and her were not close but most of the time he tolerated her because she did so much. The fact that she was almost old enough to be his mother, domineering and vocal about her opinions drove my dad around the bend at times. I'm sure as a young father he felt threatened when she interfered, especially with child rearing decisions. Helen was also, a "bible thumper", hard on everyone, including herself. She not only got involved at home life but at church as well. She had long since understood, she came to minister, not to be ministered to. As far as church went, we never considered missing any function, unless deathly sick; if the doors were open we were all there. After all, this was the "normal Christian life", was it not?

I never recall Dad saying anything bad about Helen and for that I am thankful and give him credit. Therefore, some 40+ years later, when he brought up the topic, it came as a surprise to my siblings and me. The occasion was a family "group therapy" session with Janine Shultz, our second cousin and the daughter of George Elsasser. I think her official title is "Clinical Therapist". She is the owner and the Director of "By Peaceful Waters". She and several other counselors work, primarily with adults, who require mental, emotional health counseling. They deal with a variety of issues such as grief, in the loss of a loved one, stress, anxiety, depression and struggles in relations and more. In any case, Janine often knows how to "push the right buttons", to get people to talk openly; most people that is. However it was too much for Mom and shortly into the first and her last session she left the room in obvious discomfort like any normal Gascho would have done. Dad, a typical Bast, started to share openly about our upbringing; about Helen and the early years, as if it was still fresh in his mind. He sensed the need to explain why he was absent much of the time and uninvolved. He confided that he found it easier to be silent than to argue.

As Mom slowly got stronger and we got older, we saw Helen less frequently. She usually came to visit a couple times a year, especially at Christmas and always brought nicer gifts than my parents could afford. We got new pajamas every year and when I was 9 or 10 we hit the jackpot. The boys all got a full suit of hockey equipment. Apparently she was a penny pincher when it came to her own needs but with us she was generous. This was the 50's when an orange and nuts were what you would expect in your Christmas stocking, maybe a popcorn ball. Gifts were small and few, usually clothing.

Helen did not appear to me to be very happy. She found her fulfillment in life by working for God, which in itself is not a bad thing but she seemed driven, busy with a sense of urgency. I think this outlook on life had a definite influence on me. She worked for many years at a school for the blind in Cambridge. When she finally retired she took up the job of praying for people and writing letters. On more than one occasion I sent her a large quantity of old letterhead so she didn't have to use scraps or the back of mail she received. Her letters were always positive and to the point; serve God for He is the only One worthy and will repay you in a meaningful way. One day I asked her how many letters she wrote. She told me she has written 3 or 4 almost every day, for many years, although, many of them were short notes of encouragement, often to missionaries over seas or people in the hospital. Even if you don't count Sundays, this translates into at least 20 per week or over 1000 a year. I was truly impressed and sent more paper whenever I could.

In her old age, Helen had a stroke, and became very ill. I visited her one time only, in the hospital; I was with Gerry. We went away shocked and puzzled. She had lost her faculties to a large extent and had become extremely angry and bitter and cursed God openly and frequently. Apparently this is common but I will not attempt to explain this phenomenon. At her funeral I was not real surprised but still a little overwhelmed at the numerous personal testimonies, mostly letters, from all over the world.

## Little Brother Syndrome

Art being the oldest was naturally always Dad's favorite. He enjoyed special privileges like going on road trips in the big truck and when he got his license he got to drive them. He also became a truck driver for several years, just like Dad. Gerry being the youngest, the one that required the most attention from Mom and Helen became their favorite. I guess while I am wallowing, I should mention Marilyn, the only girl; was the one Mom and Dad both loved to dote over. They must have had enough love for all of us though, because the concept of favorites never crossed my mind, that I am aware of, until much later in life. Having said that, some would argue it must have affected me or I wouldn't mention it. Regardless, "When you are second best you try harder". Maybe subconsciously, deep down, I was aware of something. All my life I have been driven to excel above my peers at whatever I put my mind to doing. The up side is that this gave me the competitive edge.

At Art's 55th birthday party at Parker House in Sudbury we were encouraged to bring a song or poem etc. Being the big talker of the family I put together my 2 cents worth. In my address I began with the fact Art was dad's favorite. I felt the freedom to relate a few early stories and even to embellish a bit to get the point across effectively. Later the host Jim Cull, I believe Cathy Fielding's husband, congratulated me on my speech. He said it was good and very funny, which was my reason for giving it. Not a whole lot of thought was given to any underlying motivation. Anyway, I went on to make up a story about the day Gerry took his first few steps in 1953. Mom couldn't wait to tell Dad as soon as he walked through the door that evening; Dad's response, "Ah, Art's been walking for years". When the laughter stopped I went on, "That's nothing, when my Mom announced to Dad that I had taken my first steps, Dad's response was, "Donnie who?" Unfortunately Gerry was not present but when I relayed to him the contents of my speech he engaged in a deep, belly laugh. I guess this probably confirms we both suffer from the younger brother syndrome. Not a whole lot we can do about it; hopefully admitting it and joking about it helps a bit.

In Dad's latter years he was plagued with severe dementia. There was little he remembered of his past; the few things he did remember he rehearsed over and over hanging on to what he could. He has always been a storyteller and his story of choice, at one point, was a source of humor to the whole family, well most of us. I am not exaggerating, as I often do, when I say we heard certain stories numerous times, especially this one.

He usually started the story with "One day, when Art was 9 years old, I said to him, 'how would you like to build a house?' Art said, 'Sure!' so the 2 of us all alone started building a house." He then goes on about the specific details of laying the blocks, putting up the rafters and Art doing all the trim work at 9 years old, no doubt. We all laughed about it and assured him that they did a great job. We teased Art about it and he usually smiled, although he may have finally got tired of the ribbing. I can't be sure. I often am not sure how Art feels about things.

## A Mix of Gascho and Bast Genes

As hinted at above, Art is a man of few words. He comes by it honestly; this is predominantly a Gascho trait. Grandpa Gascho was like that and so were 3 of Mom's 4 brothers. Uncle Ivan seemed more open and verbal about his thoughts and feelings. I find it interesting that I am named after Ivan and I am more like him, while Art is named after Grandpa John and Uncle John and he is more like them.

This has always been, not only a matter of interest to me, but of concern, also. Marja's brother Risto was like that too. Is it any wonder that our only son Ben is also? I really have a hard time with it; I don't get it. Like many of my Bast relatives, I clearly appreciate the wisdom behind just blurting out whatever is on my mind, so there is no confusion. I want it to be obvious to those I am communicating with, exactly how I feel and what I am thinking. That way they can respond accordingly. This is the way to get to know people and to cultivate close relationships, is it not? I find it troubling being with people, especially, those I love, trying to read their body language to know what they are thinking or how they really feel. When I guess what they meant by their last vague statement I am often wrong. I hate not knowing if I did or said the right thing. Like, Hello! Just tell me so we can go on to more meaningful conversation. You know, like things that are important. Like, what are your dreams and aspirations, what do you expect from our relationship and what can we do when we are together that will be profitable for both of us, seeing we are here together using up precious time. I hate wasting time. It troubles me that everyone doesn't get it and just naturally pursues this line of thinking when together.

## Big Don and the Forbecks

We had many visitors come to our house, mostly from the south, where my parents grew up. Friends and relatives were curious to discover this new frontier, first hand. Apparently, they often spent the night and a few lived with us for short periods. I don't know where they slept, maybe in our bed. If so, I don't know where we slept. Uncles and aunts were the most frequent guests. My Gascho grandparents tried to make the trip north, once a year, to see their oldest daughter, which was a little difficult because neither of them had a driver's license.

Our small house was often crowded. I remember at times all 3 boys slept in the same bed, maybe only when we had visitors. The whole upstairs was two rooms with several beds. We had no indoor toilet. At night we had a potty with a lid so we didn't have to make the trek to the outhouse in the dark. One day Gerry's little bum got stuck momentarily as he got up from the pot and it tumbled over and down the steep steps to the main floor. It was a mess; not sure who cleaned it up, probably Helen.

One visitor, my namesake, Don Forbeck found something about Northern Ontario appealing the first time he came, in 1950. He came back a few years later and lived with us for some time. I don't think it was only a job he was looking for. He had his eye on one of the pretty Moxam girls, Aldene, 2 doors down. To eliminate the confusion of having 2 Dons in the house, the family attached the title of "Little Don" to me, and "Big Don" to him. I think Helen must have scolded Don for dunking his cookie in his coffee in front of us because he often said, "look at that bird". As he pointed, he quickly dunked his cookie.

In 1954, Don and Aldene were married and they never left Waters Twsp. Don worked for Inco at Creighton Mine, as a mechanic for 32 years retiring in 1985. Forbecks attended the Mennonite Church until Don died in January of 2004 at the age of 71 after a long battle with kidney disease. Don's finishing carpentry handiwork is visible throughout the church building. Don and Aldene had 4 children Brenda, Bruce, Kenny John and Perry. Tragically, Kenny John was hit by a car and killed in 1975, a week before Christmas, at the age of 17. Bruce died in 2006 at the age 50.

## The Martin Family

The Martin's lived next door. Compared to ours, their house was big, although by today's standards, 65 years later, it is quite small. It seemed to have small windows and a small front entrance, with narrow steps. I can't remember ever seeing their back door because Rover guarded it day and night. He was big and ferocious looking but was held back by a long chain. He marched back and forth; dragging the heavy chain wearing down the whole area an inch or two lower than the lawn and barked loud if any one dared come close; so I kept my distance. Ray, the youngest son, still lives there today.

Periodically the Martin children would join us outside to play, although most of my interaction with them was in church. I guess they had chores to do and they were also very studious. One favorite game we played was called, "Eavy, Ivy, Over", for which our small house was ideal. Two teams were picked and stationed one on each side of the house. One player shouted Eavy, Ivy, Over and threw a rubber ball over the house roof. If no one, on the other side, caught the ball before it hit the ground, a player on their team had to yell out and throw it back. If the ball was caught the whole team would split up and run both ways around the house. The ball was kept hidden so the opponents weren't sure who had it until the one with it threw it at someone. If a hit was made that player now joined the other team. This continued until all players were on the same team.

I vaguely remember a few services led by Thomas in their home. An old pump organ stood prominently as you walked into the living room, where meetings were held. I don't remember anyone playing it much. The Martins, unlike many Mennonites, did not excel in music, at least from my perspective. I stood close to Thomas in church, on occasion and watched and listened carefully when we sang hymns. I am quite sure he was just mouthing the words or as we used to joke; he was singing a "solo" - "so low" no one could hear him. I also remember Paul took violin lessons. I heard him practicing close to an open, upstairs window, in the summer, and what I remember was not that melodious. I don't know how long he stuck with it. As far as I know he never played in church. Several of the children sang in the choir and still do; according to Dad they contributed well as long as they had a strong voice to follow in their section. In any event, the Martins had a profound impact on my early years.

Thomas was the church founder and the spiritual leader. Once the congregation grew enough to warrant an official "Pastor" he filled other roles such as Sunday School Superintendent. He was a tall man and his wife Elvina was very short. From 1950-1955, Sunday school and church services were held in the basement of 1A, Waters Public School. I remember walking early Sunday mornings with John Martin to set up chairs. Actually I ran much of the way because John walked so fast. He must have been a hard worker because the first time I wrestled with him I discovered he was solid muscle. Years later I found out that Paul and John both had played football for Copper Cliff High. It is hard for me to understand why I didn't know this fact at the time. When I was young I accepted the fact that organized sports were too worldly for Christians. I can see how John would have been good at tackling and carrying the ball, being short and so strong. Like Thomas, the 5 oldest children, at least, had a no-nonsense approach to whatever they did. David was born in 1955, and Ray in 1957. Being that much younger I didn't get to know them very well.

Like Dad, Thomas had several different careers, none of which were his main pursuit in life but merely supported his family while he pursued the Lord's calling to be a missionary to the community. He sold insurance for Dominion Life on the side and also operated his own cleaning business for several years. In the summer he would buy blueberries up north and haul them to the Farmers Market in Waterloo. In my late teens I made a few trips with him in his big, old van loaded to the ceiling. I did most of the driving so he could sleep.

Blueberries were plentiful up north in the late 60's. Although, smaller, they are much tastier than domestic varieties. Some places they hung in clusters like grapes. Most of the pickers I met were French. They actually lived in the bush, in tents for much of the summer with their whole family. I asked one man how many baskets he and his family picked in a good day. He told me, that he, his wife and 5 children picked about 20 eleven-quart baskets on a good day. I know this is hard to believe but they didn't actually pick them one by one like most people do. They gently "slapped" the berries with a small, broad, aluminum paddle. No matter how careful one was at slapping berries, some got bruised and did not last as long as those handpicked, so time was of the essence. We arrived Friday afternoon, filled the truck and drove through the night; our goal was to get to the market a few hours before sunrise and be set up before the gates opened. At the end of the day Thomas bartered; hauling too many berries back to Sudbury was not an option. If they sat for a few more days they would be wet and soft, good only for making jam.

Driving old vehicles made the task risky. This was one aspect of what appeared to me, as an already hard life. Thomas never seemed to complain. I figured he was used to hardship and had accepted it a long time ago as part of his "lot in life" and "the Lord's will". On one trip home from the south the fly-wheel on Thomas' old truck broke and we spent most of the day at a garage near Severn River. To keep myself occupied I spent hours carving D.F.A.C. in the rock cut a few feet away from Hwy 400. The letters stood for a common saying, not appropriate for this writing, that my friends and I had adopted from Tiny, the man who owned and operated the pool hall where we played. Several years later the road was widened and the rock blasted.

After I married and moved away I only saw Thomas a few times at special church functions. Thomas died young, with his hands dirty and wearing his work boots, indicative of his life. His inherent sense of duty and service seemed to be passed on to his children, particularly the two eldest. Paul (1941) and Erma (1942) seemed to have a clear understanding of their reason to be here; it was to do the Lord's work, not to have fun. They labored with purpose; they were on a mission and excelled at what they did. Paul, the firstborn, set the bar high. He went to university to study medicine and became a doctor. He opened his own General Practitioner office in Copper Cliff, the small town, which was head office of INCO's operations. He later specialized in the mental and emotional aspect of health and began his own counseling service. His interest in helping folks deal with these types of problems took on a personal aspect when his wife Mary began to struggle with her own problems after her mother's death.

Erma followed close behind and spent 3 years at Kitchener–Waterloo School of Nursing and received an award for highest standing in the class of surgical nursing. After she was married her and her husband David Nicol, were missionaries in Lesotho, South Africa, from 1980 – 1986. David later served as pastor of Waters Mennonite church from 2003 - 2013. They built a new home on the site where I was born next to her parent's home.

John came next; born on October 28 1945, 3 years to the day after Erma. 7 years later my brother Gerry and Joy Moxam were also be born on October 28 in 1952. The success of his 2 older siblings must have put pressure on John to excel. He also walked with purpose, like he was in a hurry to get somewhere important. He seemed to be on the same path as his older siblings but started having problems while still in high school. In his own memoir of 2008 he described his experience as, "More than forty-four years of struggle with serious depression, mental pain and nervous tension. For at least thirty-two of these forty-four plus years, I was under the care of a professional psychiatrist whom I would see between eight to twelve times a year. . . . I also have symptoms or inclinations towards manic depression or a bipolar condition, obsessive-compulsive behavior and to a lesser extent, schizophrenia. I had chronic headaches between age fourteen and nineteen. . . . I had a complete schizophrenic, delusional or psychotic break with reality during the spring of 1978. . . . By 1984 however, the psychiatrist said that my psychiatric condition had sort of shifted to manic depression or a bipolar condition. . . . More recently however, in February 2006, this same psychiatrist simply stated that I "primarily" suffer from a "mood disorder." (Yea Though I Walk Through the Valley, John Martin, Pandora Press, Kitchener ON. pg.10)

In the introduction, John mentions that teenagers made fun of him because, as an adult, he was delivering newspapers and flyers. He also records a conversation he had at church, during a period when he had no work because of his severe depression and mental pain. A "brother" piously quoted 2Thessalonians 3:10, "If any one will not work, let him not eat." I don't want to read more into this than the obvious but from my experience this kind of thinking is common in many religious circles. Similarly, Elvina was warned, that if she left her Old Order Mennonite roots she would lose her faith and her children.

From my first-hand experience, I am convinced that this self-centered, performance-oriented emphasis puts undue pressure on sensitive children. Although, in many cases mental illness seems to be hereditary, to some extent religion is to blame for mental problems. John has written much himself but does not make this connection in his books I have read. In any event, the fittest survive and excel but the weak suffer and many lose their way in life. Two of John's younger siblings also struggled with related issues, maybe not to the degree he has. Not sure why but I have always been able to empathize with and relate to these "weaker brothers" in a way that I cannot with the strong, especially the religious leaders. It seems our Lord had a similar experience; I take comfort knowing I am in good company.

John continues on the next page to address this issue by asking the following questions, "Where was God in all of this? How could I still believe in a loving God, after experiencing all of these overwhelming negative events?" He answers his own questions with "In my darkest moments of pain, loneliness and doubt, God would always make Himself known to me. In surprising and at times miraculous ways, He would come to me with His unfailing mercy and love." To hear him say this is most enlightening and comforting. Unknown to onlookers, God was near and John was aware of His compassion and intervention in his near lifelong journey with psychiatric illness. The book was inspiring, to say the least, one I highly recommend to anyone interested in this controversial but intriguing topic.

I find it fascinating John could not hold down a job, although he was able to operate at a high level in school and submerse himself in study and writing. He completed numerous university courses, a Bachelor's degree and 2½ Master's degrees. This is one of the few books I read from cover to cover. Not only did it give me insight into this subject but gave me a respect and love for the man who grew up next door. His book was a motivation to me also, as I plugged away with writing my story.

I know little about Ruth, who was born in 1946. I lost track of her when she went to University in Kitchener. She acquired a Master's degree in social work and has labored in that field since. She now operates her own counseling service working primarily with children and family issues. Ruth never married.

Mary was born on February 8, 1949, 13 days before my brother Art. Mary delivered the Sudbury Star newspaper in our area until she started high school, at which time I was asked to take over her route and gladly accepted. She received a University education, married Howard Wideman and raised 4 children. They are very involved in the Waters Mennonite Church still today and Mary is presently teaching school in Sudbury.

Not unlike the two older Martin boys, the two younger, David and Ray are a display of success and failure, according to the "worlds standards" of the day, which "Christendom" has, for the most part, adopted. Paul became a career doctor, John a life-long mental health patient and never had a career. David is a "man of the cloth" like his father. He was pastor of Manheim Mennonite Church in Markham and later of Sterling Avenue Mennonite Church in Kitchener until he was promoted to "Conference Pastor". I rarely saw David over the years. I got to talk to him briefly in 2006, at my Uncle Ivan's funeral, which was held at Sterling Avenue. I was sitting with John and Mary Gingrich who I hadn't seen since the 60's when David appeared at our table. He sat down and talked for a couple minutes, long enough to tell me of his recent advancement. The Gingrich's and I were talking about the old days, a time probably too early for David to remember, and he soon quietly slipped away.

Ray, like his brother John, was also a sensitive child and excelled early in life and then lost his footing along the way. After high school Ray received a BA in Christian Education at the Mennonite Bible College in Winnipeg and a teacher's degree at the University of Manitoba. He went on to teach school in Thompson Manitoba and later took a year of French Immersion training in Quebec to better learn French. It was in Paris France, in his late 20's, where he had his first mental breakdown. He has never fully recovered and therefore has not been able to work at a steady job since. Apparently he is able to cope fine on his own as long as he takes his medication. He still lives in the original  Martin residence on the Old Soo Road. He loves music and spends much of his time playing guitar. In fact he is a gifted craftsman and makes his own guitars and other stringed instruments. I have seen him walking on the Old Soo Road a few times and waived to him. Not sure if he recognized me or not but he quickly turned away.

Before I leave this topic I must add that this chapter is primarily for the purpose of expressing my observations, especially when it comes to mental illness. I have no formal education or training in this area and will be the first to admit I am not qualified to formulate any conclusions. Having said that, I can't help having an opinion. For whatever reason, I have long pondered these things; they are a part of what I am and how I think. I therefore spend a lot of time writing about the people who have affected what I have come to understand. The more I learn though, the more I realize how little I know about this complicated subject and how much more there is to learn.

One thing I do know, is that a religious environment and an indoctrination that offers either the prize of heaven or the doom of an eternal hell puts tremendous stress on sensitive children. Very young I was aware God was watching me and I pondered much the great contrast between the bliss of heaven and the torment of hell.

Later in life I became obsessed with trying to please the One, Who held the keys to heaven and hell. During this period I often entertained thoughts and displayed actions that can only be classified as less than sane. Some friends and relatives would agree that for several years in my 20's I went through a period of temporary insanity. I must also mention; I believe the minds of "believers" and especially those called to preach the gospel, and their families, regardless of how one interprets that call, are in a spiritual warfare and their minds are subject to an attack, in a way "unbelievers" are not.

## The Young's

In 1954 Eddie and Gloria Young and family moved in next door on the west side of us. I have a vague memory of The Patry family that lived there before the Young's. Andy, their oldest child was slightly younger than me and years later we attended the same high school. I recognized him and said, "Hi", as we passed in the hall. At the time Young's moved there they had 4 small children but another 6 would follow. Doug was the oldest and the one I played with the most, although he was several years older than me. Shirley was one year older and Roy was a year or two younger; Faye was several years younger. After they moved next door Sandara was born, then Susan, Ron, Debbie, Sharon and last but not least Eddie Jr, whom I think still lives there with his family. The Youngs like the Martins caught my attention. All large families intrigued me but there was specific factors about these two that affected me deeply.

I think Mr. Young was a workaholic. Like most of the men in the community he worked for INCO. He also had a garage in his big back yard where he spent endless hours working on cars. In the winter he played with an old tractor he rigged up with a plow for moving snow. I can still picture the way he used to put his tongue between his lips to make a puttering, engine sound the same way a child does, as he drove around on his big toy.

Eddie Young seemed to leave the childrearing responsibility to his wife who appeared overwhelmed with the task almost every time I saw her. Gloria often yelled at the top her lungs, which was loud. Her favorite target was Shirley, then Roy and down the line to slightly lesser degrees as the children got younger. Doug seemed to be exempt from her wrath, maybe because he was the oldest, a boy and was often helping his dad in the garage, where I am sure he preferred to be.

A cloud seemed to hang over their house and the smell of urine hit my nose as I approached the front door. The same feeling of heaviness was always the first to greet me. There were times when one of the smaller kids wet themselves, out of fear, standing there enduring her wrath, anticipating a swat across the ear. I think several of them wet the bed most nights. In the morning they had to clean up their own mess, strip their own bed and wash the sheets.

The way they were treated would now be classified as child abuse. Today she would never get away with it except maybe in the most remote areas. In the 50's, times were hard and people were busy trying to survive; most people didn't get involved in other's problems. It didn't seem to bother Mrs. Young to humiliate her children, even in my presence. When it came to expressing her complete anger and disgust for her children, she often lost control. She may have noticed the horror in my eyes and restricted her abuse to verbal. I could guess what happened when no one was watching and there were telltale signs to back up my suspicions. The bruises, especially Shirley's, confirmed what happened behind closed doors. The children were so beat down and discouraged I don't know how they endured; maybe because they had each other to empathize with. As far as I know, none of them excelled at school but they functioned well enough to get by. I made a point of being kind to them.

On occasion they were let out of their prison to play. I was especially drawn to Shirley and befriended her. Although she was older than me she was tiny and frail. She responded warmly and I detected a little twinkle in her eye, a sign her spirit was not broken. She called me Don Diego, Zorro's real name. This was an endearing title. In Shirley's mid teens my Mom and Helen decided to do something drastic and started seeking a way to get her away from home while she still had her sanity.

When she was 16 they quietly and secretly put her on a bus and slipped her away to Nova Scotia near her parent's hometown. She lived the balance of her life there, close to relatives. She married a good, "down home man" who adored her. They raised a family together in peace and happiness. I know she never forgot her hard childhood and I don't see how she forgave, either. I saw her only once after 1965 and we talked about the old days. All she said about her mom was that it was absolutely wrong the way she treated her children.

Doug remained an Inco man his whole career and Roy joined the Armed Forces. Roy told me his goal was to retire after 25 years of service and then to operate a small garage, maybe with his younger brother. I am not sure what the others did. I only saw them once briefly at their parent's 40th anniversary. They appeared happy and well adjusted. We don't know what demons people fight on the inside. A few of them gave brief speeches and talked casually about their parents and their past. What else could they say?

## The Moxam's

It is hard to imagine, I found another family just as unique and fascinating as the Martins and Youngs but I did. Just one house east of the Martin residence, separated by a few trees and a tall fence that was easy for boys to climb, dwelled the Moxam clan. Laura and John Moxam had 14 children, 4 boys and 10 girls, between 1932 and 1954. All but the 3 youngest were older than me. These 3 families, 6 adults and 31 children provided me an early education that formal schooling never could.

John Moxam died in 1956 leaving the largest family in our community fatherless. Vivian, the oldest, was 24 at the time. She never married and stayed home to help raise the children.

Vivian lived with her mother until the day Laura died in 1992 at 80 years old. Beverley, nicknamed Bobby, was the second oldest and then Aldene and Jackie. The first boy, Kenny was about 20 at the time of his father's death and like his dad he worked at INCO. He naturally assumed the role of father in many respects. The other boys were Barry, John Calvin, Andrew who was still born and Ross, who was my age. The other girls were Margie, Vimy, Brenda, Jeri and Joy, born on the same day as my brother Gerry. The youngest, Bonnie, was only 2  when her father died.

Apparently in the 20's John senior's father homesteaded and farmed on the Old Soo Road. The Moxam farm was later divided amongst several of the boys. John was the eldest and lived in the original log home. Elmer built a house one block west, and Jardine lived on the other side of the same block in what appeared to be old farm house but a newer style than the original farm house. Ken built his family house further down on the other side of the creek. All of these, except the old log home are still standing and some still occupied by Moxams. Another Moxam clan lived family nearby. John's uncle also homesteaded in what is now the Hillcrest Subdivision. In total these two "Old-timers" had 13 sons. So the area has a lot of Moxams

Laura and I shared the same birthday, July 7; she was 39 years older than me. I always liked her and I sensed that feelings were mutual. When she died in 1992 she had 33 grandchildren and 23 great grandchildren. I spent a lot of time at their place but seldom in the house. I enjoyed exploring the big empty log buildings out back with Ross. From the old chicken coop second floor window I could see much of the neighborhood. Another building had a steep ladder going up to a loft full of boxes of old clothes with a  unique smell that still lingers in the back of my memory.

Somewhere I heard Barry and Calvin enjoyed picking on Paul and John Martin, who were close in age. Mennonite kids were taught fighting was a sin and turning the other cheek made God happy. I suspect this made them an easy target. I also heard they enjoyed raiding the Martin garden after dark. Not that it had anything special to eat they couldn't find in their own but it was more fun. Moxam's had the biggest garden I had ever seen, which made sense; they had the biggest family. Mr. Moxam had a big two-wheeled tractor, with long handles, that he walked behind the same way you would a team of horses. It resembled a big rotor-tiller with interchangeable implements.

The 3 oldest girls Vivian, Bobby and Aldene were in their teens when the mission work began in Waters and soon got involved with helping the Bast's and Martin's in their work. Aldene along with Vimmy and Bonnie are still involved in church activities at Waters Mennonite today.

The Moxam's took fishing and hunting seriously and were good woodsmen. John had many mouths to feed and taught his boys early in life not to depend on the grocery store for meat but to get all you can from the wild. For every evening meal 10 pounds of potatoes were peeled and cooked hopefully along with fish, venison or moose meat from last falls kill.

Moose hunting was the highlight of the year, for the men. The boys learned to properly handle guns and shoot by the time they started public school. Holidays were scheduled to coincide with moose season if possible. Several days of preparation were spent at the moose camp before the season opened. Trails needed to be brushed and the area scouted for signs. Only a few birds, partridge that is, may be shot at the right location so as not to spook any moose that were nearby. Everyone who could was in camp before dark the evening before the opening of the annual, moose hunting season.

I learned young to appreciate the silence of the bush. Especially with the ground covered with a blanket of snow, it is a constant, over-powering presence. Particularly when hunting senses are invigorated with new life. The silence seems to enhance ears, eyes and even the sense of smell and any sign of moose nearby sets one's heart pounding with excitement. Often, the first time a hunter encounters a moose, he becomes overwhelmed by the rush of adrenalin, fires too quickly and usually high. Few are able to calmly and sanely take their safety off, raise their gun, breathe deeply and relax enough to fire accurately.

It is important to make the first shot count because once the rifle sounds the moose is alerted, your ears are ringing and the echo pulsating through your whole head sends you into a different world. This rush apparently never escapes even the most experienced hunter. The secret is to harness it and allow it take you into a zone where you can think and act above and beyond what is "normal". I cannot imagine what it is like to be in a war facing the enemy and fighting for your life. It has to have a permanent effect on even the strongest or hardest individual. Shooting a large, wild animal is indescribable but to be shooting at another human being especially, when they are shooting back at you is inconceivable to me, not to mention the effect of witnessing a close comrade being killed must have.

Many "animal rights" activists feel that hunters have no respect for the life of their prey. This is obvious in some cases however in the 15 years I moose hunted I did not witness this at all. The men I was privileged to hunt with had a great respect for the animals they were hunting. The few times I was involved in "the kill" I sensed a deep awe for the life we were taking. The Indians in past generations who depended on wild meat for survival spoke about a bond between hunter and prey that is powerful.

I had a keen awareness of the value of the life I was preparing to take, while toting a gun through the woods. There was a mixture of sorrow and thanksgiving immediately after the kill that is difficult to explain. It can only be properly appreciated with the understanding that the animal is fulfilling its purpose by giving its life for food to you and your family. Whether one is hunting for food or simply for sport makes a huge difference.

The Indians who depended on the buffalo for their existence harvested them in a way that they would have had a supply of fresh meat indefinitely. However, when the white man came they literally slaughtered thousands of buffalo in a few short years for the hides and some just for sport. Obviously they had no concept of the value of the buffalo or a respect for their life.

## The Lady Luck Riders

One of the big log buildings behind the Moxam house served as the clubhouse for a motorcycle club called the Lady Luck Riders. Margie and her husband Leonard Ethier (Trapper) were members of the club. I found these "bikers" intriguing, to say the least. I remember "Big Paul" in particular, who although he rode a big Hog, it looked rather tiny under his huge frame. I think it was the noise of these Harleys that left the most vivid memory. The sound that a Harley Davidson makes is different from all other bikes and easily identified to the discerning ear. The roar of more than a dozen of these bikes and the freedom they represented as they pulled out of the yard was stamped on my young, impressionable mind.

Ross was my age, and we hung around together for a few years in the 60's. Barry and Johnny (Calvin) and their families became very close friends in the 70's. Although I never got to know Kenny or the girls real well, there was something about the whole family I liked a lot. They seemed to be so down to earth; content to live their own life and I usually knew where they were coming from; that was important to me.

Unlike other houses on our road, when the warm weather came, their front door was often open and inviting. Close inside was the piano, which several of them played to varying degrees; a few of them played well, especially Brenda. They all seemed to have an ear for music and I especially remember Brenda and Jeri playing and singing the pop music and love songs of the 50's, sometimes side by side playing together. Through the screen door the sound traveled easily to my attentive ears. I was drawn like a magnet to this music and still today it has an appeal far above contemporary music. Some of it was sad but much of it was very happy music and I loved it all. It did bother me though that I enjoyed listening to this worldly music. I was also confused; I thought only singing about Jesus was supposed to make me happy.

One Sunday evening the Markstay church joined us and Art Gingrich gave the evening message. We were still in the church basement so I know I was not a teen yet. He brought a little portable record player and put on a pop record and turned up the volume. I don't remember the point he was making but I do remember that after a few minutes he shut it off and asked us, "Did anyone find his or her toe tapping to the music?" I had to admit that my foot was tapping, all right. I couldn't deny it. I loved this music even if it was "worldly" and therefore a sin to listen to. I wasn't sure how serious an offence it was. I think the point Mr. Gingrich was making was that music is music and it is normal and "natural" to enjoy it. I was afraid he was going a little too far but I admired his courage and freedom. This would be one issue that I would continue to struggle with over for years to come.

The relationships with the Gingrich, Martin and Moxam families would play an important role in defining who the Basts were, as a family, and also me as an individual. The older I get the more I am realizing the value of good relationships and the profound effect that we have on each other.

There is one more family I must briefly mention. A German couple, Irma and Alex Petrovich who lived two doors down from the Young's. I was invited over once in awhile and enjoyed the cakes and cookies her mom was famous for. Irma worked at a Hotel restaurant in Sudbury, making their desserts and often brought one of her specialties to church functions. They had one daughter Sonya who seemed to take a liking to me although she was a couple years older. I think she was the first girl that I had any kind of romantic feelings for, other than Mom, of course. I remember rolling around tussling with Sonya on their plush, living room carpet. I was about 7 and she was about 9. I never thought about it much until many years later. Alex died young; I can't remember from what.

Sonya was an honor student in school and an accomplished pianist at an early age. However, while still in high school, she became very ill mentally. She was placed in an institution and is still there today and not in good shape. I talked to Irma about her in January of 2012 and she said Sonya still remembers the Bast kids and talks about them from time to time. Sometime after Alex died, Irma married George Freisen and they resided in Sudbury. They had two children Monica and George junior. Irma still attends the Waters Mennonite Church and is her same old bubbly self and has never lost her German accent. On October 5, 2013 we attended her 90$^{th}$ birthday party. For the party she made several amazing cakes and a few other deserts. She cut generous size pieces and served all 50+ attendees herself as much as they wanted and more in many cases; not mine.

## Pennsylvania German; Plautdietsch

Both my parents spoke "Low German" growing up but never made an effort to teach us. It appears this was one aspect of their old life they left behind and they only reverted to it when they were discussing a topic that we were not allowed to be privy to. However, whenever my dad met anyone who spoke German, high or low, he could not resist conversing with them in his native tongue.

We often visited the Mennonite churches down south and after the service Dad loved shaking hands with as many old-timers as possible. He greeted them in German and talked until another man, who recognized him, interrupted. He seemed to know them all and I was surprised at how many we were related to. Once Dad got going he seemed to glow and did not want to quit. He was always one of the last to leave and we had to almost drag him out of the building. Later in the car he would explain how we were connected to the folks we had just met.

This was the part of the church visit I enjoyed the most and I watched and listened patiently. The worst was going into a strange Sunday school class. I was shy and felt so out of place. I did not at all like being the center of attraction. I realize now they must have wondered what I was doing there. They were taught young how a "Christian" is supposed to dress and it was obvious to them that I was not one of them.

I didn't mind the worship service because of the bigger crowd and most eyes were to the front not on me, besides the singing was wonderful. It was a little weird; to see so many people in the same place dressed so similar. Especially the old folks, whom intrigued me. Maybe they were not as old as they looked. The older men all had full beards, never trimmed but no mustache and they all sat together on the right side of the church. It was like seeing 100 Santa Claus, looking old men all sitting together in rows of pews one behind another. Many fell asleep during the service, which may be one reason why they seemed old and they all dressed in dark suits and white shirts hence the saying, "Black and White must be Mennonite".

On the left side of the church was a similar picture; this is where the older women sat with their dark dresses and bonnets. In the middle section, which was almost half of the seating area is where the younger adults sat with their children. Here you may find women wearing lighter colored dresses but definitely no pants or slacks. The younger women also preferred to wear a thin, white, see through head covering. This was acceptable, as long as the head was covered, especially in church, although most wore them all the time. When our daughter Star was 3 or 4 years old she identified the word "Christian" in our conversation and blurted out, "They are "Christians?" I said, "Yes, what did you think a Christian was"? She replied very seriously, "You know, one of those ladies who wears a coffee machine on their head." She meant coffee filter and that's what they look like, only transparent. Growing up my mom and many of the other ladies wore these coverings in our church services. It slowly diminished over the years at Waters but is still practiced by Conservative Mennonites globally.

Outside in the parking lot almost all the vehicles were black. I found it even more intriguing to drive by a "horse and buggy", "Old Order" or "Amish" Mennonite church on Sunday morning. There was something fascinating about a long open garage filled with horses and buggies. Only on a few occasions did I get inside these churches to attend a funeral. It was like entering a time warp but it was kind of fun. At a young age I realized there were several different kinds of Mennonites; my parents accepted them all as kin and as "Christians' so I did also.

My cousin Paul Wagler (1958), who has studied our Anabaptist roots considerably more than I have, informs me there are over 3000 Mennonite sects worldwide. I am not surprised. I knew of groups that only sanctioned cars if they were black. Others painted the chrome bumpers black, also. Some groups allowed any dark colored vehicle and so it goes on and on. I met a Mennonite man, Mr. Miller, in Grand Rapids Michigan several years ago at a Conference. When he found out my background he approached me and we shared our pasts briefly. He said he knew of a church group that split over the issue of buttons and zippers. I still see men wearing pants with buttons and no zippers so maybe it still is an issue in some circles today.

## Our Building Projects

Andy Albiani was my best friend. We spent a lot of time playing together and riding bikes. I remember getting a good laugh at peddling our tricycles, side by side, as fast as we could go calling back and forth to each other, "hey Joe, hey Joe, hey Joe" on and on down the road. We both loved exploring the bush also and spent hours playing cowboys and Indians and building things.

In 1955 with the help of our older brothers, Charlie and Art, we built a cabin. Andy and I were 5 years old and our brothers 6. As the picture shows it was a two-story frame building nailed together with whatever boards we could find, cut to size with Mr. Albiani's handsaw. Something to stand on or a boost from a friend was required to get up to the top floor, which was a convenient problem because it kept the girls out. After college, Charlie became a Construction Supervisor in Winnipeg and was probably the foreman on this job, although Art was a capable carpenter for 6-years old. Andy and I were eager apprentices.

This is not necessarily an endorsement of our individual building skills but a sign of the times. Do you happen to know any 6 year olds today who could construct that type of building? I don't!

We built many cabins, tree houses and even one below ground. It was a dugout and resembled an army bunker or foxhole. Unfortunately, it never got used long. Even though it was covered over, except for a hole to crawl in, it filled with water the first good rainfall. We were good carpenters for our age but hadn't figured out how to solve drainage problems. I preferred building above ground anyway, the higher the better. I also loved climbing big trees, as high as my shaking knees would take me. The view from above offers a much different perspective.

As a child I cannot remember a time we didn't have at least one dog, often a female. This meant enjoying the birth of puppies and observing them as they fed, played and wrestled with each other. The day "Sparkey" was run over by a passing car was a sad one. We all cried as if a member of our family had died. Our dogs were never tied and some of them couldn't resist chasing the frequent passing cars. In the 50's, the Old Soo Road was Hwy 17, the main road going west to Sault Ste. Marie and although it was not near as busy or as fast moving as today's highway, there was a steady flow of traffic. In the winter the road made a great place to play road hockey. It was usually plowed clean with high snow banks, which served as sideboards. When a car came we moved to the side and hoped they wouldn't run over our snow goal posts.

## 1A Waters - School Days

In the fall of 1956 I was thrust into a whole new world when I started public school. It was about a mile walk but I had an older brother in grade 2 and many other kids to walk with, although I didn't mind walking alone. In fact I learned early to enjoy being alone. When alone I was able to think clear thoughts. When it was very quiet, my imagination was free to scale the heights and it knew no limitations. I could do what I wanted; be what I wanted to be. I found living in my head often more exciting than the scene around me. I also had a deep sense of something more real than what I could see. Some would say it was just an imaginary world; a few may suggest it was an awareness of the spiritual realm. I didn't think about it much; I just knew it was real, a good place and exciting to explore. I now see I had simple, childlike awareness of God. I knew He was everywhere, filled the universe and was always with me. When I was all alone I felt His closeness in a special way. We enjoyed being together, just God and me.

The morning after day light savings ended, Mom forgot to put the clocks back. I was out of the house first and a bit early. I found it strange there was not one other kid in sight. I enjoyed being first at whatever I did and was quite proud of myself. As the school came into view, my joy turned to concern; I saw no buses, no cars and no kids; something was wrong. I turned back; when I got home I told Mom, who realized what happened.

On another occasion, once again a little early, walking all alone, I met Laurie James, a young neighbor man; not sure where he was coming from at that time of day. Maybe he worked a night shift somewhere but I doubt it. I said, "Hi" and was surprised at his response. I thought it was quite clever and memorized it. He answered rather quickly; "Good Morning this morning, nice morning this morning, if tomorrow morning's like this morning it'll be a nice morning tomorrow morning". He said no more and just kept walking. I looked back but he didn't. I have repeated this story, on occasion; I get the odd chuckle but few seem as impressed as I was that beautiful morning.

Miss Chevrette, later Mrs. Maki, was my first grade teacher. She was pretty and a nice lady not like some teachers I would encounter. She recognized my math skills and periodically had me tutor Albert Jarvi alone in a back corner on the floor counting blocks during arithmetic class. I knew who Albert was. I had observed his father walking slowly past our place, swaggering slightly as he made his way back home. No doubt he had spent too many hours, again at "The Waters Hotel" and too many dollars that should have been used to meet his families needs. I took an interest in the Jarvis and would get to know most of the family. I felt sorry for Albert and at times shared my lunch with him. Most kids ignored him; some teased him and a few were just plain mean to him.

After school one winter's day I observed a classmate sitting on Albert's chest just outside the schoolyard fence. This bully was scooping up snow and "washing Albert's face", as we called it, while his much older brother held Albert's arms on the ground above his head. I was horrified and ashamed I couldn't say or do anything, not that it would have done any good. The older brother and his friend, encouraging him along were at least 5 years older than me and twice my size. The whole time they seemed indifferent to the fact Albert was gasping for air, choking on the snow that filled his mouth and nose. They finally had enough fun, let him up and walked away laughing. Albert scurried off shouting obscenities as he fled. Incidents like this are forever branded in my mind.

Why was I in a state of shock while others seemed to just walk away unaffected? Was I the only one who could read Albert's eyes and share his fear? Did these boys not know how wrong it was and that God was watching. Little did I realize, at the time, that I would later become friends with these brothers, one very soon and the other much later in life.

In my own simplistic way I hated this injustice. I wished I could help Albert and also teach these bullies a lesson. Giving them a taste of their own medicine was surely the right thing to do. As long as I can remember I have been attracted to strong boys and men who had a sense of justice and were able to put bullies in their place. In Sunday school I learned how God would deal with His enemies.

I struggled with the fact that life wasn't fair, not for Albert and others. Albert's pain and plight in life hurt my heart deeply. I think the one aspect of the whole ordeal that haunted and disturbed me the most that day, was that all three of the boys seemed totally oblivious to the pain, fear and utter humiliation they were inflicting on Albert in front of a crowd of kids. I could not comprehend this. I had so many questions! What were they thinking or feeling? What motivated them to treat Albert like this? This was my introduction to some complicated issues. I didn't realize people a lot older and smarter than me have grappled with questions like this for centuries.

A few years later the two older boys were expelled from school for killing the principal's pet raccoon. Jessie Hamilton had been a teacher at 1A Waters so long that she had taught many of my classmate's parents and she would soon enough be my grade 8 teacher. She had been feeding this raccoon for some time and many mornings, during opening ceremonies, she gave us a brief report on how he was doing. The whole school and community was aware of Mrs. Hamilton's pet raccoon and got the attention of these boys, also. They couldn't resist the opportunity when it arose to vent their anger and disdain for her authority. The raccoon became an easy target.

Recess was the best part of school. Baseball and soccer were often played in the schoolyard along with peewee; hopscotch was popular among the girls. Whatever sport I played, I played to win. I have always been more competitive than most of my peers, which gave me an edge, although I learned early that winning was not really that big of a deal and I was generally a very gracious winner; but I hated losing. If I lost I couldn't wait for a rematch. I believed I could figure out a way to beat almost anyone even if they were bigger and older. I often was involved in picking sides in team sports and didn't mind having the weaker team. To me, it was more exciting because of the greater challenge, plus it made losing a little easier to swallow. Besides, winning with a stacked team is not really winning.

Attending school provided a constant forum for me to exercise my competitive nature. I was aware of the students in my class, like my best friend Andy, who were smarter than me or better at sports. Outdoor activities were always a mixed blessing because of my eczema. I often pushed myself too hard and got so hot I would go nuts with itch. To go into a scratching frenzy at home was one thing; at school it was awkward and embarrassing. The heat not only irritated my skin but I seemed to be allergic to my own sweat, especially as I got older.

Andy was a Catholic but I never gave a thought to our religious differences until a lady from our church, Mary Jacobson, married a Catholic man. Many members of the church were shocked and even at my young age I was well aware of my parent's horror. It was obvious to me that this was a terrible sin against God. When it was explained to me that Catholics pray to Mary and not to Jesus because she is the Mother of God, I began to understand the depth of their folly. Some of the older more scholarly men referred to Catholicism as a cult. I wasn't sure what that was but I knew it was serious and probably meant those in it were damned forever. Even with this new enlightenment, Andy and I didn't talk about religion. We spent our time riding our bikes and playing games.

## Grandpa Gascho's Farm

Although, I didn't dislike school per se, when summer holidays began I was elated. The freedom I sensed stepping outside after breakfast the first morning is something I will never forget. The sun was warm and the breeze was cool and I had two whole months of freedom. I could play all day, explore the bush or build cabins. Most kids loved it outside; there was so much to do. We seldom stopped from morning till dark and went indoors only long enough to eat quickly and then back out again.

One highlight of summer was going to visit my grandparents. Before we arrived we made a quick stop at a gas station so Mom could change from her slacks to a skirt. My grandparents considered it a sin for a woman to wear men's clothing. I found out later that this was not the only "dress code" issue. Mom once shared with me that in order for her and Dad to receive the "Church's Blessing" on their move north to work in a missionary effort they had to openly confess their sins in front of the church that had offered them membership. One sin Mom had committed and was therefore told to confess was the sin of wearing a coat to church instead of the accepted garb, a shoal. The "Amish" clothing she was forced to wear as a young person was a source of anger and embarrassment she never forgot. Some old pictures she destroyed, others she kept stored in boxes and wasn't thrilled when we pulled them out. Unaware of this, we had their wedding picture enlarged and framed professionally, for their 50th anniversary. It was well done; Mom looked at it briefly and as far as I know didn't comment.

When "down south" we made the rounds visiting uncles and aunts until it was time for Dad to get back home for work. It was then Art and I often got to stay behind with my grandparents, on their farm. I have many fond memories of those days. The first morning I awoke, I remember looking around at the strange wallpaper trying to figure out where I was. As soon as it registered I jumped out of bed and ran to the open window to see if I could spot Grandpa who hopefully had not fetched the cows from the field yet, or at least had not finished milking and "the chores". I put on my clothes and quickly ran down the stairs. I was always greeted with a hearty, " Good morning Donnie" from Grandma and a hug and the same question, "Did you sleep well?" Almost 60 years later, the same question seems to naturally flow from my lips, in the morning as I greet a visitor who slept over.

If I was up early enough to accompany Grandpa to the field I ran beside him, calling out as he did, "here boss, here boss". I figured this must have something to do with "cow" in German. Much later in life, I checked it out in the dictionary. To my surprise, "cow" in classical Greek is *"bous"* and in classical Latin it is *"bos"*. Maybe "Low German" borrowed words from other languages. In any event, even before we reached them, the cows immediately started, slowly, but methodically walking in single file, mooing as they went along the well-beaten path, about a foot wide.

At the barn the cows knew exactly where to go; each had their own stall. I loved the smell and warmth of the big barn. It was like entering another world. Each cow received a scoop of "chop" (ground oats) or some hay while being milked. I couldn't help stare at the cow's huge mouths and dirty teeth. Their top jaw seemed to slide across their bottom jaw and then roll up and circle around and around from side to side. I was given the job of feeding them and was careful not to make dust, which would set off an allergic reaction and force me outside sneezing, eyes watering and skin crazy itchy. At harvest time I loved riding on the wagon behind the tractor but I stayed clear of the dusty barn while they were threshing.

Other times, I loved exploring every corner of this huge building. I was particularly drawn to the view from above. Usually a few layers of last years hay bales remained, which made me feel slightly safer. As scary as it was, I couldn't resist the bird's eye view and the thrill of walking the beams. Perched on one of the big square wood beams, hugging a post, I could sit for a long time. The silo was also empty in the summer except for the pigeons that came to glean the scraps left behind. When we entered they flew up to the rafters above to safety, so they thought. I considered myself a good shot with stones and practiced a lot. I actually killed a few and brought them to Grandma who cooked them up for dinner. Grain-fed pigeons taste a lot like chicken. One day a stone came back down and hit my younger cousin Ronnie (1955) right between the eyes. I was somewhat relieved that it didn't hit him in the eye. A big lump quickly formed and I was in trouble, again; that was the end of pigeon hunting season. We also did some fishing in the creek that ran through the property. One year the water was so low we could run down the riverbank in our rubber boots and kick the helpless carp out of the water to the other bank. Apparently we ate some of them; well not me, I don't like fish.

It seems many of these activities only took place when I was around. I am not sure if I was more curious and energetic than the others or if I was just bad. My cousins did seem to have a greater respect for authority than I did. In any event, I was often viewed as the ringleader, although my younger cousins seemed eager enough to join me in my shenanigans. One afternoon I entertained them by pushing the start button on the big old stake truck in the driving shed. The engine would turn over with a roar and the truck jumped an inch or so to the laughter of my young audience, especially those brave enough to actually be in the truck with me or in the box behind. I got a little carried away and held the button one second too long. The truck, which happened to be in reverse started and backed right out of the driving shed. Unfortunately, the big sliding door behind us was not open; the truck box rails lifted the door higher and higher and up over the truck. Art and a couple cousins in the back ducked down and narrowly missed being hurt. The door slid along the top of the side racks, over the cab, flew back into place with a bang, still on its track. The door was fine but the truck loaded with kids was backing down the lane, with the girls screaming to the high heavens. Luckily, for us the truck was moving slowly and uncle Johnny happened to be close by. He heard the commotion and quickly ran to the rescue. He jumped in and applied the brakes before we hit anything. Also, lucky for me my dad was 300 miles away and no one else assumed his responsibility of applying the belt, which I surely would have received if he had been there. Besides, I was visibly shaken by the whole ordeal; Grandpa realized a sound scolding would be enough to deter me from ever doing that again.

Grandpa was a small man, almost exactly the same size as I have been all my adult life. We both peaked at about 5'8" and weighed about 140 pounds. I have now shrunk to barely 5'7". He was a quiet and serious man not unlike many of the Gascho men. In 1962, at the age of 64 he sold his farm and moved to the small town of Millbank and got a part-time job just down the street in a second hand shop. There he enjoyed fixing anything made out of wood. He once confided in me that carpentry work was his passion and only out of necessity was it that he took up farming. His handiwork was prominent in the big farmhouse. Although the main part of the house was built in the 20's he had the joy of building several additions. I drove in the lane a few years ago. The house and barn were still standing tall, now occupied by a "horse and buggy" family. I have a large picture of the farm that Uncle Johnny Metzger painted from an aerial view, photograph that brings back a flood of fond memories each time I look at it.

Mom's oldest brother, Uncle Allen (1925-2005) spent a year in "Alternative Service" as a C. O. (Consentious Objector) during World War II, working in a canning factory at Ridgetown with a group of other Mennonites. They were exempted from going to war because of their "Pacifist" religious beliefs. After the war he married Anna Mae (Erb) and for awhile they lived in the attached granny flat of my grandparent's house. Later they bought a farm just a mile away on Walker's side road. It was more of a hobby farm with a few chicken and pigs and one cow. Uncle Allen had a full-time job as a foundry worker.

Art was the oldest of all the grand children on Mom's side; I was second, which gave us a captive audience of younger cousins. Allen's 3 oldest children were close in age so we spent quite a bit of time with them. I enjoyed their company and never tired making them laugh. A Volkswagen Beetle was one of their first vehicles; riding in the hatch, looking out the back window, one rainy afternoon I named the bug "Puddle Jumper" to the delight of Rosemary and Elanore beside me. In 2014 "Gascho Gleanings, The Genealogy of David R. & Barbara Gascho" was published. The following numbers are taken from that book. Rosemary, (1951) married Harold Gerber. They have 9 children, 26 grandchildren. Elanore, (1952) married Amos Martin. They have 5 children, 22 grandchildren. Ruth, (1953) married Harold's brother Nelson Gerber. They had 7 children 11 grandchildren. Ron (1955) married Betty Yoder. They have 7 children and 6 grandchildren. Ken, (1958) married Wendy Vandermeer. They had 2 children. Miriam (1960) married Delmar Gerber and had 3 children, 5 grandchildren. Barbara (1962), married David Zehr and they had 6 children. Sandra (1964), married Brad Bender and they had 7 children. Allen and Anna Mae's 8 children gave them 46 grandchildren, 16 of which have given them 70 great-grandchildren by 2014. The potential is there to increase this number substantially. What a blessed family.

Uncle Allen, like his father was a quiet spoken man, serious about his faith and life in general. He always seemed sincerely happy to see me and greeted me with a firm handshake and big smile. He died in a tragic farm accident in 2005 at the age of 80, which I talk about later. He leaves behind a great legacy.

Art and I also visited our other relatives, mostly on Mom's side of the family. Her next oldest brother Mervin (1930) and wife Mary (Zehr) lived in Baden. Marilyn was the flower girl at their wedding in 1955. They had 3 children; Helen, (1956) married Bruce Schmidt. They had 4 children, 5 grandchildren. Brad, (1960) married Cathy Rivers. They had 3 children and 1 grandchild. Barry, (1964) married Sharon Gingerich they had 1 son. Because of the age difference I didn't get to know these cousins well, until years later, although being that much older I am sure they were watching us and heard the news, from the far north, good and bad, especially, in the 70's. Mary was my favorite Aunt, although I know I am not supposed to say that. As you have figured out by now, I do not go out of my way to be politically correct nor do I pretend to be orthodox.

One day while visiting Mervin and Mary's home in Baden I had an upset stomach that wouldn't settle. Aunt Mary suggested she fix me a drink to make me throw up, which would make me feel better. I wasn't so sure about that idea but coming from her I figured I would try. So standing over the toilet I drank it down as fast as I could. Sure enough it worked immediately, I honked my biscuits and had almost instant relief. I found this lesson very helpful, although as an adult, I don't bother with the drink; I stick my finger down my throat to induce vomiting rather than put up with whatever it is down there causing the cramps.

On another occasion, while visiting them I contracted a severe case of the hiccups or "hub cabs" as Uncle Ivan called them. It was getting quite annoying and nothing I tried worked. Aunt

Unknown to me, Mary contrived a plan and called me into the living room. As I stood there she pulled the couch away from the wall and said, "I know you have the hiccups; did they cause you to vomit?" We both stood there for a moment staring at a small puddle of vomit on the floor. I moved closer in horror to confirm what I was sure I was looking at and thought to myself, "Does she think I would pull out her couch, puke behind it and then push it back into place?" I was shocked and embarrassed. Before I could find any words, she bent down and picked a rubber, fake piece of vomit, handed it to me and asked with a big smile, "Are your hiccups gone?" I paused and thought, sure enough they were. We both laughed as I figured out what was going on. She gave me a big hug and that was that.

I remember one more significant event that took place at their home. It was in 1962. Helen was about 6 and Brad 2. We were in the back yard kicking a ball around when I accidentally stepped on it and awkwardly tripped, twisting my lower back as I fell. It hurt bad and I needed help to get into the house. When I tried to get out of bed the next morning I couldn't walk. Mary quickly made an appointment with her chiropractor. I think I went back again the next day and finally walked with much pain, which lasted a few days. I have had chronic lower back pain off and on all my adult life. On a few occasions I have found myself on my back, on the ground, helpless and alone. It took me the longest time to coax my body to relax and cooperate. First, to roll over, then get to my knees and finally to crawl to something to hang onto to get to my feet. Finally in my 40's I learned to detect telltale signs ahead of time and avoid any sudden moves or lifting for awhile. Also, the last 10 years I have been doing a 40-minute stretch routine each morning and before bed I spend 15 – 30 minutes on my electric massage chair. I still experience regular pain, especially when I work hard but since this routine began I have had no serious trouble.

Uncle Ivan (1932) my namesake and favorite Uncle, was the next oldest of Mom's siblings. He married Doris (nee Gingrich, Art's niece) in 1955. I think they eloped, cool! We stopped in for short visits regularly over the years. He was an electrician by trade but enjoyed being an entrepreneur more than pulling wire. In the late 50's they bought and operated a "SuperTest" Filling Station on Highland Road east of Petersburg. A little, front room of their house served as a small convenience store with the gas pumps out front. Aunt Doris showed a keen interest in us and maybe in all children. I always enjoyed visiting them. Their oldest child Fay was born in 1956. The next year I had somewhat of an extended visit at their place. Fay and Helen were both enjoying their first steps that summer. I have fond memories of walking behind Fay, her little arms stretched above her head holding tight to my hands as she walked from room to room. I repeated over and over "walky, walky" and she smiled and kept on motoring until one of us tired. In 1986 Fay married Andre Bernier and had 3 children. Jennie was born in 1958; married Scott Nicoll who had 4 children from his first marriage and Christine (1961) married Steve Bradley. Not sure why but Fay has always held special place in my heart. She has always been my favorite cousin but there are several close seconds.

My mom's only sister Edith (1934) married Earl Wagler in 1957 and as long as I remember they owned a dairy farm outside of Millbank. I am sure this was a factor in my grandparent's decision to move to Millbank when they sold the farm in 1962. Grandma needed to be close to the only other daughter she had, besides Mom, who was 300 miles away. Their 4 children were quite a bit younger so the only time I played with them was when they were babies. Their oldest, Paul was born in 1958 and married Darlene Troyer; our common interest in our Mennonite roots brought us together later in life. They had 3 children. Joyce was born in 1960 and married Lloyd Beachy. Darrel born in 1964 married Cathy Kuepfer. They had 5 children.

Arlene was born in 1967. At our wedding in 1971 Arlene at 4 years old was one of our flower girls, although she was not too pleased with her duties and cried all the way down the aisle. In 1994 when Arlene married Burt Kornelsen I shared this event at their reception and got a few smiles. They had 3 children.

Uncle Johnny, the youngest of Mom's siblings was born in 1939, Art the oldest grandchild was born in 1949. There is less than 10 years between the two generations. The next one is even closer; our son Ben (1972) is 5 years younger than Arlene, (1967) the youngest cousin. After this the generations start crossing each other. Ben's son, my grandson, Mahlon Jr. is older than all 3 of Burt and Arlene's children.

In the early years Uncle Johnny not being married was still living at home. It was not uncommon, at this time, for young men to be given the choice to work on the family farm or go find a job. However, if one chose the latter, which Johnny did, his wages were still handed over to Dad until he was 21 or married and on his own. Many kids today aren't even required to pay room and board; to hand over their whole pay-cheque is unthinkable.

In the late 50's, Johnny began dating Dianne Yost. A few of us older cousins naturally took an interest in their relationship. I thought it would be a good idea to start a club to spy on them and to document what we observed about this thing called "romance". At first they were humored by us sneaking and snooping around but I think they eventually got a little annoyed. They soon married (1961) and lived in Milverton. Over the next several summers Art and I often spent time with Johnny. He took us to ball games; several of his friends and co-workers played for the local team. The only name I remember was Buddy Marth. Once we went to see "Donkey Baseball". It is like regular baseball except the players are on donkeys. It makes for a slower game but a lot more entertaining. Johnny and Dianne moved out west when their 3 children were still quite young. Angie, (1963) married Robert Moore. And had 2 children. I have only seen her a couple times since they moved. Darren, (1965) married Joan Grohs. Kevin (1966) married Glenda Sayln and had 2 children. I can't remember seeing the boys after they moved.

When at the farm I kept my ear tuned for the sound of the tractor starting so I could ride along if possible or on the wagon behind if one was attached. One afternoon myself and several other cousins and siblings were allowed to sit across the front of the wagon, feet dangling, being pulled by Uncle Johnny on the tractor. I assumed Grandpa could drive the tractor although I never saw him do it. I'm sure he never drove a car; he was a horse and buggy man in more ways than one.

Anyway, on this trip Grandpa was standing behind Johnny on the tractor, as we drove down the lane heading for a distant field. Being concerned with our safety, on the wagon, he turned to face us just as Johnny made the sharp turn onto the road. Grandpa lost his balance and was thrown sideways; his leg jammed between the big tractor wheel and the fender. He was instantly hurled by the turning wheel around and over and then down on the ground. The tractor wheel ran over his leg before Johnny could get stopped. We watched half in shock and half in disbelief. I realized it was partially our fault. More adults quickly gathered around. Slowly and painfully grandpa was carried into the house. The doctor eventually showed up and must have set his broken leg and applied a cast right there in his own bed. Although the details escape me, the solemn atmosphere that pervaded that evening, is safely tucked away in memory bank.

A similar sad memory lingers from 1959. Grandma's sister, her only sibling, our great Aunt Fannie died in their home. Her and her husband Christian Roth were living in the granny flat at the time. The funeral service was held in the living room, as was common in those days, and followed by a memorial service later in their church. She was less than 5 years older than Grandma and only 61 years old at the time of her death.

My great-grandmother, Mrs. John Gerber, former Annie Yantze also died in their house in April 1951. Actually, Grandpa had built this small apartment for her when Great-grandpa died. Obviously I was not old enough to remember this event but later found it interesting to see my name and Art's in the lengthy obituary that appeared in the local paper. We were the only two great grandchildren at that time. It seems quite a few relatives lived in the granny flat over the years. I know the farm was a blessing to the whole family and a place of refuge for me each time I visited. I loved it there!

Grandma's name was also Annie, although I never knew this as a child. She died at the age of 80 on October 14, 1982. This was moose hunting season; possibly I didn't hear about her death until I came out of the bush. I can't remember; it is quite possible I just chose to hunt instead of going, which is now difficult to admit. She had suffered with Diabetes for a long time and lost one leg, several years prior to the disease. She was very unhappy her latter years and made sure her oldest daughter knew about it. The fact that Mom abandoned her many years earlier was never forgotten by either of them. I'm sure Mom lived with guilt her whole adult life. Grandma always cried when it was time for us to leave. Regardless how long we had been there, she repeated the same pleading question over and over, "Why do you have to go?" In Mom's latter years she cultivated her own haunting mantra, which I'm sure is directly connected to her Mother's. Especially when looking out a window driving, she repeated, "How did we ever get to live so far away?" If Dad was in the car she added, "Mahlon, its your fault."

In Grandpa's family of 4 boys and 2 girls, he was born first in 1898, and died last, in 1989 at the age of 91. Grandma also gave birth to 4 boys, 2 girls. A senior's residence, Knollcrest Lodge, in Milverton, his home for many years, was his last. Apparently, he was not happy there, although I don't think he complained. I am thankful relatives in the area saw him more than I did because I am ashamed to admit, I can only remember being there once.

The last years of his life, he spent hours staring out the window. I wish I would have known; I may have made an effort to share a few hours of those lonely days with him. On his last day he got up with a spurt of energy, went to the dining room, ate a hearty breakfast, which was rare, went back to bed, fell asleep and never woke. At the time I was 39 and a renewed interest in my heritage and family was finally coming alive in me, again.

At his funeral, as I mingled with and embraced his bountiful and loving progeny, I was honored to be a part of this family. I realized, this old man, I learned to love so early in life, was a part of me and a part of him lives on in all he left behind. Some of his genes are more evident in some of us than others. Not only am I about the same size as he was, we share similar interests. He also loved the outdoors and working with his hands, especially with wood. He had a quiet peaceful demeanor and talked openly about his faith to those who expressed an interest. Most of the time, he said little but possibly his silence had greater meaning than any words he could have offered.

## My Dad's Relatives

I'm not sure why but we spent less time with Dad's side of the family. It is common for daughters and mothers to stay close and for their families to bond accordingly. We did visit Dad's parents at least once a year, often in the summer and usually for dinner and an evening. Grandpa was easy going and wore a permanent smile, like his namesake, my oldest cousin David. He was the youngest of 8 children, 3 boys and 5 girls.

Grandma was a Steinman, she came from a family of 3 boys and 4 girls and she would give birth to 3 boys and 4 girls. She looked like a Steinman and talked like one. They have prominent and unique traits that have been passed on from one generation to the next. She comes from a long line of stern and serious minded people who wore their religion on their sleeve. I appreciate their openness and honesty, although a number of them had the reputation of being harshly critical of others who didn't live up to their high standard. I guess I come by it honestly but I'm not proud of it. It takes a conscious effort, on my part, not to give into this deceptive influence.

Visits and dinners were more formal with the Basts. Grandma's homemade tomato juice was her beverage of choice, which we endured with a fake smile. They lived in the town of Wellesley and had a small yard with little for bush-kids to do. Grandpa's big shinny Ford Edsel was one thing I took an interest in. It was the nicest car I had ever seen up close. Clifford Fielding drove a Rolls Royce but I never got close to it. Grandma's real name was Veronica but people knew her as Fanny. She played the piano and assumed we would enjoy being entertained by her. It was rather boring for us to listen to, and we were happy when she stopped.

Dad had 3 older siblings and 3 younger; John (1923), Alvin (1925), Suzanne (1926), Mahlon (1928), Alma (1932), and the twins Dorothy and Doris (1934). Both brothers moved away at a young age; all 4 sisters stayed in the area. Similarly, on Mom's side only her and one brother moved away the other 4 stayed close. I enjoyed visiting Dad's family but never spent enough time with them to cultivate close relationships. However, that did change later on in life, especially with Dad's little sister Doris' family. Doris married Johnny Metzger in 1954. I vaguely remember their 4 children, from the early years but they were too young for us to connect at the time; years later we did.

Most of the following is from "Bast Family History, 1821-2005". Larry (1956) married Beth Fisher; they had 3 daughters. Elaine (1959) married Leo Mortensen and had 2 daughters. Anita (1963) married Bobby Fisher and later Ikenna Uche. Julie (1971) the youngest of all the Bast cousins married Parry Herties and had 2 daughters. In Aunt Doris' family a male has not been born since 1956 but many cousins carry on the Metzger name.

Dad's oldest brother John (1923) married Helen Reimer in 1942. They had 5 children. David (1943) married Sharon Lumsden; Bobby (1945) married Anna DeMoel; they had 2 children; Rita (1946) married Bill Stanley; they had 2 children. Esther (1947) was tragically killed at 16, which I document later on. Ruth (1948) married Tony Van Kooten and they had 3 children.

Dad's other brother Alvin (1925) moved to the west coast in his 20's and never returned except for the odd visit. He married Connie McKibbin in 1953. They had 4 children. Diane (1954) married Dennis Le Vasseur; they had 3 children. Marie (1956) married Dennis Holland; they had 2 daughters. James (1957) married Mary Botel; they had 2 children and then divorced. He then married Karen Gallagher and they had 1 child. David (1960) married Ingrid Walter and they had 3 children.

Suzanne (1926) married David Bowman in 1947; they had 4 children of their own and adopted 2. Evelyn (1947) married Paul Hoffman; they had 4 children. Clifford (1949) married Elaine Martin; they had 2 children and then divorced. Clifford later married Wendy Shantz; they had 2 children. Margaret (1951) married Don Weber; they had 3 children. Leslie Robert (1958) married Elizabeth Tari; they had 1 child. Patricia (1961); has 2 children. Barbara (1967) married Ian Ross; they had 2 children.

Aunt Alma (1932) married Lester Bechtel in 1954; they had 4 children. Bruce (1963) married Diane Lichti; they had 2 children. Cheryl (1965) married Steve Gerth; they had 3 children including twin boys. Debbie (1966) married Cameron Shapanski; they had 2 children. Peter (1960) married Sonia.

Aunt Dorothy (1934) twin to Doris married Sid Rudy in 1952. They had 3 children. Connie (1953) married David Martin. They had 2 children. Pat (1957) married Steve Errey; they had 3 children. James (1961) married Margaret Erb; they also had 3.

As far as Grandma Bast's 6 siblings go 4 of them never married. Dad's Aunts Katie and Barbara, his Uncles Dan and Noah were life-long residents of Wellesley. Most of their lives they lived together in town, beside the river, near the beautiful park. Apparently the 2 girls fell in love when they were young and both had their hearts broken; it seems neither of them recovered or at least never found true love again. Visiting their home was always an interesting experience, to say the least. It was actually a little spooky for me when I was real young. The doors and windows were shut tight, even in the summer, and blinds were down making it quite dark inside. They seemed very old and a little strange although they were friendly enough and seemed extremely happy to be honored with our presence, which did help me relax.

Aunt Barbara loved music and played the piano. She especially, wanted to hear us sing. As the story goes; many years prior, her parents forbade her to marry her lover; he was a "worldly opera singer". I must try to confirm this next fact, somehow if I can, but what I was told is that her lover committed suicide after he received the news that Grandpa Steinman refused to give his daughter in marriage to a "heathen". In any event, a part of her died that day but not her love for music and she wouldn't let us leave until we sang as a family, which we did in church once in awhile, also. I guess we all inherited musical genes, although it is a little more evident in Art and Marilyn. At 83 Mom still had a beautiful soprano voice and Dad still enjoyed singing bass, especially the notes way down low. So, we sang a favorite hymn or two; they smiled as they listened intently and praised us afterward. The women never worked outside of the home, as far as I know. The men owned and operated the local Feed Mill for years and were respected businessmen in the area.

Shortly after Marja and I were married the two remaining siblings, Noah and Barbara, decided to sell the house and move into a senior's home. As was the norm they hired an auctioneer to sell their furniture etc. As was also the norm many family members attended. Their dining room suite immediately caught my eye. It had 6 solid oak, beautiful hand crafted chairs plus a captain's chair. The big table was maple so not really part of the original set. It was solid with 5 large round legs and several leaves' that would extend it to 8 feet long and seat a dozen people comfortably. The chairs were sold alone and first; I was able to buy them for $19.00 each, right under a few antique dealer's noses. I'm sure they could tell I was determined to buy them by the way I bid without hesitation, which meant they were not going to get a real bargain and this also may have discouraged relatives, if there was any interest. I know they were happy to see it stay in the family. I opened the bid on the table at $3.00 and no one countered.

I later learned the dining room suite had been a gift to our great grandparents, John and Susanna Steinman (nee Gascho) on their 25th anniversary, from their children. They were married in 1877, so their 25th anniversary was in 1902. That would make the dining room set well over 100 years old, at the time of this writing , if I have all my facts right. In any event, it is still in fine shape today, even though it has moved around some. In 1973 we gave it to my parents for their 25th anniversary. These were the days we thought God wanted us to give everything away.

Many years later my parents decided that an oval table would give more room in their kitchen. Mom talked to us about her intention and we offered to trade her for the set we had been given by Marja's parents. So the Steinman dining room suite was redeemed and became a prominent part of our home for many years after. In 2005 we sold our house and held our own auction. There were no worthwhile bids and we were not about to give it away cheap, especially to a stranger.

We were about to put it in storage with a few other possessions but Aunt Doris Metzger showed interest in it and we made a deal for $1500. She still has it in her dining room today and it looks lovely. Marja and I periodically have the privilege of sharing a meal with her and family on it. A few years before we sold it I had it refinished. It had a few scratches and scuffs and the finish was getting a little gummy in spots. I asked a friend, Ron Jones what he would charge me to refinish the 7 chairs and table plus to make an extra leaf. He offered to do it at home on weekends for $1000. I knew he would do a professional job. I had admired his handiwork for years. He worked for Marja's brother Risto as his main finishing carpenter. He spent 8 years alone working full time on Risto's large house. His beautiful craftsmanship is everywhere.

When I hesitated, he went to plan "B". If I did the sanding and prep work in his shop at Laamanen Construction, he would be there to supervise and then do the finishing in the spray booth and just charge for the hours he spent on it. At this time Risto and I were partners of Kan-tex Mfg, which was located on same property, a stone throw away from Ron's workshop. This was too appealing to refuse. My son Ben and brother-in-law Paul both worked for the canvass business. On slow afternoons they walked down the hill and worked on the dining room suite and when they were done Ron did the spraying, as planned. He also drilled a small hole down through the seats and legs of the chairs into each spindle and injected wood glue with a syringe into the cavity and clamped them overnight. They are solid and the set almost looks like new.

In 1998 when I took sole possession of Kan-tex Mfg. the issue of Ron's time spent on the set came up as Risto and I were settling accounts. This was only one of many items we had to deal with. Risto checked the books and we discovered that Ron had logged $2800, worth of wages for refinishing. I was flabbergasted and a little upset. Apparently he had allocated whole days for the several weeks the set was in his shop. I guess this was an easy way to log his time. I told Risto the story. When I was done all he said was, "Don't worry about it". Risto was like that.

You may or may not have realized that my Dad, like his Grandfather, John Steinman (1851-1942) married a Gascho, Susanna. She died in her 95th year, in 1949. She was one of Wellesley's oldest residents to date. Her father's name was John Gascho the same as Mom's father. Now you know where the saying comes from, "When Mennonites get married are they still cousins?" Just kidding; Not!

Grandma Bast had another sister, besides the two old spinsters, Mary, who married John Schmidt and they only had one child Catherine, who never married. They owned the garage and gas station in Poole, where Mom attended public school. This was a very small town, if you could even call it that but it had a road sign that said, “Poole”. Mary died in 1951, at the age of 65; I was too young to remember her. I vaguely remember seeing her husband at the garage once, in grease stained coveralls. It seems to me he was smoking, which would have been a shock.

Other than a gas station Poole had a small grocery store with a bus that traveled to the neighboring farms on Saturdays, loaded with all the necessities, including candy. We looked forward to seeing the “store on wheels” driving up the lane. The few little treats we were allowed, this one day, were special and enjoyed as long as possible. Years later we adopted a similar program that is common in Finland, called “Karkki Paiva”, “Candy Day”. When our son Ben was young he was treated to a few candies of his choice on Saturdays, which was Candy Day. Interestingly, he does not have a sweet tooth, although neither does his Mom. Other than these two all the rest of my immediate and extended family surely does.

Catherine visited us several times over the years. She was very quiet and soft spoken, even seemed quite timid to me, for an adult. Even when she did talk, which was seldom, it was more like a squeaky whisper. She worked as a librarian for many years in Toronto; good career for her, in that respect. I liked her well enough but I was a little concerned for her, or maybe just aware that others were.

On one visit, after the death of a loved one, I believe. She spent hours pacing the hallway, back and forth in silence, deep in thought or maybe praying. This seemed odd. Grandma Bast’s third brother our great- uncle, “Enos”, whom I only remember seeing a few times, had 6 children, I believe. The only two I remember are Irene and Ruth. Ruth married George Elsasser, the parents of Janine who married Bob Shultz.

Uncle Dan was the next to die, in 1960, at the age of 76, while visiting in our home at 49 Moxam Drive. I will never forget what he looked like. He wore an extra large, square, Steinman jaw with distinction and had a rather large nose to go with it. Actually, he was a big man with a big head and a big voice. I seemed to have inherited a mixture of Bast, Gascho and Steinman traits. I often joke that the advantage of having a big nose is you only need to take one breath in the morning and you're good for the whole day. Actually my nose is not half the size of Uncle Dan's. I think it may be a Bast trait that causes me to talk like this: anything for attention. Aunt Catie died in 1964 at 84. I vaguely remember the service. The church was packed with mostly "horse and buggy" Mennonites. I felt like I was in a time warp. Uncle Noah lived to 87 and Barbara to 92.

I remember very little about my Bast cousins, during this time. Because John and Alvin moved away I very seldom saw their children and 3 of Dad's sisters children were too young to be of much interest. Aunt Suzanne and Uncle David had 3 children around our age. Evelyn was a few years older, Clifford was Art's age and Margaret was Marilyn's age. These cousins we got to know the best because we spent the most time with them, usually in Dorking where Uncle Dave owned and operated a feed mill. After grandpa died in 1974, at the age of 79, Grandma Bast moved in with the Bowman's and she died in 1976, at the age of 83.

## Humbugs

I must mention one more very old gentleman that Uncle Mervin took us to visit a few times. Charlie Schaefer lived in Poole behind the school that Mom and her siblings attended. I was fascinated with him mainly because he appeared to be the oldest person I had ever seen; besides he gave us candies. Immediately after introductions and handshakes he turned and headed for a nearby dresser. The second time we visited him I knew exactly where he was headed and watched with interest and anticipation. It took what seemed a long time for him to slowly and methodically shuffle across the floor of his bachelor apartment and pull open the top drawer. There he retrieved a small bag of humbugs, one of the little pleasures of life he still enjoyed. I could tell he was delighted to share them with us.

I sensed our visit had made his day and Uncle Mervin's, also, who grinned from ear to ear because we were so intrigued by this old man and his gift. The humbug was also to remind us to come back again, soon. Although we didn't stay long this was Uncle Mervin's way of keeping in touch with his old friend as he did with many other folks in the area. Wherever his travels took him with his dump truck there was always someone along the way he could stop to visit. A couple of my aunts told me that he dropped in on a regular basis, just to say hi and enjoy a wedge of homemade pie, which he knew would be almost always readily available.

## Jesus Died For Me!

I was very familiar with many Bible stories and was taught to memorize Bible verses at a very young age. We were also taught right from wrong; what displeases God and what makes Him happy. I took these things seriously and Mom told me I was not shy about informing others also. Apparently, as soon as the telephone repairman came down the pole, I shared with him that God was not pleased with him smoking.

I have one memory of my early years in our first house that stands out above all others. I was probably 7 years old because I turned 8 the summer we moved. My mother and Helen were both there; one of them read the "Crucifixion Story". My siblings must have been present also but I don't remember but I will never forget the story. I had heard about Jesus dying on the cross numerous times, although I may not have been read the complete Bible account before.

For whatever reason, I was ready to hear it in a way I never imagined possible. The tragedy of the murder of the "man of sorrows", the only-begotten Son of God gripped me powerfully. I can vividly recall the pain in my chest that was so incredible I thought my heart would burst and I rained tears uncontrollably.

Even now I get a lump in my throat and can't hold back the tears, as I write. It is impossible for me to express in words what happened that day but something took place inside my heart that caused me to realize the grace of God in truth, like never before. Since then my "knower" has known that I have been set apart for Him. The knowledge that I am His and the awareness that His spirit took its abode in me that day has never left.

Even through my most rebellious and dark days I was aware of His closeness and assured of His love for me. My understanding, my attitude and my behavior have wavered to and fro, over the years, from one extreme to other but through it all I knew I was safe in His arms because Jesus died for me and I was His child. He didn't leave me when I was lost, bad or just plain stupid. Pleasing Him or walking worthily of His love is another matter separate from this realization. How I have done in this area I cannot say, yet. That is in His hands and when I finally see Him face to face, I'm sure He will let me know.

# CHAPTER 2

# Age of Innocence: 1957 - 1964

## Times Were Different

In the spring of 1958 Dad bought a bush lot at 49 Moxam Drive across the road from our new pastor, Menno Ediger's house. This location was also one block away from the church but on the west side. That summer with the help of a few local men Dad built, what to us, was a big house. It was an 1100 square foot, 3-bedroom, brick bungalow. For its time it was modern. It had a basement, an indoor bathroom with a flush toilet and a bathtub. My sister, Marilyn had the luxury of her own bedroom, next to ours. There was an opening at the top of our closet above the hanging clothes where one could climb up and then crawl from one bedroom to the other if one was small enough and spry enough and so inclined. Young boys can think of a few reasons why they would take the time and effort to do that.

Although, I still had to share a bedroom with my brothers, we eventually all got our own single bed. This was luxury. All 3 were lined up against the back wall with just enough space to walk between. However, for the first few years we shared two old style double beds with steel frames and sharp corners. This fact is still prominent in my mind. One day, Gerry, following his big brothers, jumped from one bed to the other. He was a little smaller and didn't quite reach his destination; instead he gashed his head open on the corner of the bed frame and spilled his blood all over the floor. It seems Gerry and I both got hurt more than Art. Not sure what that means. Art was bigger and probably smarter than we were and also more cautious. On another occasion Doug Young throwing Gerry up into the air dropped him. He fell hard to the floor landing on his head. That night he slept with Mom. She set her alarm and woke Gerry up every hour all night, just for a few minutes. Apparently, if one has a serious concussion and sleeps too long they sometimes don't wake up. I was happy to see his smile the next morning.

Most of our basement served as our recreation center. Hockey was our favorite sport and "shots on net" was more fun than a hockey game with 3 players. We had a space of 6' wide at one end between the freezer and the chimney where the shooter could wind up and slap a ball as hard as possible. The net was about 20 feet away where the goalie was equipped with a goalie stick in one hand and a baseball glove on the other. Shin pads and helmet were optional. We spent hours taking 10 shots at a time at each other logging how many goals were scored. This not only improved our hockey skills but also gave us good baseball, fielding practice.

Our new house was closer to my best friend Andy Albiani and his brother Charlie. The open field between our homes is where we played football and baseball. Mr. Albiana liked his boys to stay close to home so I often played with Andy in his yard. We played peewee a lot and got quite good at it. We had a slight advantage over most other boys because we knew how to make a paddle the right length and diameter and good little sticks, very pointed. We decided to play something more exciting one day, darts. Throwing them at the board became boring so we took turns running by the big garage wooden door, while the other hurled darts from about 20' feet away. Andy got me first in the calf of my leg. I pulled it out; it bled and it hurt but I got him back. Unfortunately I shot a little too high. The dart stuck right in the side of his head. That was the end of that game.

On another occasion, during a winter snow ball fight, Andy peeked up above the wall of his fort just as my snowball arrived. It got him right in the eye. Mrs. Albiani was very upset. She scolded me and sent me home. Andy was a south-paw and in his early teens played for the local baseball team. He was one of their best pitchers, so I'm not sure why I got more direct hits than he did. Maybe I took the games a little more seriously.

Mr. And Mrs. Albiani called Charlie "Drago". This was probably his Slovenian name, but he made it very clear to me this name was not what anyone else called him, especially if they were smaller than he was. His dad was a hard worker and muscular. He worked for Inco his whole career but was also a carpenter, a brick-layer, and a jack of all trades on the side. He built two fine brick houses in the neighborhood although they lived in the first one all the years I lived at 49 Moxam. I frequented their home regularly; they had a TV long before we did. Most of the time we played outdoors but I was intrigued with television and gladly went in when invited. Mrs. Albiani (Mary) was polite and seemed to watch her son's Mennonite friend with curiosity. She was a devout Catholic.

There were times I was there over lunch when Andy was served a large bowl full of homemade French fries, Wow! I never experienced that kind of meal, ever. On occasion I was offered some and they were good. When his dad came home it was time for me to leave. I never even considered asking to stay even if we were in the middle of a show. Kids generally were not that bold in those days besides he was a rather stern, disciplinarian type of father. I saw him loose his temper a few times and literally throw a shovel or a concrete block in fury. I would never consider getting on his wrong side. I timidly said, "Hi" on my way out and kept on moving.

This is the time and place I discovered and fell in love with cowboy shows like Roy Rogers, Gene Autry, Hop Along Cassidy and The Count of Monte Cristo, to name a few. Even to this day I prefer a sub-average "Duster" over almost any other movie. In these shows the "good guys" and the "bad guys" were obvious, to even the youngest viewer. The good guys usually wore white hats and often rode light colored horses; of course the bad guys had black hats and dark horses. Good always prevailed without exception and the hero always won the heart of the pretty girl. Evil was always harshly punished and bravery and honor rewarded. There was even good Indians and bad Indians.

I have repeated the punch line of a joke many times over the years that I am sure you have heard a version of. Anyway, this is the way I heard it; the Lone Ranger and Tonto are being chased by the "bad Indians" and came to edge of the steep cliff with a large river below; the Lone Ranger looks at his Indian partner and asks the question, "What do *we* do now Kimosobi?" Tonto replies, "Who's *we* white man?" On TV they ride their horses over the cliff, fall into the water below and the horse swims to safety with the rider still on his back.

I shared a few of these old flicks with my children when they were young. They said the acting was phony. I knew that but it still hurt ever so slightly to hear it from them. They still bring back a flood of great memories. Today, for a movie to be of interest to me it has to either be from the frontier days or earlier or take place in the wilderness, preferably with animals. I particularly like horses. I will tolerate a modern day movie if the setting is primarily outdoors. If it takes place in a modern day city but is based on a true story I may consider starting to watch it to see how it goes. More times than not I head to bed half way through, to my wife's displeasure, "Sorry Dear!" Now that I have lost some of my hearing it seems easier to prefer my much needed sleep over most movies.

My brothers and I often climbed the mountain south of our house with our friends. There we played cowboys and Indians, picked blueberries and carved our initials into the flat rocks hundreds of feet above the neighborhood below. We could literally see for miles; I was intrigued with all the uncharted bush. Also up there, it was easy for me to imagine I could fly.

One day a big field several miles away caught my attention. We guessed it was past the Santala subdivision and Pentney's Service Station, probably north of the V.L.A. I think that stands for the "Veteran's Land Act". After World War II the soldiers who came back home alive were given a lot in this particular subdivision, for free, I think, or at least cheaper than normal, as a reward for their service. Good idea! Anyway, we often talked about this large grassy meadow and wondered if it would make a good "happy hunting ground". We purposed, some warm sunny morning, we would pack a lunch and ride our bicycles to find this field of dreams. One Good Friday morning, because there was no school, we decided this would be a good time to go exploring. Charlie and I got up early and headed west on our bicycles. I know Andy didn't join us and I forget if Art came along. This detail is overshadowed by what I do remember. Being Good Friday all "Good Catholics" go to Mass, all except Drago (Sorry Charlie) on this particular Good Friday. I don't think he missed another one, at least, not for a long, long time.

I don't know what he was thinking that morning as we headed out. Maybe he forgot or thought he could be back in time. In any event, he was not there when the family left for church. When Charlie did get home he was in big trouble, to say the least. Mr. Albiani lost his temper and literally chopped up his almost new bike with an axe. Charlie and I talked about this event at Carl Albiani's funeral in 1996. Charlie said, "This was one time my father went too far because this bike was bought and paid for by my own hard earned money". This was a hard pill for Charlie to swallow, although it seems he and Andy both learned from the lessons their dad put so much energy into teaching them. As they grew up, both the Albiani boys, were more focused and more disciplined, through high school and beyond, than Art and I and many other students were. Andy became an Optometrist and Charlie a Construction Supervisor.

## Music: Piano lessons

Once in our new place, we bought a piano. Mom wanted us to learn to play and arranged for a teacher to come to the house. Because of my love for music, and because I was captivated by the sound of someone who could play the piano well, I endured it for a couple years. The pull to go outdoors was just too strong for me to stay at the piano long. It soon became apparent I wasn't practicing enough to justify the expense of lessons. When I got married I bought my own piano, with the hope the inspiration to play might seize me. Our children took lessons for several years. Marilyn's girls became quite good at playing and we often had sing songs around the piano, especially when Art and, or Paul had their guitars with them. Heidi usually played the piano. We had other guest who played also. Barry Bird, a paraplegic Indian man stands out as one I particularly enjoyed. Even with the brakes jammed on, his wheelchair still moved backwards because he pounded so hard. After every song he had to move closer to reach the keyboard. Jimmy Swaggart or his cousin Jerry Lee Lewis had nothing on Barry. He played a pretty good violin in the same fashion. I could listen for hours. I often thought about taking lessons again but there were too many more urgent things to be done in life. The years from 2008 - 2014 would have been ideal; my niece Marja, a piano teacher, lived 3 doors down but by then we had sold our piano.

## The Strap

I can't even remember who my teacher was in grade 2 or 3, which is odd. Anyway, I did quite well in all subjects, all the way through public school, but always excelled in Mathematics. I loved times table contests. I can still impress my grandchildren with how fast I know them. Today, kids use calculators.

Discipline, at home and in school, also was very different then. I don't remember getting the strap in school until grade 6 but it seems to me I got it on 3 occasions. If so, the first time would have been in grade 4 because my teacher, Mrs. Crawford, was much tougher than my first 3 had been. It wasn't in grade 5 with Mr. Smith because he was too gentle to strap anyone unless you provoked him to the limit. Now!, Mrs. Fortune, in grade 6 was another story. She was a big, strict lady who seldom smiled and ruled her domain with a rod of leather. Now that I look back, I think she was trying to compete with or at least emulate Mrs. Hamilton, who was similar in size, personality and in her approach to no-nonsense teaching. I know I got the strap from her at least once, for "whispering in the cloakroom", if you can believe that. That is correct; not a sound was to come from our lips, going out or coming in for recess or lunch break. We were to hang up our coats in complete silence. We were to be seen and not heard unless spoken to, period. I have relayed this story to my grandchildren and the look on their face speaks volumes. I'm pretty sure they believe me; I have never outright lied to them but they cannot relate at all.

Every student knew what the strap was and most feared it to death and avoided it at any cost. I've heard everyone has their price. The fear of the strap tended to reduce the value most kids put on valor and friendship. On the other hand there were a few boys who seemed to get used to it or at least didn't go out of their way to avoid it. Possibly they just couldn't resist the temptation to push these contemptible, authority figures to their limit. I understood this well enough but the terror of the strap usually kept me from going there. As I mentioned Mrs. Fortune was a big lady, at least twice my size and with the mighty strap in hand, a "righteous anger" overtook her. For those who are not familiar with the strap it was a piece of leather about 2" wide, 1/8" thick and 16" long. Both hands had to be fully extended, palms up and whatever you do don't pull back when you see it coming. If you do, the teacher gets the sting of her own weapon in the shin and immediately discovers a new level of angry.

The penalty for first time offenders was 3 whacks on each hand. This was plenty to sting severely and leave a lasting impression. We often heard the slap of the strap and the subsequent screams of pain all the way down the hall if the door was open. That was enough to deter most of us. All, but the toughest, would leave with hands burning red and tears streaming down their face. The pain did not subside for a long time. You may think teachers would be afraid to send kids home with bruises or any signs of the strap still lingering. On the contrary, in most cases, children didn't want their parents to know. Some would get it again at home if their dad found out. Most parents just said, "Good, you must have deserved it".

## My Friend Robert Ransom

My classmate and friend, Robert Ransom, got the strap often and I never heard a peep from him or saw any tears as he returned to his seat. He had failed at least once and was therefore older and bigger than most of the other students. He was tall, dark and handsome and muscular. Apparently one of his duties at home besides splitting and carrying firewood was to haul water from the well. I heard he had to carry two 5-gallon pales of water suspended from a pole across his shoulders.

On at least one occasion I know Robert pulled his hand back at precisely the right time, to ensure Mrs. Hamilton got a taste of her own medicine. For this I was proud of him. Of course this would mean several more stripes. His pain would subside long before the memory of his sweet revenge and perhaps he hoped the sting would be permanently branded on her mind. This made it worthwhile, besides it may cause her to let off just a little in the future, not knowing when he might do it again.

I thought about Robert and others like him. Although he was a very likeable guy, his anger seemed to be ever present, just lingering below the surface. At times it would consume him in a way that the pain didn't even seem to register; not the way it did with us softer, more "normal kids". I felt sorry for him and admired him, at the same time, and I think he knew it. He was well aware I considered him my friend.

There were a few times we teamed up in the school yard in what we called "horse back fighting". This was a game where the biggest and the toughest boys became the horse and chose a smaller, lighter boy as their rider. There were few rules other than no punching, kicking, scratching and no biting. The goal was, by any other means, to knock the other horse and rider down or pull the rider off the horse. Robert was strong and sure on his feet and I was light and wiry; forgive me for mentioning it again; I was very competitive, also. We made a good pair. The last horse and rider left standing in tact was the winner. I enjoyed winning well enough, although not near as much as I hated losing.

Only one time do I remember getting on Robert's wrong side. It was during a lunchtime baseball game. Willy Jacobson, a big heavy set boy, was the pitcher and Robert the batter. Robert got angry with Willy for whatever reason and threw the ball back at him and made a hard, direct hit. Willy, although he had never failed a grade, was big for his age. Being the proud Finn he was, his automatic reaction was to retaliate. A scuffle ensued until the teacher on yard duty broke it up. Because of my innate sense to restore law and order and my big mouth I got involved, as did my best friend Andy, before the teacher arrived. We were all sent directly to the principal's office. We knew the strap was coming but for who and for how many we were not sure. We all told our side of the story. The sum of all these accounts, clearly added up to proving Robert's guilt, in Mrs. Hamilton's mind, at least, which was convenient for the rest of us.

I'm sure everyone's testimony was carefully articulated with one goal in mind; to deflect blame away from self. We never intended on making Robert the sacrifice; although he was the obvious choice for a scapegoat. Our only concern was to avoid the dreadful strap. When the dust settled Robert was the only one who got it and this time, in front of the rest of us all. After administering 5 blows on each hand, Mrs. Hamilton sternly asked Robert if he had anything to say to us, hoping for an apology as confirmation that her severe disciplinary tactics actually worked. He said "Yes I do, I'm going to kill you guys after school." I instantly realized there was something I feared more than the strap, that was the vengeance of Robert Ransom. Mrs. Hamilton kept Robert after school long enough for us to make our getaway.

The next morning I had one goal in mind; to get to school without being spotted by the boy I admired and now feared. Before this turn of events he had been my friend. I looked both ways heading out onto the Old Soo Road, as I began the long walk to school. I made it safely all the way to Jacobson's store beside the Water's Hotel. I decided to step inside for a minute, as I often did, not looking for a treat but reinforcements to accompany me on the last leg of the trip, to safety. As I opened the door and took one step in, there was Robert sitting on the steps, elbows on his knees; I froze as our eyes met; before I could turn and run a broad smile formed on his face; I was so relieved. He was truly my friend and the expression on his face that morning settled it in my mind once and for all.

Richard Charbonneau was a year or two older than Robert and one or two grades ahead of us. Before he had moved on to high school, he had been the undisputed toughest kid at 1A Waters. There had been several who had challenged him over the years and lost. Others had no interest in challenging him to a fight but ended up on the wrong side of an altercation, for whatever reason, and learned real quick not to mess with Richard. He was not only older than Robert he was also heavier and about the same height. I'm quite sure Robert was not looking for trouble; he had his full at school and at home. The problem was his reputation as the new, tough guy at 1A Waters, preceded him to high school. Richard made a special visit to challenge Robert, who was not accustomed to turning the other cheek. He was not about to start now. Besides, as I have already said, logic seems to leave the scene when hate and anger fill the mind.

Richard had come prepared. He pulled two thick, heavy elastic bands from his pocket and secured them tightly over the bottom of his pants to keep his rubber boots from flying off. Kicking was a big part of his arsenal. A solid kick to the stomach or a little lower, could end the fight in one blow. Punches were the preferred tactic because black eyes and scars on the face left a lasting impression on the victim and were telltale signs of who won the fight, sending a message to others, to beware.

I'm quite sure Robert must have been afraid, to some degree, as he contemplated and prepared himself mentally to face this wild beast that had just showed up from nowhere. I detected something else in his eyes, other than fear. Another master captivated his mind and overshadowed all else, even his fear. For some reason this challenge touched a nerve and he took it personally. It may have had to do with his relationship with his father and the treatment he received at home. Whatever it was Robert was instantly smitten with a disdain for this big brat he hardly knew. With little regard, if any, to his own danger he focused all his energy on one thing, to give this bully a taste of his own medicine, which he obviously deserved.

The fight went on cautiously for several minutes both sizing up their first time opponent. They glared into the other's eyes, the window of their soul, looking for a sign, a hint of a weakness. My heart pounded as they eventually began trading blows over what seemed a long time. Robert's few punches and kicks were hard enough to let Rick know he was not going to walk away unscathed, if he pushed too hard and too long. Robert was in better shape and I suspect, he easily had more stamina for the long haul if need be.

As it turned out, no one got a black eye or even a bloody nose that day and I don't remember either becoming the undisputed champion. I guess something got settled in their minds but I am not sure what it was. All the outward activities seem to have been overshadowed by what I was observing on the inside of my good friend. Apparently, this showdown needed to occur and now that it was done and over, Robert's life could go on. He had stood his ground and got in a few good licks; in that respect he won the day, in my mind. I felt closer to him after it was over than I had when it began but what could I do, how could I help? I could continue to be his friend that's all.

I was keenly aware of the gap between what I perceived as right and wrong and picked friends accordingly; maybe everyone did. I was attracted to those with a good sense of what was fair, especially the big and strong, the ones equipped to enforce justice in the school yard. Tom Scarf fit into this group. He was the tallest boy in the class, quiet and unassuming unless something rubbed him the wrong way. He didn't look for trouble but when it appeared he was compelled to stand for what was right. I admired that. Brian Nadjiwon was another schoolmate I befriended. His dad was Ojibwa and his mother Scottish, although race didn't matter a hoot to me then and still doesn't much. However, I found myself attracted to anyone who was a part of a minority group. Of course I didn't know what that meant, at the time, or even why I was drawn to them. It was possibly because I grew up viewing my ancestors, my parents and therefore myself in the same category, a minority. I was well aware that I was also different and like these other kids I didn't feel like I fit in; therefore we shared a kinship.

## Indians

The first minority group I became aware of was the local Ojibwa Indians. The Reservation was a few miles west, near Naughton. Now known as Whitefish Lake First Nation. Every summer they joined other bands from the area and lived in teepees along Hwy 17. They congregated there to pick blueberries on the low rocks nearby. I stared out the window whenever we drove by on our way for a picnic and swim at Simon Lake or Morrison's Farm on McCharles lake. During the day there was not a lot activity because most everyone was out picking berries. In the evening they gathered around the campfire socializing and eating as the brown skinned kids ran around playing.

The local Indians attended 1A Waters and I befriended a few of the boys. Most of them were shy and quiet but not lacking in skills when it came to sports. I took note and was impressed. Dennis Wabegijig was in my class and I liked him. In high school his little brother Cecil and I were in the same class. Dennis was probably the best soccer player in the school. He had a kind and gentle manner and was rarely noticed until he got control of the ball on the soccer field. I could tell he loved to run. School was not his forte and as soon as he could he went to work for Inco. He married Bertha Nebenionquit, raised a family and never left Naughton. Dennis died in 1995 at the age of 46. On his obituary, his 7 brothers were listed. 3 of them predeceased Dennis, including Cecil. I hurt for his mother who lived to see ½ of her 8 sons buried. There is something terribly wrong with this picture.

## My First Hospital Sleep Over

Although I visited doctor's offices many times because of my eczema some of which were at the hospital, I never endured the horror of staying overnight until May 1960. I was 10 years old in grade 5. For a few weeks that spring, on my way home from school, I had been enjoying swinging on a wire that hung from a hydro pole, perfectly placed on the side of a hill. From the top I could run, holding on to wire, and fly in a half circle over the road and around to the hill again on the other side of the pole. This was great fun until Dennis Moxam decided to take me higher and grabbed the end of the wire as I flew by. I hung on as long as I could and then fell to the paved road below landing on my right arm. My wrist was broken badly and quickly swelled to twice its size. I tried to sit up but my arm would not move. It felt like it weighed 100 pounds. Somehow, with a lot of pain, my arm and I were transported to the Memorial Hospital.

My introduction to Anesthesiology started wonderfully because it immediately took away my excruciating pain. The nurse told me it was "ether" but I am not sure if she used the word ether as a generic term or not. In any event, I have had a bad taste in my mouth for the word ever since. When I awoke several hours later my arm was the least of my worries. I had been sick before many times and had spent hours in bed quietly moaning to myself, praying for the pain to subside but when I awoke after my operation, I discovered a new level of stomach cramps and pain. After I had vomited myself empty the cramps continued. All night, alone in that hospital room, I repeatedly tried to vomit thinking my insides would surely come out.

Sometime before dawn, after the worst night of my short life, I fell asleep. At the sight of Mom coming into my room , later that morning, I totally lost it as a flood of emotions overwhelmed me. I wailed like a baby. I was so happy to see her but so hurt she had not been there for me. Like any good mom she got the message loud and clear; comforted me and got me out of there as quick as she could. I finished my school year in a cast. Mrs. Smith gave me the final exams orally and I did very well. I had another problem; the itch under the cast was unbearable, especially as the weather warmed. When mom was not looking I took a coat hanger apart and stuck it inside the cast to scratch my arm. The pain was much favored over the itch.

I have been "under the knife" and put to sleep 5 times since then with no ill effects. Each time I asked the nurse if they still use ether and was assured, "not". There is no way to know but I have wondered if ether is the reason I have had "gut" problems since my youth. Even if it is, this may have been a partial blessing in disguise. I have never been able to stomach much beer. I tried hard in my teens to get the elusive buzz my friends enjoyed but I always got sick just as I started "feeling good".

## Danny Hood

When Petrovich's moved away from Waters the Hood family moved into their house. Danny their only child, was 2 years younger than me. Danny's dad was a tough looking, war veteran with tattoos and scars. From my perspective, he appeared to have a drinking problem. Danny told me his parents often spent hours at the Water's Hotel and left him alone in the car. Every once in awhile his mom would come out to check on him and bring him fries or junk food and a comic to read.

Mr. Hood died young; Danny and his mom moved to Creighton. Very few times did I ever stay overnight at a friend's house but after Danny moved I was invited to his birthday party and I stayed overnight. The party was a new experience for me. We played many games, which was common, but the winner of these games got a chocolate bar. I was good at games! I'm sure I ate more chocolate that day than I had my whole life previous.

In the middle of the night I was awakened by a loud and awful sound. I had no idea what it was or where it was coming from. I had never heard this sound before. It sounded, kind of like, an animal trying to gnaw a hole through the wall but not exactly. I listened for a while and then realized I better wake Danny up, so I did. I shook him and asked, "Do you hear that sound?" He lifted his head and listened for a minute and replied, "That's just my mom grinding her teeth." I found this extremely hard to believe but was in no position to argue and no one to argue with; Danny quickly fell back to sleep. I tried to ignore it but was so intrigued by how it was possible for someone to make a loud sound like this with their teeth and not break them. I eventually went back to sleep and never slept there again. I did go back for a few day visits; to play hockey with Danny on the outside rink. He had several friends that were good hockey players. Warren Anderson and Ivan MacFarland were two I remember.

## Ross Moxam

In the early 60's one of Ross Moxam's older siblings, probably Kenny, bought him a horse. Ross didn't participate much in the games and sports the other neighborhood boys did. I think his family wanted to help him find a constructive way to occupy his time. Apparently, his older brother, Calvin struggled in his teens, to find direction in life, without a dad, which is understandable. This has got to be one of the most difficult pills for young boys to swallow. I heard by the time Calvin was 17 his mother and older siblings were very concerned about him. As the story goes Kenny, at one point, took him to the back shed to give him a stern talking to. I also heard there may have been bruises left after the talking was done. Shortly after, Calvin disappeared; I learned he had joined the army. He came back 3 years later a changed man.

Ross took a keen interest in his horse. The best place to ride him was around our block because it was a dirt road and there was less traffic than the Old Soo Road. I loved watching the big bay, quarter horse gracefully gallop by, always going around the block turning to the left. Seems to me this was also the case at public skating. This may be one reason why I preferred playing right wing even though I shot left. I found it easier cutting to the net from the right side because of all the practice skating that direction. In any event, this horse was huge and strong and had done some racing. I got the opportunity to ride him a few times and it was fun. He required little prompting and took off. I loved the sensation of riding, especially around the corners. He naturally leaned to the inside and I hung on; this was in the category of "scary fun", my favorite kind. Unfortunately the horse stepped through a broken board in the barn floor and broke a leg. That was the end of Ross's new friendship and the end his diversion from lesser productive activities.

## Hockey

In my opinion, and that of many other Canadians, hockey is the best game ever invented and early it became a passion of mine. During the summer there was so much to do outside I did not want to go indoors. In winter there were a few things to do but nothing compared to playing hockey. Road hockey was good but as soon as the ponds were frozen we would clean the ice and put on our skates. I could play hockey all day long on Saturdays or holidays if I had someone else to play with.

Hours were spent cleaning snow off a pond or a rink, by myself if need be, in the hopes that a hockey game would break out; "If you build it they will come". I have years of experience moving snow. Since 1998 I have had the pleasure of using a truck with a plow but the principal is the same. All different sizes and shapes of driveways or parking lots require a different strategy. I have thought about it and experimented trying to figure out the most efficient way to clean an area. For the more complicated yards there always seems to be room for improvement.

Every town, of any size, had their own outdoor rink with boards and often lights. The closest community rink was about a 10 minute walk from our home, across the road diagonally from Jacobson's grocery store. I often made my way up there and stayed until my hands and toes almost froze. I didn't want to quit because I was having too much fun. I remember Mom came to find me on one occasion, because I was so late. She knew I was freezing and wrapped her long coat around me and held it with one arm, as we walked home together. With her other hand she rubbed my fingers and wiped my tears.

## The Maple Leafs

Most of my friends were Leaf fans. This was the "Hometown team" even though Toronto was 250 miles away. Most of the French kids, and there were many, cheered for their archrivals the Montreal Canadians. My brother Gerry and a few others I knew began cheering for the Chicago Black Hawks after they acquired superstars, Bobby Hull, Stan Makita, Pierre Pilotte and goalie Glen Hall. With this core group, they managed to win the prize of all prizes, the coveted "Stanley Cup" in 1961. I didn't know anyone who cheered for the lowly Boston Bruins or the New York Rangers until I was in my 20's. My dad liked Gordie Howe and the Detroit Red Wings. After Toronto, Detroit was my 2nd choice. By the late 80's it became apparent there was no point in expecting the "Maple Laughs", as they were called, to ever win the cup again and Detroit became my team.

Saturday night was "Hockey night in Canada" and Toronto seemed to always be playing. I can still name many of the Leaf players from the last Leaf, Stanley Cup winning teams of 1962, 63, 64 and 67. Those years I was elated; when Montreal won "The Cup", I was devastated. During a close playoff game I was a nervous wreck. I find a little comfort in the fact thousands of other fans took it that personal, also. Staying home from church Sunday night, even during the playoffs, was not an option but as soon as the final Amen was uttered, I was out of there, home in time to listen to the last period on the radio and later on TV.

When I stayed home from school because I was ill or snowed in I spent hours organizing my hockey coins. I formed my own power plays from each team and graded them. One coin used to come in each box of "Jello". We all liked Jello and soon had the whole set of 6 teams. Toronto and Detroit were proudly displayed above my bed in the plastic plaques provided but there was something even more valuable than the hockey coins and cards I collected. Remember the days when Beehive Corn Syrup came in a round, blue, metal container? In the 60's it came with a thin cardboard ring over the spout that could be redeemed for a 5" x 8" black and white hockey picture. We all liked corn syrup also and collected over 100 of these photos.

Years later when I needed some cash I emailed Gerry and Art to see if they felt they were partners in this collection, deserving of their third of the proceeds, if I sold any these coveted pictures. They both replied that they had played a role in forming this collection. I guess they ate their share of corn syrup, although I knew who was the passion and driving force. This is why I saved and protected the coins, cards, books and pictures all this time. They had probably forgotten about them years ago but I didn't argue. I bought a copy of the "Canadian Sportscard Collector" magazine and picked out the 25 most valuable pictures and sold them for $600.00, which we split three ways. Later, I sold a few more through "T and T Auctions" but was only getting around $10.00 each for them, so decided to keep them awhile longer.

## The Stanley Cup

Hockey playoffs were the highlight of my year. When Toronto was not playing I cheered for anyone playing against Montreal. I vividly remember the Islander and Oiler dynasties of the 80's. I also, have memories of a few painful Montreal championships. The wounds have healed but the scars remain. A few years ago, I picked up a hockey book with a list of Cup winners since the beginning. As I reminisced past battles fought over the coveted Cup, I realized that I could remember which team won the cup many years. I also discovered when I drew a blank it was probably Montreal, again. This was the case for two reasons.

Firstly, I was trying to forget about Montreal's victories and secondly, they have won the League championship more times than any other professional team in any sport, a record 24 times. With this realization I decided to make the effort to fill in the few blanks where I had forgotten who won the cup. It seemed like a good idea at the time. I rationalized, even if it is useless information, at least it is good exercise for my brain. Today, I am a little hesitant to inform certain folks that I can rhyme off who won the Stanley Cup every year since 1947. If I haven't thought about it for awhile I may need a pen and paper.

## New Neighbors

Along with our new house came new neighbors. A few of them not any less captivating then the 3 families we left behind on the Old Soo Road. Our next-door neighbors were Dora and Wilbert Burrell. They had 4 children together the oldest Marsha several years younger than me, then Kathy, Lester and Carter. Besides these younger children, Dora had 2 big boys, from her first marriage to Mr. Frank James who was now deceased. Her sons names were Frank (1941-2002) and Laurie (1943-1983) James. In some ways they reminded me a lot of the infamous James brothers, Frank and Jessie James.

To me, Frank and Laurie were no less notorious and they were still alive, which was convenient. They were good looking men but they were rough, tough and seemed to periodically get in trouble. It was always a newsworthy event when a police car pulled into the driveway next door and gave the neighbors something to talk about. Frank spent time in a penitentiary and Laurie frequented the city jail on occasion. Lauri especially often wore battle scars and black eyes from his riotous lifestyle.

One day they were given the job of digging the hole for a new septic tank in their front yard. After they had managed to dig a rather deep hole; somehow an argument started; then it got interesting. I watched them wrestling on the muddy lawn; bare back; tattoos visible; muscles flexed; each trying with all their strength to put the other into the hole.

In the early 80's shortly after my long, "dark day of the soul", I had a most meaningful talk with Laurie. I was renting a fairly new, brick, bungalow in a quiet subdivision. He drove the garbage truck for Water's township, at the time. That night he been drinking and openly lamenting his miss-spent life. I tried to assure to him I could relate to how he felt; I also regretted how I had lived much of my life. His reply to me was, "I know where you live and the car you drive". I reminded him of my rather dubious past, of which, he was well informed. I let him know that I was no better than he was. His reply this time was, "You don't know me, Donnie, I am nothing but a punk".

He died a few years later, at the age of 40, when he fell down his basement stairs drunk. Rumor has it, he had been fighting with his wife, again and there may have been a tussle at the top of the stairs. The police may have suspected the worst. It wouldn't have been the first time they had visited their home. They also knew it would never be proven in court and frankly I don't think they really cared. As in many events documented in this writing, I take the liberty to document hearsay, gossip and assume other details by filling the blanks. I think it is called "Literary License" and I hope, right or wrong, I am not over stepping my boundaries.

Frank was a couple years older than Laurie; he was also bigger and a more handsome. Although, he seemed to have less of a chip on his shoulder, he also had been in trouble with the law and did "real time" at least once. He babysat us a few times and told us some far out stories. One day he came over to use our phone to call his favorite police sergeant. I guess he didn't want his Mom to hear; he didn't seem to mind if we did. He left the office door open and I overheard him express his increasing distaste and impatience towards a couple of bikers who were teasing his new girlfriend as they tried to have a peaceful drink together at the Coulson Hotel, downtown. Frank went on to say, "one of these days one of them is going to push me too far; how would you feel about that?" When he hung up I asked him, "What was the sergeant's response to your question?" Frank replied, "He said, just don't leave any fingerprints".

I knew the James boys were not a good influence but I was fascinated by their carefree, confident and rebellious attitude. I also found it interesting that Frank had befriended the police sergeant and felt comfortable enough to call him. I guess he realized the police were not "the enemy". In fact, in this case, they had a common foe, which made them friends, in a strange way. Frank died in 2002, at the age of 61.

Another new neighbor was at the corner of Moxam Drive and the Old Soo Road. Here Jordine Moxam, younger brother to John, lived with his wife Jan and their 3 daughters. Evelyn was a couple years older than me, Kathy a year younger and Marlene was the youngest. Their house was old but more modern than the original Moxam farmhouse, where John and Laura had their 14 children. I was told Jordine and Jan's house was built on the site where the original pigpen used to be and was probably the 2nd oldest in the area. As far as I know Jan still lives there. These 3 pretty girls were from a world altogether foreign to me. Their parents often had weekend parties, especially in the summer. There was smoking, drinking and dancing; music and laughter could be heard all the way down the street.

I knew I shouldn't get involved with "non-Christian" girls but I was so innocently and subtly drawn, especially to Kathy. She was bubbly and outgoing, always busy organizing activities. She taught us a couple games I found enticing, like spin the bottle and a version of hide and seek. We usually played this in our basement, after dark, with the lights off. We would wander around in the dark and when we bumped into someone, of the opposite sex that is, we had to give him or her a kiss. Kathy and I seemed to bump into each other quite often and I didn't mind at all. We knew my parents would not approve so we didn't tell them. Before going to sleep at night I told God I was sorry and asked Him to forgive me for feeling the way I did towards Kathy and for playing the games that aroused me this way. However, a few days later, when the opportunity arose, I couldn't resist the temptation; the lights went out and the games began.

By the time I was in grade 8 I had a serious "crush" on her. I think very few parents talked to their children about the "birds and bees", mine didn't. My infatuation for her was quickly extinguished when other boys started hanging around and she lost interest in me. Her cousin Ross and his friend Harold Yanchuck were two regular visitors to her house. It was obvious they were bad news; I saw them smoking and I heard them swearing. They showed little respect for authority and openly put down and made fun of parents and teachers. I watched them, curious to know what they were up to.

They surprised me one day when they invited me to come to their secret hideout, in the bush, across the tracks. I was surprised again when I saw the camp they had constructed. It was better built then I thought possible for these two misfits. The walls were constructed out of small poles standing vertical and nailed tightly together like the old, frontier forts. It had smaller poles for roof rafters; these were covered with many branches that helped keep out much of the rain. I could sense the freedom these rebels enjoyed having their own hideout, far away from all adult influence. I knew what they were doing was not for me but there was something appealing about it.

I guess, I was beginning to experience, for the first time, what I had been warned about, “the pull of the world”, which I always assumed I would be exempt from. My dad was gone a lot; when he was home he tried to keep a tight rein on his 3 sons but I needed more than that from him. Pastor Ediger did his best to help; he provided us with a regular dose of the fear of God. Menno didn’t wear a black suit or a long beard but he was stern and preached hell fire with the best. For this reason I looked up to him. I saw him as God’s strong leader and was determined not to get on his wrong side. I once observed his holy wrath poured out on some irreverent boys and admired his boldness. He reminded me of the prophets of old who slew the enemies of God. I knew God had put “a call” on my life, also and deep down I had a strong desire to be like the pastor.

## Delivering the Sudbury Star

In the fall of 1962, Mary Martin, who had been our “paper girl”, started high school. That summer I turned 12 and took over her paper route. I had about 30 customers spread out for a mile each way up and down the Old Soo Road and around our block. In those days papers sold for 10cents at a newsstand. Sudbury Star charged 45 cents a week for home delivery, which I had to collect and hand in. That worked out to a little over 7 cents per paper; there was no Sunday paper in the 60’s. I earned about 1 cent a paper, plus tips, which were good near Christmas. It may not sound like much but I was able to save near $2 per week and in the spring I bought a brand new, red CCM bicycle.

A few customers were hockey fans, like myself. When the playoffs began they introduced me to "hockey pools". I had the perfect job for selling tickets and started making my own pools. This made my job more interesting and kept my mind sharp working with numbers. I knew this was kind of gambling and a sin. I hoped it was a small sin and God would overlook it.

Around this time the Seniuks moved into the house across the street where Edigers had first lived. They came from Creighton Mine, the Inco town where Dad had worked. They had two boys. Lornie was a little older than Art and Fred was my age. In Mom's 1962, Christmas newsletter she made a request for prayer for Lornie who had been in Toronto Sick Children's Hospital since early October, with Bright's Disease. He was sent home with little hope. Lornie died on December 29, 1962 at the age of 14.

Many years later I was amazed as I read a letter dated January 1965, written by Isabel Seniuk to Mom regarding the death of Lornie and the dread of another upcoming trip to Sick Children's Hospital. Fred had also been diagnosed with the same disease. I had viewed this woman as a lost heathen who knew nothing about God and was not interested, either. She was even a smoker. I often accompanied Fred to the store to buy her a pack of Black Cat, cork tip cigarettes. In her letter I saw things from her perspective for the first time. She candidly spoke about her struggle to depend on God and accept His will. She pondered the same questions "Christians" do when going through similar situations and expressed a firm faith in the only One Who knew what was best. She acknowledged He was also the only One Who could help. In time of need it seems most people turn to God in prayer because they cannot help it.

After Lornie's death I often played outside with Fred and was regularly invited inside his house to watch television. Although their house was always full of smoke, which was not good for my allergies, I felt more welcome, now that Fred was an only child. Mrs. Seniuk in particular was happy for me to come in and play with Freddy. She introduced me to the world of playing cards, real cards. Cards were not allowed in my parent's homes growing up and neither ours but slowly they were shedding the "Old Order" ways, one by one, and becoming more tolerant of such things.

My time with Fred was a love / hate relationship, to say the least. He desperately needed a friend but I would never be able to replace his big brother and he continually put me down. He made fun of me because I didn't know the name of an actor on T.V. or any detail a Conservative Mennonite kid would never be privy to. He would chuckle and mutter to himself, loud enough for his mother and me to hear, "He doesn't know anything?"

I didn't like Fred's attitude but went back for more punishment each time I was invited. Now that he had moved to Waters, and his brother was gone, I became his so called "best friend", actually his only close friend although he often talked about all the good friends he left behind in Creighton.

I felt sorry for him and we did have some good times. Besides I was so intrigued by the TV, which was always on and enjoyed playing cards immensely. I was good with numbers and caught on fast. Beating Fred was a sublime pleasure indeed. It was around this time that my parents, attempting to keep us at home more, gave in to our pleading and bought our first television. They also allowed us to bring playing cards into the house and I quickly taught my siblings the games I had learned.

## Tragedy in the Bast Family

In the summer of 1963 my dad's brother John, Aunt Helen and our cousin Esther were all killed in a car crash in Vineland near their home. John and Helen were in their early 40's and Esther was 16. My 4 cousins; David who just turned 20, Bobby 18, Rita 17 and Ruth 15, survived them. Rita, who normally drove to work with them had a toothache that morning. The newspaper read, "Identification of Mr. Bast was almost impossible after his torn body was extracted from the mangled wreckage of his car". The driver of the truck that hit them was unhurt. I had only met these cousins a few times before. At the funeral, I felt close to them and was aware of their shock and pain, although I couldn't begin to imagine what they were going through. It was good they had each other. I took an interest in relatives, especially those a little older than me. Now that their mom, dad and sister had been taken from them I took special notice. Over the years, since this tragedy, I have only visited with Bobby and Ruth a few times. Rita I would see a little more frequently and David I saw a lot of because he moved to Sudbury a few years later.

This was the first time I met Dad's other brother Alvin and his wife Connie. Alvin had moved as far away from home as he could, all the way to the west coast, at the age of 25. He never returned except for the odd visit, or times like this. In fact this was the first time my parents met my Aunt Connie. They would however visit them in BC quite a few times. I don't remember them visiting our home.

We had many visitors in the 60's. Most of my Uncles, Aunts and older cousins, at one time or another, came north and stopped in. Several came regularly. Often visiting preachers also stayed at our place and some held extended revival meetings. In 1963 George Elsasser, who had moved to McAurthur Mills, returned to hold a series of services in our new church building. My Mom referred to this time as a mountaintop experience. In her annual letter, she wrote "God really blessed during this time, moving many hearts in Waters Township to be saved." And she also requested prayer for new believers.

In June of 1964 I graduated from public school with good grades and would be off to high school in the fall. This was the end of my "Age of Innocence". 7 years had passed, since God's grace had overwhelmed me with faith and love in Christ Jesus, Who died on the cross for my sins. I had spent these years by my parent's side, rejoicing with then, in God's goodness, singing the old hymns, from the front pew, at the top of my lungs, week after week.

It was now time to enter the next chapter of my life. Ready or not, I had arrived at what I had often heard called, "The Age of Accountability". This is the age I would have to decide for myself what I wanted to do with my life. How would I stand the test of being true to my faith in high school? How would I handle the peer pressure of so many worldly kids my age? I was soon about to find out.

Moe, Joe Lavigne and Me

"Bringing in a couple of ki's"

Grade 11

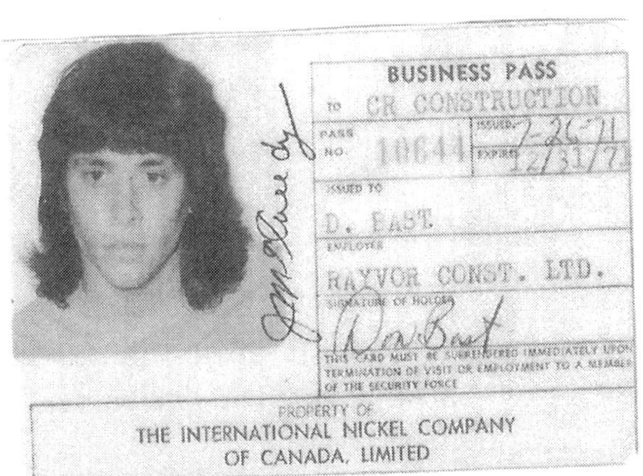

BUSINESS PASS

TO CR CONSTRUCTION

PASS NO. 10644 | ISSUED 7-26-71 | EXPIRES 12/31/7

ISSUED TO

D. EAST

EMPLOYER

RAYVOR CONST. LTD.

SIGNATURE OF HOLDER

THIS CARD MUST BE SURRENDERED IMMEDIATELY UPON TERMINATION OF VISIT OR EMPLOYMENT TO A MEMBER OF THE SECURITY FORCE

PROPERTY OF
THE INTERNATIONAL NICKEL COMPANY
OF CANADA, LIMITED

1971 Inco Pass

DON & MARJA BAST
JULY 10, 1971

# CHAPTER 3

# 1964 – 1971: The Age of Accountability

## Joining The Church

Like my older brother before me, I was baptized and became an official member of Waters Mennonite Church at the age of 14. This was the same year Menno Ediger resigned from his position as pastor at Waters and moved to Oklahoma. At his going away celebration, during his final address to the congregation, he said that if the congregation had asked him and his wife to change their minds and stay, they would have done so. I am not sure why he told us, but I knew he was serious and I knew this was important for someone to hear. The fact I remember this detail reminds me, that at the age of 14, I was paying attention when a "man of God" was speaking. Mr. Ediger, in particular, who had been our pastor for the last 7 years, had a profound influence on my life. This would become much more evident to me later on in life. I wonder if the absence of his strong leadership made it easier for me, over the next few years, to finally give in to the ever-increasing pull "of the world". In any event, when the tight reins that had held me secure, this long, were severed, I sprang free like a calf being released from the barn in spring.

We spent a year without a full time pastor. Henry Schroeder filled in between the summers of 1964 and 1965. I had such a hard time relating to him. His preaching did little for me as did the odd duet he sang with his wife June. Maybe it had more to do with me than him but I was losing touch quickly with the reality of church life. I found Henry and the whole scene becoming increasingly boring. My dad was driving for Aldershot Poultry and worked long hours and often spent nights on the road. My Mom also worked at the Husky Restaurant for 5 months that year, so we were frequently left on our own.

I was supposed to grow out of my eczema by now but it wasn't happening. My parents took me to Toronto for skin tests the summer of 1964 and my mom and I stayed with Catherine Schmidt for a few days. A serum was prepared and a nurse at Dr. MacGruther's office in Creighton took on the task of administering weekly shots. Attending high school meant I had to stay on the bus, a little longer, once a week, and get off in Creighton, wait for my needle, and then hitchhike home. The shots would gradually be required less frequently over the next 5 years. I was getting so many needles these days that the nurse had to keep trying to different spots and changing arms because the skin was getting tough with scar tissue.

The high school I attended was Lo-Ellen Pack Secondary, on the south end of town near the "Four Corners". Because of my good grades at 1A Waters, I was registered in the 5-year Arts and Science program. This was the program for the smart kids, whose goal was university and therefore needed grade 13. This was a new school that had just opened the year before. Most of the kids were bussed in from the out-lying areas like Waters, Naughton, Whitefish and Burwash, the little town established around the prison farm 20 miles south of Sudbury. I recall seeing the signs on the highway on both sides of Burwash not to pick up hitchhikers because they may be escapees.

At Lo-Ellen it quickly became evident to me how different I was from the other students. I felt so awkward, like a fish out of water. I was not only a Christian, I was also a Mennonite, but I told no one. It seemed everyone, students and teachers alike, had come from a different world with a different mindset. They seemed totally unconcerned with "pleasing God" and oblivious to the fact there was a hell and judgment day was coming. The school did have a "Christian Club" that met periodically and I may have attended one meeting. The group was comprised of what I identified as boring intellectuals and sissies that held no attraction for me. Not one student from my grade 8 class was in my grade 9 class. I made no close friends that first year; I didn't seem to fit in anywhere. This would be by far the most difficult year of my short life. The decisions I made and the direction I chose in grade 9, would drastically impact the rest of my life.

For the first time in my life I became keenly aware of my looks, the clothes my peers were wearing and hairstyles. I realized I was short, skinny and not good-looking, which made me more self-conscious. Eczema afflicted my face like the rest of my body. I had very little eyebrows because they were worn off from constant rubbing and scratching my itchy face. Looking at old photos Art's 2nd wife, Sue, who didn't' know us when we were young, blurted out, "That's Don?" Realizing I heard her, she stumbled on looking for the right words to clarify her shock. After a moment she finally said, "Time has been kind to you!"

The mid 60's, the time boy's hairstyles started getting longer, I quickly realized the more of my face that was covered the better I looked. Long hair in front covered part of my missing eyebrows and provided a distraction from the rest of my features. Several times Dad and I had a serious, power struggle at haircut time and he had to practically drag me downstairs to cut my hair. Gerry recently told me he remembers Dad being very angry with me and in the middle of a rather heated discussion he lost his temper and began yelling at me. I don't remember this event but it may well be it was over cutting my precious hair. By the time I was 16 he gave up and left me lone.

At school, I couldn't concentrate on studying and did poorly in most subjects except for math, which came easy. After an exam one morning with several hours to kill until the bus came, Paul Groves, a classmate invited me to walk to his nearby house to play pool. I was immediately intrigued by pool or billiards as we called it; I soon got hooked and played whenever I had the opportunity. Unlike schoolwork, I was good at concentrating at pool and I could get lost in the game and improved quickly. I even talked my dad into going with us to play a few times.

When the results of my grade 9 final exams came, I had failed. This was so uncharacteristic of me; I had always done well in school. My marks were just slightly below a passing grade and I was allowed to go into grade 10 on "probation" until Christmas. At that time my report card would determine if I stayed in grade 10 or was sent back to grade 9.

I didn't take my second chance serious. I found it easier and more fun to provide smart-ass comments, in the classroom, than the right answers, which required work. The negative attention from the teachers seemed to meet a need in me and also gained me some popularity among the students. Well not all the students, not "the sucks" as they were referred to. More and more I was attracted to the rebellious students and felt the need to be accepted by them.

## Back to Grade 9

When the second semester started, the powers that be, decided that I should not only go back to grade 9 but that I would be better suited for the 4 year, Science and Technology course. Although they knew I was smart enough to go to university they figured that was not going to happen because I was not willing to make the effort. It seems each time I had a teacher interview or visited the principal's office I was reminded I had a very high IQ and the ability to do much better if I would only apply myself.

Back in grade 9 my confidence level increased substantially. I was now a year older than most students, and had one year of high-school experience under my belt. I was also a bit of a novelty because I had come back from grade 10. I thrived on the attention and found satisfaction in being the "class clown". I was not alone in this pursuit. There were a few others who actually had years of experience at acting up in class to get attention. It became a competition to see who could get the most laughs. The second time around, in grade 9 was fairly easy and I found that the 4-year grade 10 curriculum was not difficult either. School was easy, my marks were acceptable and I thought less and less about God and more about having fun.

At church, we finally got a new pastor, Gary Harder, who was a breath of fresh air. At 23, he was only 8 years older than me, fresh out of university. He had never sensed God's call on his life to preach the straight and narrow gospel road message. He had gone to university to prepare for a career in music. He had not even considered being a pastor until he was asked to go to Waters as an interim pastor for 1 year. His wife Lydia Neufelt had been here before they married. That year she had been my Summer Vacation Bible School teacher. I had fond memories of her. Gary was a big man, and one I could relate to. He was not at all like the hell fire and brimstone preachers I had endured my whole childhood. He had no Amish or Old Order roots. He often played football with us Sunday afternoon and we had regular "Young Peoples" activities every Friday night. We even went on a few tours together to perform Christmas plays in other churches as far away as Ottawa. So now school was fun and church was fun also.

Walking home one evening, in early November of 1965, after spending the afternoon playing pool, I was informed by a neighbor that my brother Gerry had been taken to the hospital. He had an accident with fire and had severe burns to his face and neck. I immediately realized I was to blame for his tragedy. It was my fault for spending the afternoon in a "Den of Iniquity". My heart wanted to ask God to be merciful to both Gerry and myself but the guilt and shame was over powering and I was in a helpless state of shock. I knew the pain of fire because I had burned my hand badly, a few years earlier, when I accidentally grabbed the stovepipe in the church furnace room hiding on a friend before Sunday morning service. The pain was incredible and Dad sent me home to be alone. I quickly went outside and put my hand in snow, which did help for a while but back inside I went wild running around the house holding my wrist and crying until church was out and Dad took me to the hospital.

After I heard about Gerry I hurried home and they rehearsed the story how he had made a little fire, which was not a big deal seeing he was 13 years old and it was November, not the dry summer season. However he made the mistake of trying to get the fire going better by emptying the last few drops of a gas can on the small open flame. The can blew up and flames engulfed his upper body long enough to do the damage. He was very sick for a few days and stayed in the hospital for two weeks. After a month or so he returned to school 10 pounds lighter and with permanent scars. My mom wrote in her year-end newsletter, "This experience was a trying experience yet one of drawing us closer to God and realizing how good He really is. We truly thank Him for sparing his eyesight and that it wasn't more serious." I guess it did draw me closer to God, for a short time but the guilt wore off and it appeared that Gerry's scars would slowly disappear, as did my renewed interest in God.

## My First Jobs

When I started high school Gerry took over my paper route and I began looking for part-time work. The first job I landed was at the local grocery store stacking shelves and carrying out groceries. David Jacobson was the owner, the son of Charlie the long time owner and operator of the first General Store beside the Waters Hotel. The new, bigger store was on the other side of what is now Regional Road 80 across from Tim Horton's. I was paid 80 cents an hour. In 1965 this was good money for a 15 year old living at home.

My friend Brian Nadjiwon was pumping gas at the Husky Service Center across the new Hwy 17 close to our home. He got me an interview with Harry Kovalchuck the owner and I soon left the grocery business and began pumping gas and changing flat tires. Here I was able to work more hours, evenings and weekends and was paid $1 an hour plus I got the odd tip. One night a guy asked for $2 gas, which was not uncommon in the 60's. I pumped it, took his $20 bill and went inside to get change. When I walked back outside, there he was, gone and I had just received my biggest tip, ever. One day a truck driver asked me for $50 gas and when he came to pay he gave me his company credit card and said charge me $100 for fuel and give me the other $50 in cash. I had no idea how that would work; my boss was there so I said, "Please wait a minute" and I went to ask Mr. Kovalchuck about the request. He said, "Fine as long as we get paid, I don't care". I knew the guy was ripping off his company and I didn't like being a part of it but I was just following orders. I also pumped gas for a while at the Esso Station in Whitefish. The owner Ben Bourne was a member of our church.

In the fall of 1966 I tried out for the school junior hockey team. My mom wrote in her annual letter "Donald worked hard to make the school hockey team and is enjoying it". It is true, I never got cut from the roster at the try-outs and continued to be invited to the practices however, I don't remember ever playing in an actual game. I guess I was kept on as a spare in case of injuries. I was glad to be able to get out early with the team and I enjoyed attending the games, even if I didn't get to play. We had some good players like the Scharf boys, Tom my friend from 1A Waters and his little brother Ted, who went on to play for the Edmonton Oilers of the World Hockey League as an enforcer. Much later he became the president of the Kitchener Rangers Hockey team.

In the school washroom one morning Brian Wolfgram, a grade 11-student, also from Waters, began teasing Ted who was in grade 9. Brian was a fun-loving joker but had a mean streak that came out once in awhile. A tussle developed and before we knew it Ted had Brian's head in a toilet bowl. I don't think he messed with Ted again. On another occasion, Brian who had a permanent reservation on the back seat of our bus was telling jokes and acting up as he often did. This time his target was Bill Mason in the seat directly in front of him. Brian was teasing this big, quiet guy who usually didn't bother anyone or get involved. I had worked with Bill at the grocery store and had gone up against him a few times in horseback fights in public school. I knew he was strong but I also knew he was not interested in fighting with Brian or anyone else. What I didn't know, at the time, Bill's father was a career guard at the City Jail and may have given him some training on dealing with bullies.

Anyway, as we got closer to Brian's bus stop, at Hillcrest drive, the taunting challenge got loader and more persistent. Brian openly dared Bill to get off the bus with him at his Hillcrest Street, stop so he could teach him a lesson. I could tell Bill was embarrassed, although he continued to say nothing and kept looking straight ahead. To my surprise he finally spoke up and invited Brian to stay on the bus and get off with him at his stop. Bill lived near the end of the school bus run, several miles down Black Lake Road, in the bush. I knew Brian wouldn't consider going there with no way home but this put the ball back in his court. In frustration, just as the bus began to slow for his stop Brian nailed Bill hard in the back of the head with his fist. It must have hurt both Bill's head and pride and Brian's hand also, but not as much as what happened next. Without hesitation, before Brian stood up to get off, Bill turned around and labeled Brian square in the side of the jaw with a solid punch. Brian was not only in pain but also in shock. As he got up to leave he muttered a threat about, "a next time" and walked off the bus never to bother Bill again, as far as I know.

I was always one of the smallest in my class and really never had to worry about the tough guys flexing their muscles my way. Neither did I have any interest in fighting. The closest I ever came to fighting was a tussle in the schoolyard in grade five. I can't even remember who it was with. Once in high school I threw one quick boot, without even thinking, at the crotch of a schoolmate who kept punching me in the arm and wouldn't stop. I don't think I connected real good but hard enough for him to get the message and he left me alone after that.

For me it always made sense to talk my way out of fighting. One reason was because I had a lot more experience at talking than fighting and I figured, even when there is a declared winner, in a fight, both get hurt and that makes them both losers. Besides, I grew up in a pacifist home and church; turning the other cheek was the right thing to do, although I don't think this had much to with my actions. I was motivated more by fear and common sense. In any event, I admired the guys who stood for what was right and were strong and brave enough to put the bullies in their place when called upon to do so, just like the good cowboys of the Wild Wild West in the movies I loved.

## Stumbling Towards Manhood

When I was 16 I started smoking. This was a definite statement regarding my lack of common sense but also of my need for independence. I was now officially letting everyone know I was making a clean break from being under my parent's wing and the church's authority. I seldom went to church, anymore but agreed at times to keep peace in the house. I still needed a roof over my head. I worked as many hours as possible in order to have my own money for cigarettes, pool and other necessities.

I had taken a few puffs before with the Moxam girls but found nothing appealing about it. When the time was right it seemed like the natural thing to do. I was with Doug Young and his Mother's younger brother Russell Hirtle. Russell offered me a "Mark 10" cigarette and I took it and that was that; I started smoking. Russell and his brother Doug both came from Nova Scotia looking for work at Inco. They had heavy accents and used words I never heard of. It was like a different language and I had to concentrate to understand them. Russell stayed around for a short time; Doug got on with Inco, bought a house, raised a family and stayed in Waters Township until he retired and then he and his wife Eleanor moved back home again.

That summer I got my driver's license and Art and I bought a motorcycle together, a 250 Yamaha. I drove it a few times but felt insecure on it. On the highway at 60 miles an hour it seemed to float all over the road. It was not a big bike but still heavy for me, at 125 pounds. I laid it down in some loose gravel one day and although there was no damage done I decided I would rather drive my parents car instead of a bike. Art gladly took over the bike payments and responsibility. He would soon outgrow this bike and move on to bigger more powerful bikes. He became a very good rider and I often regretted not sticking with it. Many times over the years I considered getting a bike but the older I got the more I realized, when you are young is the time to learn to ride and I never did get another bike.

1967, Canada's centennial year, would also be a monumental year of change for me. I guess life went on as usual in my family and Water's church but I was becoming more and more severed from both as I struggled with becoming an individual. Gary Harder left to go back to school and John Zacharias took over as pastor. My mom wrote in her year-end letter that 3 new members, including Lorraine Moxam, Barry's wife were added to the congregation by their confession of faith and baptism. I often attended to keep Mom and Dad happy. I went and tried to put on a good face but had a hard time relating.

One Sunday morning service Wendy Bourne brought her new longhaired boyfriend to church. He wore big work boots and left his long doeskin shirt hanging out. After the service I heard him talking to some of the "elders" at the back of the church. He said something like, "this place is dead man; I felt like stomping my boots and yelling as loud as I could to see if you guys were just sleeping or what." He went on to say that he wouldn't have cared what kind of a response he got as long as he got one. Now that message I could relate to, but I wasn't blaming anyone for the direction I knew I was headed. An unseen force was driving me and I was just hanging on, trying to enjoy the ride.

Now that I had made the break from being a "Christian" other sins were easier to indulge in. Pool became an addiction and I spent weekends and as many school days in the Norland Billiard Hall as I dared. I periodically got there around 9:00 am and played until 11:00 pm and caught the last bus home. By grade 11 I started skipping school on a regular basis. In grade 12 I was 49 absent, (7 x 7). God has a sense of humor, I guess, although I didn't think so at this time. I often fell asleep at night realizing I was displeasing Him. I made many vows to change my ways but each new day brought new challenges and more exciting temptations; I had no power to resist.

## The Movers and Expo

The summer of 1967, in particular was a turning point in my life of enormous proportions. Art and I with 4 school friends made a trip to Expo 67 in Montreal. Art convinced my parents to let us take Dad's car. It was on this trip we decided to form a club called "The Movers". Billy Parent was one of the boys along and had a couple nicknames, "Mover" being the most popular one; hence the idea of our club name was born. We never gave it much thought and didn't realize the name would not only stick but that the Movers would become well known at Lo-Ellen Park Secondary. Besides Art and I, Bill, Larry Rootham, Dennis Hauta and Greg McGuigan were along on that life-changing trek.

I was excited to be associated with these cool guys. They were all confident, full of life and popular in school for various reasons. Bill was big for his age, played football, was outgoing and very funny. Greg was tall dark and handsome and popular with the girls and played basketball. Larry played both football and basketball and was good at both. Dennis didn't excel at any sport; he was more interested in chasing girls. Like many young men, he was particularly attracted to large breasts but Dennis was very vocal about it and also about any aspect of sexuality. He often would greet one of the boys with a big kiss on the cheek or he would grab their right hand and put their fingers to his nose to see if he could detect any lingering evidence of last night's activities.

Actually, on the trip to Expo, 7 of us headed out that fine summer morning. Larry's cousin Mike tagged along because he needed a ride back home to Ottawa. So the first leg of the trip was crowded, with 4 big guys in the back seat. On the way, someone lost their gum and it ended up in Mike's hair. He took a temper tantrum and we would have not thought twice about letting him out on the side of road, right there, if he hadn't been Larry's cousin. The "Movers" would learn to tolerate a lot from each other over the next few years but would increasingly have less and less patience with others, especially a screaming brat.

Montreal was a big, busy city with a lot of crazy drivers. Our response to the impatient, rush hour traffic was a practical joke. Driving down a main street, bumper-to-bumper, Art sat behind the wheel with a newspaper spread out in front of him, blocking his complete view, as I held the bottom the steering wheel and told him when to brake. We continually tried to think of ways to make the others laugh. I think I was good at it and cherished their approval, which only encouraged me all the more.

We found a trailer park close to the Expo site and quickly set up two tents and made a trip to the corner store to get supplies. We were tickled we could buy beer at grocery stores in Quebec, in brown quart bottles, no doubt. As we blew into the store Billy, who walked with a skip and a hop, when he was excited, boldly approached the store manager and asked, "How old do you have to be to buy beer in this country?" His answer was "Your age". Billy was big for His age and looked older than 15.

## Buffalo Girls Won't You Come Out Tonight

I have only a few clear memories of Expo that linger. We heard some good live music, spent a lot of time at "La Ronde" where we met a couple pretty girls and won some big prizes. The first morning we split up into 3 pairs. Not sure why but Art and Greg paired off, as did Billy and Dennis. Anyway, Larry I headed to La Ronde. I noticed a booth similar to what I had seen at midways and fall fairs and had tried it before with mixed results. It involved throwing a baseball. The bilingual worker kept yelling at the top of his lungs "Knock em down" and then, what I presumed was the French translation, something that sounded like "Billay Tomebay". Whatever it was it stuck and became a household term at school. I guess the other students figured we knew what we were saying and many just copied us. On any given day, for the next few years, you could hear "Billay Tomebay" echo through the halls of Lo-Ellen Park Secondary, followed by the same response at the other end of the hall.

Anyway, Larry and I stood nearby and watched for awhile as the participants tried to knock down 6 stuffed cats standing in a pyramid formation with 3 balls for a quarter. I always thought of myself as a "good shot" when it came to throwing a ball or stones but now was the time to prove it. After a few tries I managed to knock them all completely off the shelf and won a huge stuffed animal. Although we really didn't want to lug extra baggage around the rest of the day I couldn't resist trying again. Sure enough, I soon won another one and gave it to Larry. By now a small crowd was gathering. Among them happened to be a couple pretty girls who had been watching me and one of them asked me if I would throw for her. I proudly agreed and sure enough after a couple tries, won another big stuffed animal to her delight. Well I was her hero and so the four of us spent the day together and ended up trading phone numbers and addresses. Betsy was the name of the one I connected with and I forget the other one's name. All I know is they were pretty and Jewish and from Buffalo. When we all met later that afternoon Dennis and Bill were with a couple girls also, French girls. Dennis's new friend had "Voluptuous Orbs", as he called them, and as I already mentioned, that was important to him. The next day I showed up at the booth again but the attendant refused to let me throw any balls. He said I was banned from competing. I was disappointed but realized, this was the best complement I could expect from this guy and wore it with pride.

We spent several days at Expo and had the time of our lives. A few of the guys attempted to stay up all night drinking beer; not me. I had some time ago accepted the fact I had an allergy to beer. I remember telling someone about my problem, years later, and his response was "I wish I was allergic to beer", inferring he couldn't control himself and often over indulged. I also needed some sleep or my skin would be a mess if not. So some of us slept on the tent floor while the others partied on. I remember waking up soon after daybreak and saw Billy sitting there with a brown, quart bottle in hand.

Our last night in Montreal, we got a little carried away and made a rather large bonfire with boxes from a garbage bin. This prompted an early morning visit from the City Police and an escort to the outskirts of town, to the highway heading back to Ontariariario, laughing all the way.

That fall Larry and I contacted the girls from Buffalo and made plans to visit them on a particular weekday. They said they would take the afternoon off from school and so we picked them up there. We drove off heading to a nearby bowling alley. Things were going along fine; I think I was falling in love, when suddenly a posse showed up led by Betsy's dad who was raving mad. He strongly suggested we head back north across the border ASAP and never come back or else there would be big trouble. We really had no choice but to leave and head back home. Seems we were making a habit of getting run out of town. I can't remember if we ever heard from them pretty Buffalo Girls again or not. I know we never saw them again.

## A Sense of Belonging

I didn't give it a lot of thought at the time but the stronger the bond got between this group of boys the looser my ties became with my parents; quickly the security of home and church was being replaced by a new family. As I drifted further from my roots, I experienced a sense of belonging that I seemed to need so bad. Most of the movers were not close to their fathers, either. Some were alcoholics; others workaholics. A few seemed to balance both acts at the same time leaving little time and energy for family. The companionship of the Movers seemed to meet a need in them also. Almost 50 years later, the core of us still share a special bond; getting together periodically to catch up on what is new and to reminisce the good old days.

Nicknames were created for all the boys. Mine was "Shark", as in "pool shark". The pool hall was the most common meeting place in town and billiards was a big part of our recreation. At this time there was about 10 pool halls within the downtown core, with an average of 10 – 6' x 12' tables each. On Friday evenings it was difficult at times to find an available table. My dedication to the game soon became evident, although a few of the other boys were good players also.

Art's was tagged with the handle St. Paul because of our religious background and the fact that he was the only one of us that wore a beard. Somehow the connection was made to saints of old and beards. Dennis became know as "Hickey" and later as "Hoot". When we called him, especially from a distance we dragged out the word, "Hooooot" in a high falsetto voice. This was another sound often heard ringing through the halls of the school. Greg's handle was "Tommy's Boy", named after his dad. Larry was called "GDR", which stood for his common expression you are "G_d Damn Right".

The 6 of us that went to Expo made up about half of the Movers, although we never created a formal club membership because that wasn't cool. I used to say, "the real Movers know who they are." Among them was Murray Rantanen, known as "Big Mur"; Danny Desjardins, "Daniel" or "The Frenchman"; George Parrett we called "Georgie" or "Pierrite" with a French accent; my other brother Gerry, was just called "Gerr"; Pentti Hanninen, "Hern"; Jamie Flowers, "Frank", after his dad; and Randy Howard, "Herb", after his dad. Others came in later and a few seemed to come and go. Also, a few others had close relationships with one or two of the Movers but really didn't participate in group functions, such as Phil Pagnutti known as "Pagut" or "Pheel", Rick Ahola known as "Rikku", and Dave Ham who went by "Davie" or "Ham'.

Billy became my closest friend and was my best man when I got married, also. He was one of the funniest guys in the school and a popular figure. He was voted "Mr. Lo-Ellen" one year. I have no idea what influence we had on school life at Lo-Ellen but we did make, an otherwise boring experience, a little more fun for quite a few, usually younger, students and ourselves.

In 2012, Helen Grant, one of Mom's caregivers introduced herself to me. She told me she had attended Lo-Ellen in the late 60's. I looked at her intently trying to remember what this, tall woman would have looked like 40+ years earlier; I think I did vaguely remember her but that was the 60's. This is where yearbooks come in handy. Anyway, she said, " I remember you Bast boys, you were notorious". She also remembered the Movers. I am a little reluctant to admit it but I still take comments like that as a compliment. I think from the way she said it, that is the way she meant it. We all want to be remembered for something. This is a key motivation behind going to all the time and effort to write ones life's story; no use pretending otherwise.

## The Music of the 60's

Something about the 60's music spoke to my soul and spirit in a powerful way. It captivated my whole attention; I was able to get lost in it, in a similar manner, as I did in my early years, singing the old hymns. In a peculiar way, the music opened up something deep and wonderful in me. It took me a long time to figure out what this was that invaded my consciousness through the music. I now see that the music was expressing the cry and longing of every human heart, including my own, for reality and love. Through the music I shared a deep awareness of our common plight, the "human condition".

Of course there was a lot of different music in the 60's; some of it I had no interest in and some, like heavy metal was actually annoying to me. Old Blues, Soul, Country and Bluegrass I could enjoy periodically in small doses as I always have Classical music also. There was however, a specific kind of music that grabbed me and overwhelmed my soul. This music is what I call "Folk / Country Rock". A few favorite groups were Buffalo Springfield; The Band; Crosby, Stills and Nash (and Neil Young); The Byrds, Gram Parsons and The Fallen Angels, and The Flying Burrito Brothers. The lyrics of many songs were good; they expressed a craving for truth and for God and confirmed what I was feeling but it was more the music itself that grabbed me so profoundly.

At first I bought the popular records of the "Peace and Love" movement, music my friends listened to and the songs the underground FM radio stations played; bands like The Beatles, The Stones, Bob Dylan, Moody Blues, The Cream, The Doors, Jefferson Airplane, Van Morrison, Jimmy Hendrix and Janis Joplin, Simon and Garfunkel to name a few. I also went to every live concert I could and was exposed to a variety of music. In a period of about two years I collected 300 albums, which were displayed in order of importance. I started at the top left, the way a book reads, with my favorite and preceded to the right and then down.

Growing up in a Mennonite church and a musical family I early developed an ear for music and learned to love it. In my opinion, the human voice is not only the most diverse and interesting but also the most beautiful sounding instrument there is. Although I am not sure if this will be true in heaven. I know we will be singing but we may be accompanied by angels. In any event, I never tire listening to the unique voices of the members of the groups mentioned. The only thing better than a raw, beautiful, single voice is the harmony produced by two or more voices, especially when the sound is gushing from a deep well of sincere emotion.

Rick Danko and Richard Manuel from The Band are probably my favorite duo. They produced more than a harmonious sound. It was a harmony with a vulnerable openness and honesty. They were not afraid to bear their soul and expose their weakness through song and it was powerful. Eric Clapton said this of Richard Manuel, "He had an amazing power to move you with his music, voice and with his presence. Just coming into the room you felt really drawn to the energy that was in this guy. He was very shaky, fragile and scared. In some reverse way it had a lot of power that drew you and attracted you". Robbie Robertson said this about Manuel, "There was a hurt in his voice, a certain element of pain. You didn't know if it was because he was trying to reach for the notes or if he was just a guy with a heart that had been hurt." All I knew was my heart connected with theirs and the release of my pent up emotions was a powerful experience.

Emily Lou Harris and Gram Parsons are a close second when it comes this kind of harmony. After almost 50 years I still get shivers down my backbone, especially if I am alone and the music is cranked up. When I listen to certain songs in particular, I sense the Lord's pleasure in a unique and mighty way. I am sorry if this sounds sacrilegious to you. I realize this is a deeply personal matter and I usually keep it to myself. I also realize, what is good for one person may not be for another. Music is music. It is all comprised of 7 notes. Now that I realize the Lord has been attentively listening to the cry of every human, all through history, and someday will mend every broken heart, and wipe away every tear music has taken on new significance.

My brother Art, who is the real musician in the family, calls much of the music I have just referred to as depressing. I know what he means. I realize many songs by some artists like Gram Parsons, Emmy Lou Harris, Lucinda Williams, Kris Kristofferson, Leonard Cohen are not happy but they are real and they move me. All my life I have been drawn to this kind of music.

More recently I have been captivated with the music of Townes Van Zandt, Tom Waits, Ray Lamontagne, Ron Hynes and Fred Eaglesmith. I admit I do have a limit to how much I can take of the songs of trouble and heartbreak and then I need to sing the songs that announce the solution to the human dilemma. But by recognizing that I am made of the same stuff I can more fully appreciate God's love for them and me. Sharing their pain and sorrow for a few minutes causes my heart to rejoice knowing there will be a glorious deliverance and celebration for all when God makes all wrongs right and wins every heart.

I hope someone; hopefully one of my children or grandchildren will listen to "my" kind of music in a little different light, after reading this. Before I leave this topic, I must add, I find it interesting, much of the music of the old hymns, I grew up singing in church, were played in pubs a long time before organized religion accepted them, changed the words and made them their own. The 7 notes are not evil in themselves. To the pure everything is pure; but not in all is this faith. There will be a higher music in heaven, for sure and it may have more notes, if possible but the Bible is clear, there is even now music around the throne of God and will be in the future. I look at it this way; when we make a joyful sound, especially with thanksgiving, singing and playing music in our hearts, to the Lord, regardless of the order of the notes, it is at these times we are joining the heavenly choir, praising God for His greatness and His goodness.

## Contract Bridge

Larry Rootham lived in Lo-Ellen Park a block from the school. I ended up at Larry's house on several occasions and got to know his parents. Elsie and Harry were a little formal than I was used to. I guessed they had both gone to university. Most important they were friendly and enjoyed playing bridge. I had learned a lot of card games by then and had heard that bridge was the ultimate. As the saying goes, "Bridge to all other card games is what chess is to checkers". I was eager to learn and Mrs. Rootham was glad to teach me and maybe happy to have a fourth. I think she was a pretty smart lady and I liked her a lot. She told Larry and I we would likely see cigarettes out-lawed and marijuana legalized in our lifetime. Not bad for 1968!

She gave me a 200-page book on contract bridge. I think this was the first book, other than kid's books, I read from cover to cover; and was happy to put into practice what I had learned. I taught my brothers the basics and several Movers but I seldom got to play. Most times there was not four of us together who were able and interested. I guess it was too much like work, for most card players to learn. For me it was no work, all just play.

I also visited Dennis' home regularly and spent the odd night there, which was a few houses down from the school, and I was fond of his parents, also. Matti was Finn and Betty was from Newfoundland. Dennis was the youngest of 4 siblings. 3 boys and 1 girl like the Bast's and the Parent's. 8 of the Movers were the oldest child in their family. My brother Art was the first-born of us 4, Billy, also of 4. Danny of 6, Larry and George of 5, Rick of 3, Pentti and Murray both had a younger brother. I am sure this is significant but I will not even begin to surmise how, except to say all of them were strong individuals and leaders in their own way. Most of them later excelled in the careers.

Pentti lived on Esther Road; we always felt welcome at his house and went there to play cards periodically. Pentti's Mom, Sisco, drove the school bus and felt comfortable with kids our age and also spoke her mind. I met Bill's mom, "Big Red", several times. His dad and all the other Movers' parents I only met once or twice. They all seemed to like the boys. I guess they could tell we were from good stock and I don't think any of them suspected that many of us were headed deep into the drug culture; some deeper than others. Most, but not all, would survive and from all outward appearances, unscathed at that. Many other parents and children were not so fortunate.

## Mover Clubhouse

We never had a clubhouse pre se but next to the Norland Pool Hall, 49 Moxam became a favorite hangout and a regular place for the boys to crash. They always knew there was a bed for them at our place. Bill, Dennis and George slept there quite frequently. Our recreation room in the basement became my bedroom. It was quite a large room, bigger than some bachelor apartments. We could smoke and drink there but we did open a window when we smoked grass but I know my Mom could smell it upstairs. She consoled herself knowing we were safe here and put up with a lot more than most other parents would.

Many years later she wrote us a letter apologizing for "loving us too much". She knows she should have disciplined us more but didn't know what to do. My dad was not around much of the time to lend a firm hand. Although he tried to hide it, we knew that he also struggled with his own tobacco addiction, over the years, and probably carried the guilt of his children following in his footsteps. I am in no position to criticize my parents for their method of discipline or lack of. I knew they loved us and did their best to show it. I am ashamed of the way I treated them and responded to their love. When I had children of my own, I did things much different. The Just Judge will someday requite us for all we did good or bad. I do know my parents left a good impression on several of the boys and their girlfriends also.

## Live Music

Next to the pool hall dances were the place to meet in town. This is where the live music and action were, every weekend. As much as I loved music and being with the boys, dances were always a little awkward for me because I didn't dance. Dancing was one of the more serious forbidden sins young Mennonites were warned to avoid. Dancing led to sex, pre-marital sex. For this reason alone, I never learned to dance when I was young and later avoided the dance floor like the plague. Many of the boys started dancing very young. Larry, Pentti and Greg, in particular were and still are very good. All the boys were good dancers, compared to me, because I didn't dance .

Dennis and Billy, in particular attended the local dances in town in their early teen years. At that time they were nicknamed "Memphis" (Billy) and "Mud" (Dennis). Billy used to joke that he often spent the night dancing with a university girl and at the end of the dance she might ask, "Do you want to go somewhere to get something to eat?" Billy had nothing better to do, so he naturally agreed. Often the next question would be "My car or yours?" Billy would reply with a smirk, "Yours I am only 14."

## Grade 11

In grade 11 my complete afternoons were spent in shop classes, mostly in Mechanical Drafting, my major, except for the days I skipped school to play pool. My friend Ken Kaksonen had a car and was a pool shark. Like myself, Ken, by this time had figured out that playing pool would be time better spent than going to class. I did spend enough time doing drafting to learn how to print very neatly. I enjoyed doing drawings, especially of building layouts but when the opportunity arose to play pool, I couldn't resist. Playing with Ken was an experience. He was a natural and easily excelled. I never saw anyone shoot so hard and accurate. The sound of the balls hitting the back of the pocket resounded through the pool hall. When he "was on" or as they say in sports, "in the zone", which was often, he hardly lined up but put his cue down on his hand and fired hard, one ball after the other. He kept a poker face, shot after shot, unless I starting laughing with amazement; he then had to grin.

Even with the added interest in the school curriculum, having fun was still the main priority. In grade 11, our class was blessed with several entertaining and funny guys, John Marshall, Greg McGuigan, Randy Howard and Murray Rantanen, just to name a few. Each class presented a new contest to see who could make the class laugh the loudest. At least this caused us to pay attention and to stay alert most of the time.

I did fall asleep once in a while because of my late nights getting home from the pool hall. A few times the teacher walked quietly over to me where I was sleeping with my head on my arm and banged something as loud as possible a few inches above my ear. I woke up quite startled and a little embarrassed for a moment but enjoyed the attention and being the one who got the whole class laughing. In one Physics class while studying convex and concave mirrors Randy put up his hand. Mr. Darling who was at the front of the class holding a large mirror, said "Yes Randy". Randy replied in his innocent childlike manner "Sir I can see right up your nose". This comment, made the teacher blush as the whole class roared in laughter.

My whole purpose in life was to have fun, although deep down it stemmed from my longing to be accepted and to belong. We had a lot of laughs that year and good enough grades to pass and look forward to spending our last year at good old Lo-Ellen Park, together. If it was not for this aspect of school, I don't think I would have gone back, even though I knew I would probably need a high school diploma some day. I don't know why but I hated the whole education system and by grade 12, I couldn't get into it at all. I only went for the social life. I never did homework or studied or tried to improve.

## Moe Moran

In the fall of 1968, I arrived at school as ready as I could be for grade 12. Dennis' girlfriend Ruth Gudrunas and her best friend Maureen Moran decided to leave Sudbury High School and attend Lo-Ellen. Moe, as she was called, had long black hair with a slight curl, deep dreamy eyes and a sweet, sensitive smile. At school her and Ruth were inseparable, which Dennis seemed to accept or at least tolerate. I quickly took a liking to Moe and she responded favorably. I started hanging out with the 3 of them, which was especially convenient for Dennis.

Ruth's father Victor owned the Prospect Hotel, on Elgin Street, down town. He was a tall, thin, stern man who apparently put down a 26 oz bottle of vodka by noon each day. Ruth's older brother Peter hung around with a group that I understood to be the original "hippies" of Sudbury. Ruth had her own room in the hotel and this is where she lived. It was there her and Maureen introduced me to marijuana, or "pot" as it was called. Of course I had heard about it but I knew little about it. This was a new phenomenon, to me at least.

I was already a smoker so trying pot didn't seem much different. I almost immediately felt more relaxed and confident. When I was high it was easier to have fun. Everything seemed funny and we spent hour after hour cutting up and laughing. In my last year of high school Maureen and I spent a lot of time together, almost everyday. I was 18 years old, almost a man and for the first time in years I felt I belonged. I had good friends, purpose in life and I was in love, nothing else mattered much. Everything and everyone outside of my bubble seemed rather insignificant.

I had purposed in my heart not to have pre-marital sex because this was a serious offence against God. Somehow I understood that this kind of intimacy was so special that it was wise to save yourself for that "one and only". By the end of that school year I was sure Moe was going to be my wife and I slowly started convincing her that having sex wouldn't be so bad. How could it be avoided? We spent so much time together and often alone. She had been brought up Catholic and was also taught it was best to stay a virgin until married. She finally agreed that if we were going to be married, anyway then it was probably okay.

So, for the most part, we had a healthy start in our relationship and did things right. We got to know each other first; we spent a lot of time together and became best friends. Over the first year together we slowly got more intimate before having sex. As much as is possible, for an 18-year old, who was smoking pot everyday, I had a healthy love and respect for her.

We had something beautiful, something neither of us had ever experienced before. Our care for each other seemed to increase when we started making love. We grew closer and it looked like we were meant for each other. Her parents were often gone for the weekend and I would stay at her place. When I got there Friday evenings she would pamper me. Food was served and the bath water was run for me. She often scrubbed my back. I had never experienced this kind of attention and soaked it up. We knew this was not acceptable conduct, according to our parents. Her mom possibly suspected foul play and periodically sent Moe's older brother to check up on her.

One Sunday morning he made an unexpected visit and I almost got caught but quickly hid in the closet. Standing there in the dark, listening to the conversation on the other side of the door reminded me of something that is only supposed to happen in movies. It was comical but I didn't dare laugh out loud until "Big Brother" had made his exit. The excitement of the whole episode was indeed "scary fun". It seemed I needed a steady dose of this kind of stimulation in my life and was continually drawn to situations that offered this adrenalin rush. Besides, these close calls provided another funny story to tell the boys.

## Oh God, Please Don't Damn the Pusher Man

Everything seemed great in our relationship, although our sense of perception was more than a little clouded by our frequent pot smoking, not to mention the so called "mind-expanding" chemicals we took on a regular basis. LSD was definitely mind altering and it gave the delusion of expanding ones awareness and intelligence. On LSD we thought we were smarter; did that mean, therefore we were?

We continued to go to school fairly regularly and somehow I managed to pass my grade 12 exams and received my diploma. The fact my final report card said 49 (7x7) days absent, I find most interesting. Is this one small way God is now confirming to me that He was control all along even when it appeared that I was totally out of control?

As usual, the only subject I achieved a good mark in was math. One test, besides the regular exams, I did very well on. It was an annual provincial government exam. Each spring all grade 12 students in Ontario had to write an English and a Mathematics test set by "The Ontario Institute for Studies in Education". The results were calculated as a percentile. Instead of grading by the percentage of answers correct, marks showed what percentage of the students we scored a higher mark than. In English I got 48%ile and in Math I got 99%ile. This meant I was in the top 1% of all grade 12 students in the province. This was my main academic accomplishment for the 5 years I spent at Lo-Ellen, other than the grade 12 diploma. I still have the little report card; over the years it has periodically provided some bragging rights, for whatever that is worth.

I probably should not have passed grade 12. I may have had a little help, not from my friends, but from the school board.

Major curriculum changes were in the making for the drafting course. In my final year the grade 11 students in the same course began on the new system and our grade 12 class was the last class to use the old curriculum. It would have been complicated to integrate students from the old curriculum, who failed, into the new format, mid-stream. This may have helped me get my diploma. I didn't care; I passed; I was now free.

Smoking pot became more than just a daily habit; often before I got out of bed, in the morning, I lit up. Because of my math skills it didn't take me long to figure out how I could smoke pot free. I got to know many of the downtown hippies and befriended a couple of the main dealers that had connections in Toronto and Montreal. I knew where they lived and I trusted them. The product was readily available and there was a market. I bought an ounce of hash or a ½ pound of weed, sold 60% of it in grams or lids, recouped my money and smoked the rest free.

With little effort I had an ideal set-up. I spent most weekends in town and slept at Moe's place after a day at the Pool Hall, which was a popular hangout for many Lo-Ellen students. I could play pool all day and keep my stash up, under the table. My customers were, for the most part, kids I knew. I didn't even have to go looking for them; they came to my office, as it were. I didn't see myself as "a drug dealer", surely not a pusher. I didn't push anything on anyone. I was just providing a service for my friends and ex-school mates. Without me they would be at the mercy of the street dealers, the real pushers. Some were just plain crooked; some were strung out speed freaks with no scruples. Some of them were under-cover Narcotic's Officers. All of them were strangers to the students of Lo-Ellen Park. I was none of these things.

Tiny, the owner of the Norland and I became good friends. His real name was Nicholas Sedenow. He was anything but tiny. He was huge. He had the biggest head I had ever seen, even bigger than Uncle Dan's. I think he viewed me as a son. He let me run up a small tab, which was rare. He knew I would pay him back. Often after my opponents paid for the table, because they had lost, and then left, Tiny would look at me with a big smile, eyebrows raised and a little twinkle in his eye. He said nothing but put up his right hand, rubbed his thumb and index finger together, asking if I had won any money.

There were several "hippie houses" I was invited to regularly. One was on Drinkwater Street, which is now Paris Street, between Elm Street and Van Horne. Hughie Gillis, Rainer Funk and Victor Djursack or maybe, Peter Gudrunas lived there. Joe Lavigne and Ivan LePage had there own place on Bancroft and there was another in Gatchel on Clemow St. This is where the hippies lived and congregated. There was also a network of speed freaks, dealers and the other undesirables; I trusted them about as far as I could throw them.

Rainer Funk grew up in Waters Township on Black Lake Road, about a mile from us. He managed to work for INCO for a year or so after high school but quit and was now collecting pogey. He was a proud German, neat and tidy, and organized. Every morning he would go to the bank and take out $5.00. That was his spending money for the day. Rainer was not the most handsome guy but he made up for his lack of looks in other ways. He was confident, out-going and put a lot of effort into being funny, which he was good at. He had a rather long, pointed nose and long, straight, blonde hair. Although he was quite skinny it didn't stop him from wearing tight jeans with huge bell-bottoms or very short leather shorts when it was hot.

Rainer and I ate lunch together a few times and he cracked me up with his antics. He would choose the table closest to the prettiest girls and as we ate he would act downright silly. Anyone close could not help but see him and were distracted from whatever else they might want to see or talk about. During the meal he repeatedly winked or made funny faces at the pretty girls. He would put food on his spoon and pretend he was going to shoot it at them. After he finished eating he would put several cigarettes in his mouth and pretend he was going to light them all. Sometimes he stuck them in his ears or nose and didn't care who else was watching as long as he could entertain the girls. He had practiced tricks with a lit cigarette for hours. He could lay one on his open hand with the lit end just elevated enough not to burn his palm and the filter sticking out past the end of his fingers. He would then hit his wrist with his other hand and flick the cigarette through the air; it would softly land between his lips and he then nonchalantly took a drag, blew several perfect smoke rings and then grinned from ear to ear. Some folks wanted to see it done again; Rainer gladly obliged.

Milt Thibeault and his "speed freak" brother had their own place with a couple other guys. I once noticed his brother, in his room, laying face down, flaked out on his mattress on the floor. Apparently, he had just completed a several day run of speed and was now catching up on sleep. I happened to come back the next night and walking by his open door noticed he was still there in exactly the same spot and position as if he had not moved in the last 24 hours.

I felt sorry for those addicted to speed; it was like they had a death wish on their life. I tried to reason with Mike Peters one night at a party about him slowly killing himself with the needle. He seldom ate properly, was skinny and looked terrible. His answer to me was shocking. He admitted speed would likely kill him at a young age but without it he said he had no life. He said, "Speed is all I have; this is what I live for!" This only reinforced my determination to never stick a needle in my arm.

Hughie Gillis and Joe Lavigne were two of the main street dealers in the beginning and both were interesting characters. Billy and I spent a lot of time with Joe and Ivan LePage his partner and often frequented their apartment. This was where we partied and this is where I got my only tattoos. Joe put a small peace sign on my right hand with a needle wrapped with thread. I thought two would look better than one and did the left hand myself. I was in no shape to do any kind of intricate detail and didn't realize the mess I made until the next morning. Most people don't notice them and I forget about them for months at a time. When someone does mention them, I tell them, "They are a reminder of my miss-spent youth".

When a shipment of weed came in Joe indulged us. He would glue many cigarette papers together and then roll a foot-long refer, an inch thick; we smoked ourselves silly. For whatever reason, unlike drinking, I could smoke with the best. Joe introduced me to a couple members of Sudbury's notorious bike gang "The Plague", Billy the Biker and Rags. Rags seemed like a decent guy not unlike some of the other bikers, once I got to know them. He took me for a ride on his chopper, which was cool. I met him at their clubhouse one day and was outside talking to him when, fellow biker Soper, happened by and growled what's he doing here. Rags replied, "He's okay". I quickly blurted out, "Yea I'm okay Soper". I thought he would be impressed that I knew his name. He was not, and replied, "Don't get smart kid," Rags said, "Don't worry about him", and so I didn't. One night Billy Parent and I invited Billy and Rags to a drive-in movie. We smoked so much they needed our help to get out of the back seat of my car when we dropped them off.

On another occasion Joe had arranged a big party which, had rumors of becoming a smoking contest between the hippies and the bikers; cool! There were wall-to-wall people sitting around the large, almost bare living room smoking and listening to music. Joe was a good host. He had a big stereo and many of the latest records. As the night wore on, bodies were strewn all over the floor. We had to literally step over people to get to the washroom or kitchen for more food. In the wee hours of the morning sometime, there was only a few of us hippies still conscious and quite amused at the sight in front of us. I guess we won; at least that is my story and I am sticking to it. You will be hard pressed to find anyone who disagrees.

In the early 70's my dad owned a produce store called Mel's Green Acers" on Lorne Street. When he received a large shipment, he asked me if I would be a night watchman to guard the pallets of fruit and vegetables in the parking lot. One night Billy and Rags showed up and we had a few tokes and sampled some of the fresh fruit. Rags pointed out a large strawberry to Billy that was covered in white fuzzy mould and said, "Yummy". Without hesitating Billy put the whole thing into his mouth and he chewed up and swallowed it. Rags said he could anything. Billy loved the attention. Story has it he had been offered a pad from a girl on her period and he ate that also.

One day I joined friends at the Coulson. At the table there was a muscular ironworker who had eaten 6 draft glasses in his day. I suppose it started one night, after many rounds of draft; he thought he would show off by taking a bite out of his glass. He chewed it up real fine and washed it down. Seeing it went okay he continued to eat the whole glass. The bottom is very thick on these glasses and it takes strong teeth and patience but he was up for the task. After the first time he got a reputation and was talked into it several times after that. It is amazing what people can do if they only set their mind to it, especially when they are drunk. Apparently, in the Guinness World Book of Records there is a record of someone who ate a bicycle.

One day, Joe got a brainwave. He suggested 6 of us should join forces; Billy and Rags, Joe and Ivan, Billy Parent and I. We made some big plans and called it "Operation Takeover". That was joke but it sounded impressive. We rented a car and Rags and I drove to Montreal to talk to a Mafia contact he had. Nothing ever became of it that I can remember, although that was the 60's. There is a saying "If you remember the 60's you weren't there". Not sure what that says about this chapter.

## ***L*** **ucy in the** ***S*** **ky with** ***D*** **iamonds**

Although I did LSD quite a few times and other chemicals, I never sold anything except "smoke" either pot or hash. I tried snorting and dropping heroin, mescaline and MDA. I never yielded to the temptation to stick a needle in my arm. I knew I had to draw the line somewhere. Friends like Mike Peters were a constant reminder to me of where that line was.

LSD, the ultimate mind drug, was in a class of its own. Unlike most drugs, it was not addicting like speed and others that gave your body an euphoric feeling. I knew a few guys who appeared to be addicted to LSD, maybe not in the same way but they couldn't seem to get enough of it. I'm sure Dave Ham took LSD hundreds of times. I don't think anyone, including Dave himself knows how many. We spent a lot of time tripping together in his little 2-seater, MGA. The car was built more for Europe than Northern Ontario but fun in the summer. On a cold winter day the back axel used to freeze and seize up. We had to push it until the wheels would quit sliding and actually turn. Once we got going he was a wild and crazy driver, kind of like brother Art. One night we were driving along, south on Hwy 69, both of us better equipped for space travel, when Dave yelled out, "You see that?" I answered, "No man I didn't see anything". He said someone just ran across the road in front of us and we drove right through him. I said I didn't feel anything either. I think we can just blame that one on the LSD.

I first tried LSD on a road trip to Wasaga Beach. Art was driving his big 65 Ford with a few of the Movers along. I ended up laying on the back window ledge of the car looking up at the stars. As the car weaved back and forth along the winding road I was amazed at the sensation. I would have been terrified if Art hadn't been driving and even at that, I checked with him a couple times to make sure everything was "normal". He assured me it was, although it didn't seem like it to me. I could see the car stretch and bend around the corners like they did in the cartoons. When we got to the beach area they had these six-foot high concave and convex mirrors that distorted your shape and size. This spectacle was almost too much for me.

On a cloudless summer night I enjoyed laying on my back on the grass and watching the stars dance, weaving in and out of each other in a beautiful pattern. All the trips were not good though. I did end up in public on a few occasions while on acid and it was scary. Everything was so exaggerated, the good the bad and the ugly; people's voices; their facial expressions and every move. Beauty became much more beautiful and evil became grotesque. I seldom enjoyed the first hour or so on an LSD trip. I usually got paranoid and needed calm and quiet until I leveled out and then the whole night could be spent grooving on music and enjoying friendships or meaningful conversation. I soon learned it was best to take acid only when planned ahead, in a quiet secluded place and with close friends.

On one of these particular nights, Billy and I and a few others took an acid trip together. An hour or so after dropping; I had forgotten about Billy and was just beginning to enjoy myself when I thought I could hear Billy's voice above the music. It was more like a moaning sound but I could distinctly hear, "Donnie, Donnie". I got up, looked around and found him lying on the floor behind the couch by himself. He was obviously having a bad trip and softly crying out for his buddy. I sat with him for a long time and held his hand assuring him that everything was cool. He eventually mellowed and enjoyed the rest of the night. It was at times like this a bond was formed that still exists today.

At another party, at Ruth's dad's cottage, in the French River area, I ended up on the cottage porch roof stoned on acid. It was the middle of the night and I was there alone. I didn't know where Moe or anyone else was. For that matter, they didn't know where I was either or they would have checked me out. Anyway, I stood there for a long time mesmerized by the light of the moon on the lake. I could recall swimming there earlier that day and had a rough idea of the lay of the land, but now it was all jaded. I loved diving from heights and was being so strongly drawn to the air and the water below. Even though I could recall there was at least 50 feet of rock between the lake and camp, it now looked so different. As I stood there I argued with myself about what to do. Finally, I submitted to the right voice and came down. The Lord spared me the disastrous outcome of what could have been if I would have given in to my strong urge to dive and fly.

## The Quarry

About a mile from my parent's house in Lively was the formidable quarry. It was an ominous place but so intriguing, perfect for my kind of scary fun. My dad often took visitors from the south there and we got to tag along. This was a deep, hard rock, mining wonder. It was a long narrow hole, full of water, hundreds of feet deep with straight rock cut walls on each side. Divers had gone down at least once and I was told they never found bottom. The rock wall, at the west end, where the path from Santala Road led was actually only a couple feet high. From there two rock walls gradually inclined about 100' apart. Both sides were straight and steep and peaked at about 70' above the water and narrowed to about 15 feet apart in some places. There were "keep out" signs but no fence. This was a sight seeing wonder and a favorite swimming hole for the brave and the reckless.

We took the Movers there on many hot summer afternoons to just hangout, smoke a few joints and learn to fly. The water was freezing. The closest and best spot to set up for a picnic and campfire was about 12 feet above the water on the south side. Here there was a large flat level rock. From there you could make your way up the path to any height you dared. Most guys jumped feet first but I always dove. My favorite rock for diving was about 30 feet above the water. Even those who jumped from that height had to make sure they pointed their toes down so not to land with flat feet. If one did the slap of the water left your feet red and stinging, which was mild compared to the pain if you happened to turn your head down, to take a peak, at the last second before contact.

Many times I made my way to my perch and stood there looking down, with toes curled over the edge, for what seemed a long time, as if having a staring contest with the black water below. I breathed deep for awhile to calm myself; finally, ever so slowly, I began to lean forward to the point of no return. Falling head first down I opened my arms wide like wings and for a few exciting seconds, I was flying. Just before touching the water I brought my hands together, locked thumbs and held on tight. The impact tore my hands apart and threw my arms back up over my head violently; then it was down, down, down into the dark, cold water. I could barely hold my breath long enough to turn around kicking and paddling my way up to the surface for air and possibly an applause.

I heard stories of guys diving from much higher heights and would have loved to see them but this was as high as I dared to usually go. On 3 brave occasions I ventured higher. One day I decided to go up the rock cut on the other side to a perch about 45′ high, just to have, “a little look see”. Once up there, I went to the edge and stood for a long time, and found my body slowly leaning until it was too late to turn back. I did it 2 more times and realized it was too dangerous. Also from that height it hurt too much. There was such a fine line between a perfect dive and getting seriously injured. I reminded myself that I was a 130-pound weakling not a strong athlete in top shape.

As it was, an afternoon, at the quarry was often followed by a night of interrupted sleep. Nightmares of hitting a “dead head” and busting my skull open awoke me in a sweat. Once awake lying there, I reasoned, “That is probably what I deserve” and often fell asleep pleading with God to be merciful to me a sinner. A dead head is a “waterlog” piece of wood that floats a few feet below the surface undetected from above. Although we discovered the odd one swimming we seldom checked before jumping or diving. No one ever died there, as far as I know, but there were several close calls of people almost falling in. A few years ago, INCO finally blasted the sides in and filled the mammoth hole. I have not been back since to see what it looks like; probably like a pile of rocks, not near as impressive as it did then. Some day I will make the trek to check it out.

Looking back I can see how quickly my perception in most areas of life was so deranged. In just a few short years I had slipped constantly further away from the reality I once knew. I know the Movers were a big influence but I can't blame them. I was as much an instigator as any of them. We were tripping together just holding on and trying to enjoy the ride. An unseen force was carrying us along, doing what we did. Was it supposed to all make sense? I remember one day one of the boys hung a moon, out the car window, going through town just for a laugh. One night we stole the flag off the courthouse pole.

We knew a few guys from the street who conveniently worked for Sudbury's Parks and Recreation; one of their duties was taking care of the plants around town. They often bragged about how they got paid to grow their own marijuana plants in the city greenhouse. We believed them and late one night decided to check it out for ourselves. I was the driver of the getaway car and therefore exempted from actually breaking into and stealing city property. For this I was thankful. Sure enough they had some big healthy plants growing in big pots. I got to keep one and transplanted it in my parent's back yard. In the fall I stripped the leaves and dried them in the oven. This was the only time I knew for sure that I was smoking clean, uncut, untainted, home grown weed.

## Lotus Land

As the cold winter of 1969 set in downtown activities for hippies almost came to halt. I hated the cold and jumped at the invitation to go to the "West Coast" with Dave Ham. Two guys originally from Sudbury, John and Evan, had room for us in their apartment. At the last minute we invited Pentti. He said, "Sure", packed a bag and on December 29th 1969 we boarded the train for the coast, Lotus Land. A brave new world of music, drugs and warm weather was only 3 nights, 2 days away.

Our "Student Standby" train fare was $33.00 each. I enjoyed the trip immensely. What a great way to travel and see our vast country. We played cards and spent hours in the dome car observing the ever changing landscape. Periodically we went outside between the cars to have a toke. Smoking cigarettes in the train and anywhere was still allowed in those days. One of the highlights of my train ride to freedom was going through the Rockies. Leaning on the railing with the wind blowing through my long hair, staring at the little, blue, winding ribbon of water hundreds of feet below is a site I will never forget. There was a musician riding in the same car that had his guitar and sang a bit. One night the train lost its electric power and the lights were out for a couple hours. We sat in the dark as our musician serenaded us. It was special.

When we arrived in Vancouver it was warm. I couldn't believe it; this was the beginning of January, in Canada. A single bed was set up for me in the living room under the window overlooking Broadway Street. They were very organized and it was good experience for me to be living on my own. Everyone was assigned duties. We chipped in grocery money and took turns cooking one good meal each day, usually supper. I loved Vancouver and regularly went to Rock concerts. We took in gigs by many big bands like Iron Butterfly, Sly and the Family Stone, Paul Butterfield Blues Band and many excellent local bands. We played soccer in the park and went to a few private parties. I missed Moe and never considered cheating on her. It snowed once that winter enough to cover the ground but it was 57 degrees Fahrenheit the next day, amazing.

The first day in Van we met with our friend Rainer Funk, who was living here. Dave had something to do so Rainer invited me to tag along with him for the day. Seeing it was raining as it often does in the winter the first thing we had to do was to get me my own umbrella. Rainer often carried his and used it as a walking stick when it wasn't needed. We walked into a store he was familiar with and he led me directly to a bin of umbrellas. We quickly looked at a few; he took one out and said "you like this one?" I said "sure." He said "good, let's go" and started walking towards the cash, so I thought, but went straight out the door instead. I followed him, using my new umbrella as a cane, also and headed down the street. He shot me a quick smile, said nothing, and never looked back. I was a surprised at his smooth and bold tactics but was more than a little troubled by what I had just done. Being a drug addict was one thing; I always took pride in the fact that I was honest. I had never stole anything like that before and my conscience was pricked but I did nothing about it; I just kept walking and that bothered me.

The next thing on the agenda was to get registered for welfare. Rainer took me to the office told me what to say and also to collect my $15.00 food vouchers to keep me until my first $90.00 monthly cheque came in. To get an idea how much money this was; gas was under 45 cents a gallon or 10 cents a liter compared to 2014 where it hovered around $1.40 a liter. BC had the best Social Assistance Program in the country and the highest number of unemployed, many from Ontario and many hippies, apparently all of us looking for work. Pentti was not really into the hippie scene; he didn't smoke pot or even cigarettes, for that matter, he never did. He soon got restless and hit the road. He hitchhiked south to California and then over to Florida and back home. In the fall he registered at Selkirk College in Castlegar BC and became a commercial pilot. He retired a few years ago after flying for almost 30 years with Canadian Airlines, which later became a part of Air Canada.

Maureen was back at Lo-Ellen, in grade 12. We wrote a few letters back and forth and she called me often on the phone. She told me a few friends were asking for me to send home a care package of good stuff; so I did and she passed it on to Billy, who knew what to do with it. Somehow her mom got wind of it and informed the local narci-dicks (RCMP). By the time they did some checking the delivery was made safely, the goods sold and the money made. I spent the rest of the winter there, although compared to Northern Ontario it is not really winter at all. I was determined to move here as soon as I could. I wanted to spend the rest of my life, on the west coast in beautiful Lotus Land.

The love for my girl and the lure of Northern Ontario spring called me home. Walking down Durham St, a few days after I arrived back in Sudbury, , an unmarked police car slowly drove beside me for a long distance, checking me out. Not sure if they knew who I was before this but I was sure they did now. From now on I would have to be much more careful, not only with my dealings with Maureen's mother but also on the street.

Ida Moran now knew what kind of a young man her daughter had been dating for 1½ years and was determined to get me out of her life. She confronted me at her earliest opportunity about dragging her daughter into the drug world. I was caught off guard and my self-righteous pride quickly came to my rescue. Instead of apologizing for my influence on her daughter, I assured her it was Maureen who had introduced me to drugs not the other way around. Not sure how I thought this information would help the situation. It was a dumb thing to say, although, it was true.

Mrs. Moran was not impressed and things quickly turned ugly from there. She started yelling and calling me a dirty drug dealer with few choice adjectives for emphasis. Swearing was one thing I was good at and I responded accordingly. Actually this is one of the few times in life I completely lost it, said things I never should have, and deeply regretted it later. Well, this sealed my fate and I had to leave immediately and was ordered never to return. Several years later I wrote Mrs. Moran an apology letter. She never felt the need to reply.

Although, Maureen and I were not deterred; it did complicate our life together. Looking back I realize this was probably the beginning of the end of our relationship. I decided to get a job and at least appear to straighten out. Hopefully, this would reduce the heat coming from the RCMP and Ida Moran. During my first job interview I was asked, "Why should I hire you?" I told him that I realized with long hair it will be difficult to find another job so I would work hard and do my best for him. I thought that was kind of clever, apparently he didn't!

Shortly after I got hired on at Crane Supply driving a 5-ton truck, delivering pipe and plumbing fittings. It was hard adjusting to getting up early but I loved bombing around town in the big rig with a stick shift on the floor. Plus I was proud to have an real job, earning honest money for a change. I don't think Mrs. Moran or the RCMP were overly impressed but I felt a little better about my situation, not a whole lot but a little better.

## Street Fights

After I witnessed a few fights, I tried to avoid them because I didn't like them. One Sunday night I stumbled upon an ugly one at the Caruso Club's weekly dance. Although I didn't dance, I loved the live music. When the band took a break we went outside to smoke a joint. We heard shouting in the distance and noticed a gathering of people across the parking lot. We walked over to check it out. A tall slim guy around 25 years old, (the name Wayne Hamilton comes to mind), was yelling at a young kid, probably 18 years old, to leave him alone. The kid, who was obviously stoned, had a beef with Wayne and was challenging him to fight. Wayne said he didn't want to but couldn't just walk away with his peers watching, besides he was an experienced fighter. A few quick punches and the kid went down, which wouldn't have been too bad but Wayne lost his temper and starting kicking him in the stomach and then in the face yelling at him, "I told you to get lost!" like it was all his fault. No one lifted a finger or said anything. I guess they figured the kid asked for it and got his fill. That is the way it was. This kind of scene made me feel ill; I couldn't understand how insanely furious someone could get to want to inflict such pain. I guess I had a lot of love growing up and was sheltered from such anger. What did this have to do with grooving on music or the hippie movement of peace and love?

Another time a similar situation almost erupted but I stepped in and narrowly stopped it. Joe and I were enjoying a quiet game of pool one evening when a tall, young Indian boy staggered into the pool hall and over to our table. He was looking for a cigarette and possibly some company. He started chatting with us while standing a little too close to the table. There is an unwritten rule when it comes to a serious game of pool; "Stay back at least 4' from the table". Joe was a little abrupt with him and told him to get lost. The kid was surprised and just smiled; he was in a happy mood. He jokingly put up his fists and slurred out, "You wana fight?" and barely touched Joe's chest.

Before I knew what happened Joe's 220-pound frame tightened like violin string and then exploded. He landed 3 hard punches on his chest knocking the kid back, hard against the wall. Without thinking I quickly stepped in front of Joe and put my hands on his fists, reassuring him the kid was drunk and meant no harm. Joe froze for a minute, staring into my eyes and then looked back at the kid; he took a deep breath and relaxed. I gave the kid a smoke and he left and we went back to our game.

After Joe calmed down he looked at me and said, "Don't ever do that again". He went on to say he could not be responsible for what might happen if I did. Joe was usually a jolly guy who was fun to be with. I knew he had been in street fights when he was younger but I had not witnessed his mean streak surface before, not like that, and not again.

## The Bikers

I had limited first hand experience with bikers; mainly the short time I spent with Billy and Rags; I knew well enough not to mess with them. I heard stories about them and knew the names of the ones who hung around downtown. One day Ivan Lepage told one of them about a guy who had "ripped him off" in a small drug deal. He was just informing him, as far as I know, not asking for any favors. The bikers who were gaining interest in the downtown drug business maybe thought guys like Joe and Ivan could be of some assistance. For whatever reason, late one quiet evening, several bikers paid a visit to this particular persons house, who happened to be hosting a few friends. At the sound of the choppers rolling into the yard a few scurried upstairs before the door was broken down. The bikers found their man and began to beat him mercilessly as his friends jumped out of the upstairs window and ran for their lives.

Most people thought the bikers were plain mean and I guess some of them were. The ones I got to know personally were a little wild but had no bigger chip on their shoulder than many others I knew. Others thought they were crazy. Everyone knew they stuck together like family. This oneness and the perception of their crazy meanness was the secret to their strength. They didn't pretend to be the smartest or the strongest individuals and probably many of them would not have fared well, one on one, against a seasoned street fighter, but that didn't matter; they seldom fought alone. I found out years later that Marja, who would later become my wife, was a friend of "Cat" the president of the Plague, around this time. She told me he was a very quiet and timid guy. I think his real name was Sylvester, which explains his handle, "Cat". He had a brother in the club also, Theodore, who went by Teddy. One day riding the city bus together with him, a tough guy started heckling Cat and making fun of him, Marja said he did nothing, said nothing. He later shared with her how afraid he was. She also said he had a reoccurring dream of dying young, which did come to pass.

I witnessed one fair fight, if you could call it that, involving a biker. Rags approached me in the pool hall one night; he needed a ride, right now, in a car, to the clubhouse and back down town. He knew I was driving my dad's car. When we got to the clubhouse I realized why they didn't take their bikes; they quickly grabbed a few chains and pieces of pipe and threw them on the floor of the back seat and ordered me back downtown. A fight had just been arranged between Jim Risling and "The Judge". Jim was a new member of the club, probably striking. He was maybe only 20, but he was big and strong with a reputation that preceded him. The Judge was a black man in his 30's, old compared to the rest of us; a little shorter than Jim but much heavier and with a long resume of fighting experience.

The growing drug market was creating a territorial struggle. I remember when I began letting my hair grow long, it was rare to see another "longhair" on the street, and especially one I didn't know. Although, not all druggies were longhairs, things had changed, the demand had increased substantially, in the last few years. The Jamaican's had come to Sudbury because Inco was hiring but they had connections back home and wanted a piece of the action.

This showdown was going to settle something; I think the bikers wanted to send the message to "Blacks" they were infringing on their territory and as bikers they had the means and the will to enforce it. I just wanted to do my own thing and so far had gotten along with everyone. I didn't choose to be on one side or the other but just got caught in the middle this lovely summer evening. I had nothing against Black's; I had two good friends, that were black, Willie Byers and Peter Jackson. Anyway, the fight seemed to start fair enough; then the pipes and chains came out and more people got involved from both sides. The police quickly arrived and broke it up before any real damage was done. I guess a statement was made. I don't know if this event changed anything.

Also, around this time, the Plague, looking for more respect, decided to become a chapter of "The Choice", "Satan's Choice". As a club, they would have a probation period to determine if they were worthy to wear the colors of this notorious bike gang. This "Striking" process is not unlike the period all individual members went through to join an outlaw motorcycle club and to then be honored to wear the clubs colors. I had no idea what was required to be accepted. I heard to join the Choice one was required to take the life of an opposing gang member; that may be completely unfounded. I am sure there were specific, heroic activities to be performed, most likely, illegal.

From what I could see and what I heard on the street they now became wilder than ever. For weeks The Choice colors could be seen on the backs of bikers rumbling through town on their hogs. I didn't know if they were here to motivate the Plague members or just to monitor how they were doing or both. As a club The Plague never were accepted, partially because many members ended up in jail, during the striking period. I heard a body washed up on the shore of Lake Ramsey; guess who was suspected? As far as I know charges were never laid.

I never really thought about my brief association with the bikers until one day in the pool hall. I had just beaten Barry Palomaki, a big Finn, in a game of pool. It must have been for a bit of money or carried some importance and therefore attracted a small audience, which normally brought out my best game. The pressure helped me concentrate in a way I couldn't normally.

Barry was a cousin to the Jarvi's in Waters. I had known him for some time and often played pool with him. After the game, he came up to me from behind, stooped down and wrapped his big arms around me and squeezed hard but careful not to squeeze too hard and hurt me; just hard enough to make the point that he could hurt me whenever he wanted. He then spoke softly into my ear, "You have your buddies the bikers to protect you, aye?" I never thought of my relationship with the bikers in that respect but found it interesting.

There were a few others I knew, beside the bikers, who wanted a bigger piece of the pie. Actually, around this time my brother Art quit his job at Inco and had some cash saved and decided to get involved. He hooked up with a couple other guys; Gary Baker for one, who had contacts in Toronto and he and Art put together a couple deals. This news must have traveled quickly to the bikers and word was they wanted to nip this new source in the bud. When Art heard he was on their hit list he didn't appear to be overly concerned but Art was hard to read. In any event he wasn't going to immediately give in to their pressure. He would continue on as if normal and see what happened, although he did start sleeping with a loaded shotgun at the side of his bed. This was not normal behavior for Art. He was usually more rational than I was and has therefore been able to avoid problems in life that I didn't. Art also had a stubborn streak and maybe he just decided he wasn't going to be pushed around.

## The Bank Job

Hughie Gillis, being one of the main street  dealers had dealings with the bikers, also. Apparently he owed them money. I don't know if he had a legitimate debt to certain Plague members but the story was they wanted 5 or 6 grand by a certain date or else. In 1970 this was a large sum of cash for a young hippie boy, dealer or not. I heard about his on going problems with them and his inability to keep them happy. Dennis Hauta had become one of Hughie's best friends but was saying very little. In fact I heard nothing about their plan about to go down, a job that would rectify the problem before the fast approaching deadline. I had heard about one failed heist that Hughie almost got away with. Apparently he had a local business' safe almost loaded into the van when they were spotted. Anyway, Hughie's life was in jeopardy; and so another plan was in place.

I had been at the "Hippie House" where Hughie lived the night before the deal went down and still heard nothing and didn't clue in. The next morning, news was quickly circulating that the TD Bank at the 4 corners had been robbed. Two masked men went into the bank and got away with between $7,000 - $8,000. A little inside inquiry provided all the details. Our fellow Mover Dennis and Hughie were the two who went into the bank with nylon stockings over their heads carrying sawed off shotguns. Two friends, Ivan and Danny guarded outside to warn them of any danger. They ran across Paris St. to nearby Nepawin Lake and made the getaway in a waiting boat. Some money was stashed; the bulk went to pay the debt to save Hughies' neck.

Not unlike many of us, Dennis never was good at holding on to money. Now that he a pocket full, well a bag full, combined with the urgent need to destroy the evidence, he was anxious to spend it fast and not in Sudbury. "The Express Concert" was scheduled for the upcoming weekend in Toronto and Art was driving down with his big Ford. So Dennis, Ruth, Moe and I climbed in. Dennis needed to make a quick stop on our way out of town, near Lo-Ellen Park. He got out of the car, ran into the bush and returned in a few minutes carrying a brown paper bag and said, "Let's get out of here". As we drove away he opened the bag, displayed $2,000 cash and said, "The weekend is on me!" We drove to Toronto and checked into a fancy hotel. For a couple days he wined and dined us, blowing his money on anything his heart desired. A good time was had by all but this is not the end of the story; all was not well back home in Sudbury.

One of the guns for the robbery had been borrowed by Johnny Ovis, a friend of Dennis, from Lo-Ellen Park. It had been thrown in the lake, during the getaway and found by the RCMP. No one noticed the word "Ovis" carved into the barrel in fine print. John was the first to be picked up and hauled in for questioning. The police had quickly put 2 + 2 together and were quite sure they had their 4 men. The RCMP had known Hughie for a long time and watched him closely. Plus they had informants; knowing what was going on was the easy part. The hard part was proving it or catching the criminals red handed. If John would have known Hughie the way I got to know him, he would have known Hughie would never talk. According to Hughie the police had no evidence other than the gun. If everyone would have stayed quiet, nothing could have been proved in court.

It didn't take long and all involved were charged with the crime. Hughie and Dennis were booked into the Sudbury jail. Hughie was sent from there to Penatanguishene for assessment and Dennis got out on bail. It would be months before Dennis' trial started and almost a year before he was sentenced. He got 3 years and served the minimum, "2 years less a day", from the summer of 71 to the summer of 73. In January 1971, while still out on bail Dennis and Ruth were married.

Many years after Hughie served his 6-year sentence and moved to Vancouver he called my home on a regular basis, usually around midnight BC time, 3:00 am our time. He never knew what time it was; in his mind it wasn't late, especially for an alcoholic on a binge. 20+ years after the matter, he was still obsessed with why he had to serve hard time, which changed his life dramatically. He repeated over and over again that they would never have been sentenced if no one would have talked. He provided few details and I asked few questions but he openly expressed his anger towards John and Dennis. I never asked Dennis about it. I figured if he felt the need to talk about it he would. I can guess how it most likely went down.

Once the police were quite sure of the key guys involved they brought John in; told him Hughie had confessed and named him and the others. They then offered John a deal; sign a statement confirming how the job went down and we will get you off with only probation and no jail time. The police then showed Dennis John's confession naming him and the others. They offered Dennis a relatively light sentence to sign a similar statement. Once that was done they had the main man they were after.

When I first met Marja I had no idea her and Hughie had been good friends. They never dated but Hughie was like a little brother to her. She was one of the few friends that visited Hughie at the Correctional Center, in Penetanguishene a maximum-security facility for the so-called "criminally insane".

Actually, Marja was involved in one of Hughie's previous busts. He sent a care package to her from out west, because the RCMP were closely watching him. As soon as Marja got home late that night they were at the door with a search warrant and found the package, which hadn't been opened. She spent the night in jail and was charged with possession of marijuana with the intent to traffic. Her dad bailed her out in the morning. In court

Hughie took what in US is called, the "Fifth Amendment". I think in Canada its called, "Protection Against Self-incrimination". This allowed him to give evidence, which couldn't be used against him. Even though he admitted it was his package and he had mailed it to her, he got off and Marja was charged only with possession of an illegal substance. She was put on probation and paid a fine. She has lived with a criminal record since.

Whenever the phone woke me in the middle of the night I knew who it was. Hughie always asked for Marja, and the first few times she took his call but soon started refusing because it was so hard for her to get back to sleep again. I felt sorry for him and listened to his rambling stories, as best I could, half asleep. He had been married and his ex-wife and two sons lived nearby. He had the boys over frequently. He told me he was manic-depressive, bipolar. When he drank too much he didn't take his medication and it was at these times he called. He had remarkable tales to tell; much of which I believed.

I sent him money a few times, to bale him out of his current dilemma, which he was always vague about. I didn't know what else to do for him, no one did. In 2000 I organized a Mover Reunion at Pentti's farm in Chilliwack, BC. Several of the boys lived there and my longing for the coast had never left. I told Hughie about it and he let Jacques and Mimi Gingrass know, who were from Sudbury and close to Hughie. All three of them showed up, along with Hughie's best friend, a large Husky.

They brought tents and set them up in Pentti's yard; Hughie and his dog at the edge of the hazelnut orchard. Hughie seemed lost, in his own world. He sat on the grass most of time mumbling to himself or the dog. I never saw him again and he died a few years later. The autopsy report said the cause of death was a blow to the head. The police told Jacques that it was most likely a homicide but the chances of proving it were almost nil. To them Hughie was just another one of BC's many statistics and one less problem for the police to worry about.

This is only one of the sad stories from those days; there are many. Some followed the same path as Hughie as drug addicts or alcoholics and died young. About half of the guys I knew from downtown, who moved to the coast, in the late 60's, are dead. Besides Hughie, Dennis Botson, Paul Hyne, Ron Belrose are a few I recall. In 2006, while spending the winter in B.C. I tried to find Rainer, John Bell and others. In the beginning of April, I finally contacted Nick Menican, who was also from Sudbury. I had fond memories of Nick and he was happy to hear from me. We agreed to get together in the fall. I was scheduled to leave in a few days and didn't want to take the time to rush a visit before I headed back east for the summer. I wanted to spend at least one whole day with him but couldn't fit it in now. Two weeks later I got an email from Nick's wife informing me that he died. I was looking forward to seeing him and would have gone to the funeral if I had been in BC. When I did go back I checked phone directories, asked people and kept my eyes open for John and Rainer but never did find them.

As bad as the news was about Dennis and Hughie robbing the bank, I was also fighting my own demons. So far I had escaped the pitfalls they fell into but I couldn't keep going down the road I was on. Something or I should say, some One was shaking my life to the core and I knew Who it was. I also knew that Maureen would never understand the "call of God" on my life I had been running from, for so long, and would soon have to answer. I never considered this a factor in our break-up. I didn't really expect any girl to be able to understand what was going on inside of me. I didn't even know how to begin to talk about it. I was still trying hard not to think about it myself. For reasons unknown, my love for her turned to obligation and drudgery.

Early in June Maureen was informed she had to write her grade 12 final exams, even though she had high enough marks to be "recommended" and exempt from writing. She had missed too many days of school, often with me, and they were concerned she was not prepared for grade 13 or college. She arranged for a tutor; a fellow student, Chris Priest, came to her house and she started cramming for exams. Her mom liked Chris and told her. Neither Maureen nor her mother wanted her to repeat grade 12; this is one project they saw eye-to-eye on. For several weeks I saw little of Maureen, which made it easier for us to start separating emotionally. She wrote her exams and passed.

## Other Girls

By late summer 1970, I realized Moe and I were not going to get back together. I was the one that had been drifting away from her all along and I didn't know why. This is one area I have a big blank. To this day I can't recall a fight with Moe, any arguments or disagreements but something happened I had little control over. Dr. Laura says it takes at least 1½ years in a relationship, to really get to know someone. Maybe our honeymoon period lasted a bit longer. Possibly if we had been married we would have worked things out. But we were not married and after being with my first love for 2 years, it was over, even though there was no other girl in the picture.

I did start noticing other girls now that I was a single man again. Chris Moore was the first one I had a crush on. She owned a red TR6 sports car and I often saw her bombing around the Durham - Elgin St. loop. She was a cute little thing with a twiggy haircut. Her father owned Minute Car Wash where I worked for a short time. He probably bought her the car as a reward for getting accepted into university. Although, she didn't appear to be romantically interested in me, I let her know I liked her a lot. She was polite enough and I talked her into letting me drive her to Chicago when she started school in September. Actually I talked to Murray Rantanen about taking a road trip and he agreed. It seems unlikely, but I can only recall the 3 of us making the trip with Murray's orange mustang, *"Moosetange"* (rhyming with the French pronunciation of orange), as we called it.

The only thing I remember of the trip is we got rear-ended by a black lady in a big car in downtown Chicago. To make things worse, even though she was at fault, for running into us, she threatened to sue Murray for stopping too fast. I don't think anything became of it and there was minimal damage to the mustang. Murray never heard from the lady again and I never heard much about Chris after that, either. I know she married Larry Frappier and they moved to Florida. Apparently they just recently broke up after almost 40 years of marriage.

I also dated Yolanda LaMothe a short time, maybe only one date. So much is a complete blur from those months. She had a lovely disposition and a sweet smile. I remember going with her to one function, a wedding reception, I think. Yo had been one of the original hippie chick's downtown. I saw her around with her boyfriend Victor Djursick. On occasion they would dress to the hilt and walk around town, her in a long dark dress and him in his tuxedo and top hat; I thought it a little strange but cute. There were so many colorful and unique individuals these days. I heard a saying, "Kids, today try so hard to be cool; in the 60's they just were". There may be some truth to this but it seems to me some in the 60's tried quite hard to be cool, also. I liked Yo but sensed no real chemistry between us and I never pursued her after that.

It wasn't just my feelings for Moe that had died; something more was taking place in me. I was getting tired of my life and restless for a change. Even working, driving a truck all week, so I could party on the weekend, seemed a waste of time. Actually I was getting run down and tired period. I knew I couldn't keep living this lifestyle much longer. I was now ready for something new; actually, I was desperate for change.

## We Met at The Coulson

One sunny evening, after work, the fall of 1970 I formally met my wife to be. I was standing outside the Coulson Hotel in my work boots, waiting to see who would happen by. Sure enough, Joe Lavigne and a couple others came strolling along heading for their favorite watering hole. They naturally invited me in and I had nothing better to do. With them was a beautiful Finn girl, Marja Laamanen. I had seen her before on the street a few times and at a party or two with Jerry Penttila, I thought.

We all went in and found a table and ordered a round. It soon became apparent there was not going to be a drinking contest tonight, which happened periodically. One reason was, no one around the table, especially me, would consider trying to keep up to Joe. Drinking was something Joe was good at. He was a heavy-set man with a rather large head and neck. He could tilt his head back, open his throat and literally throw back a glass of draft as fast it would pour. He could do this over and over again, especially, if someone challenged him by trying to keep up.

Many serious beer drinkers often drank their own case of 24 beers in the course of a night but I never met anyone who could drink as fast as Joe. He also had a high tolerance level and could drink hard stuff, like tequila shot after shot. I had learned the hard way that 3 or 4 drinks was my limit. I knew better than to challenge the sensitivity my gut had to beer.

Joe, also had other talents and this night the competition had a lot more to do with the lone pretty blonde girl at our table. At first I didn't even consider entering this contest. I was just along for the ride, trying to have some fun. I had long ago accepted the fact that some girls were out of my league. She was not only older than me, she was also a bartender at the Holiday Inn, and beautiful. She wore high boots and a long purple leather coat. She was also well read and could talk politics, religion or current events with the best. Although, I had no illusions of winning her there was something about her that captivated me.

We drank, talked and laughed. As the night wore on, one by one, all left the building except Joe, Marja and me. With only the 3 of us left, things changed dramatically. Now that the other suitors were gone; not sure if there was any serious ones; her attention turned more my way. We sensed a kinship, a common thread we didn't identify specifically that night. We would later learn that we had similar backgrounds and we were playing the same game of tag, learning, "You can run but you can't hide".

Being the honorable young man I was, I wasn't going to leave her alone with Joe Lavigne, if I could help it. Like a knight in shining armor I had to at least try to rescue this poor damsel in distress. In a gallant act of bravery I played the only ace I had in may hand; I had a car, if you could call it that and I offered to drive her home. To my delight, she agreed. Joe gave me a look, as we said good-bye and the two of us left together.

Marja told me years later the one thing that first caught her attention was my work boots. They reminded her of her father and were a symbol of hard work and stability to her.

She didn't seem to mind that I was driving a purple Volkswagen Bug that I had bought for 3 grams of hash. It had no back seat. I forgot the passenger seat was not bolted to the floor and took off a little too quickly and she ended up in a heap in the empty, open space at the back. She was not hurt but I was embarrassed and apologized. She seemed to take it in stride.

We drove off together in the wee hours of the morning, never to be the same two people again. What happened the rest of the night was beyond my control. I was in no shape to be driving, let alone be on my first date with my future bride.

That night, even in our drunken stupor, we instantly fell in love and latched on to each other like magnets. Somehow I drove home safely and woke up late the next day, hurting physically but on an emotional high. My whole outlook on life had been transformed and I prayed to God that Marja felt the same way.

As happy as I was, my life was now a bigger mess than ever. I knew I was not going to marry Maureen. I stole her virginity, broke her heart and then left her. I had betrayed my own conscience and broke the commitment I made to both God and Maureen and seemed helpless to do anything about it. The fact that I was smitten with love, like never before, made it easier to block everything else out of my mind, for the time being.

A song by Kris Kristofferson, quickly became my favorite. Some of the words are so fitting. My brother Art and Bob Sloan sang it at our $25^{th}$ anniversary. I still love it.

Loving Her Was Easier

I have seen the morning burning golden on the mountains in the skies.

Achin' with the feeling of the freedom of an eagle when she flies.

Turnin' on the world the way she smiled upon my soul as I lay dying.

Healin' as the colours in the sunshine and the shadows of her eyes.

Comin' close together with a feelin' I've never know before, in my time.

She ain't ashamed to be a woman, or afraid to be a friend.

I don't know the answer to the easy way she opened every door, in my mind.

But dreamin' was as easy as believin' it was never gonna end.

And loving her was easier than anything I'll ever do again.

I drummed up enough courage to Marja and was delighted that she wanted to see me again. Later that day we got together and the rest is history. Some of my friends were blown away at my catch and openly showed their approval of my new girlfriend. What were the chances this relationship would last, though? The chances were slim unless of course God had ordained our union.

Over the next few weeks we shared our similar, religious and secure start in life and how we had both seemed to lose our way with no direction home. Deep down we both had the common desire to turn around and escape the inevitable crash if we continued in the direction we were heading.

## Moe Moran Revisited

Moe heard I was with Marja but contacted me and wanted to talk one more time; I owed her at least that! She came to my parent's house and we talked; she cried and I tried to comfort her. She was willing to leave home, her parents and Sudbury to start a new life together, even though she knew her mother would disown her. I instantly saw things through her eyes, shared her pain and was smitten with guilt and shame. It was awful, worse than awful. This was the worst predicament I had ever gotten myself into. In the emotion of the minute I said I would reconsider what I was doing and said maybe we could get back together. As we held each other, I realized we still had a strong attachment; in a way we had become one.

The fact that we ended up in bed that afternoon reminds me what a thick fog my brain was in. What was I thinking? How the mighty had fallen. This young, proud, Mennonite boy was in a lot worse shape mentally and spiritually than he imagined possible. What had I done? What was I going to do now? I was in a state of shock and my head was swirling.

The next day as soon as I got together with Marja, the fog instantly cleared, my mind was settled, my heart was steadfast. This was the woman I wanted to spend the rest of my life with but what a mess I was in. I didn't want to hurt Moe anymore but didn't know how to prevent it. I avoided her and never called because I was too embarrassed to face her.

Now as I am writing, a Buffalo Springfield song haunts me. Not all the words apply but some are right on; kind of eerie, almost.

## Go and Say Goodbye

You ask me to read this letter; That you wrote the night before.

And you really should know better; Now she's worth a whole lot more

Brother, you know you can't run away and hide

Is it you don't want to see her cries, is that why

You won't go and say goodbye

You said the fault was yours; When you really were to blame

'Twas as if to close the doors; And to hide away in shame

Yes, and why, tell me why; Can't you see that it's not right

It's a lie, it's a lie; Don't hide your sorrow in the night

And you know the pain is double; But for her it's even worse

You must face her with the trouble; 'Though it's hurting like a curse

(Stephen Stills)

I continued to self-medicate in order to block God out my mind and now Maureen. The days turned into months, the months into years and I never called her. She had no choice but to go on with her life, without Don Bast. She went to college and started a career with the RCMP, believe it or not. She became a scientist, in the forensic department, and often had to attend court providing incriminating DNA evidence against bad guys. I went on preoccupied with just living, trying to sort out where I belonged.

Marja and I were both convinced we were meant to be together but it was not easy. I was very jealous from the beginning and found it difficult when we ran into old boyfriends, especially if they were older, more confident and better looking than me. I reminded myself this was the 60's but it hurt. I was determined to keep her. I was a desperate man. Wherever we went I didn't leave without her. Others had pursued her and thought they had a hold on her but she slipped away. This was not going to happen to me, if I could help it.

I loved being with her and was content to take her home to be all alone. We listened to music and mostly drank. I discovered whiskey; her drink of choice was easier on my gut than beer. After a couple of months, we had empty 26 ounce bottles lined up along the whole back wall behind the furniture. Most nights we crashed into bed drunk and exhausted. Often I fell asleep immediately after making love, sometimes still on top of her, unaware that she stayed awake for hours until she finally cried herself to sleep. She was so afraid that this relationship would end like the others before but never said a thing and I was oblivious to what she was going through. She was always so confident and out going, especially after a couple of drinks, which made her more attractive, not only to me.

## Fender Benders

My little old purple bug had been in a few accidents and was getting quite beat up. Driving Dennis home late one night, turning left onto Loach's Road; the direct steering locked up just as another car approached the intersection. I was going too fast for the shape I was in and banged into the side of the car. I quickly put into reverse, backed up a few feet and took off in a hurry, barely stopping long enough to let Dennis out and took the all too familiar back roads home through the bush. These events didn't seem to bother me at all as long as I didn't get caught. They simply became another funny story to share.

One day, Frank James borrowed my bug and had a similar incident. Driving down the Kingsway he started to turn left onto Barrydowne Road and the wheel locked up again; the car turned so sharp that the bug rolled over on its side. When he told me later what happened, I asked him, "What did you do?" He said, "I got out and lifted it back on its wheels and drove away". I know the bug was light and he was a strong man but I think he must have had some help but failed to mention this detail. The purple bug was laid to rest shortly after.

One warm Sunday evening I was driving Art's 65 Ford, passed the Caruso Club, arm out the open window, head turned to see if I could recognize anyone standing out side. I veered a little to the right and the door handle grazed several cars, leaving long scratches along the whole side from back to front. Realizing what was happening I quickly turned the wheel to straighten out and kept driving as if nothing happened.

At this point I decided to bite the bullet, get a loan and buy a better car. Even though I was working, I needed a co-signer. My dad agreed and after shopping around we found one I liked. It was only a few years old, an ex- OPP cruiser for $1500. In those days, when black and white OPP cars were traded in, they were not painted; the car dealer just wrote "DEALER" on the front doors, in big letters, to show it was no longer owned by the police but was for resale by a car dealer. It was a Chev and came with the fastest 350 cubic inch engine available. I was so tickled but of course couldn't let my dad know what I was thinking. This was too cool, me the drug dealer, driving a police car with "DEALER" written on both sides.

Friday after work we went to the bank to get the money, then to the Insurance Company to sign papers and picked my new "Dealer" car. I spent Friday evening and Saturday driving around town showing it off.

I always tried to pick up Marja at the Holiday Inn after work. We usually then had a drink or two before heading home between 2:00 and 3:00 am. This Sunday morning, driving up Larch Street through town minding our own business, I didn't slow down at Durham Street because the light was green, it was late and there were few other cars around at all. However, there was one other car downtown full of teenage kids from Quebec speeding down Durham Street with windows open just having a grand old time. I took a quick glance and thought they were going a little fast but that is how most kids drove downtown from one light to next. Instead of stopping the driver sped right through the red light. By the time I realized they didn't even see the red light or me, it was too late. I slammed on the brakes and skidded into the intersection as they smashed into the front corner of my big, new, dealer car and totaled it.

The police soon came and both parties told the same story, "We had a green light". Believe it or not, there was one lonely gentleman from England obviously with his internal clock messed up, walking the street. He told the police officer that I indeed had a green light. The other driver was charged but my big dealer car was history, less than 48 hours after I had picked it up. I guess God didn't think this dealer car was as cool as I did. He continually caused things to happen to remind me He was in control and I was heading in the wrong direction. Now as I look back I can see how He had been preparing me, all alone, for a complete turn about but I still needed to suffer a little more before I was ready to make the leap of faith.

To make things worse, the insurance company refused to pay for my car because they claimed they hadn't processed the paperwork yet. Worse yet, the young French kid decided to fight the charge. At the court case the only witness was back on the other side of the ocean. We both told the judge the same story and because there were no witnesses he threw it out of court. So now I had my first car loan to deal with and no car. I faithfully made my monthly payments for 18 months and then to my surprise received a cheque in the mail for $950.00. I guess the law finally caught up with Bretlaff Insurance who had been gaining a reputation for not paying out claims.

After the accident I bought a 1964 Comet station wagon from Wilbert Burrell for $75. One evening, Marja and I picked up John Bell and his girlfriend Louise Dignard to go to a movie. Crossing over the bumpy railway tracks at the bottom of Beattie Street hill the Falcon screeched to a halt. I stepped on the gas; it wouldn't move. After scratching my head for awhile, I looked under the car and realized the emergency brake cable was as tight as a fiddle string. I pulled on it and couldn't get it free. I got my pliers and cut the cable and presto we were off to the movies. We smoked a joint and had a good laugh about it.

On our way home a few hours and tokes later, crossing over the same tracks, to our surprise the identical thing happened again, exactly the way it had earlier that evening. This was too much! John in particular, was beside himself laughing so hard but I could tell he was more than a little freaked out, as we all were.

We sat there for a long time talking. I had no idea what to do now. I had no emergency cable to cut. The car wouldn't budge an inch so we left it on the side of the road and walked to their apartment and called for help. At the garage the next day the mechanic told me the whole rear-end of the car was rotted out and ready to fall off. Both times I went over the bumpy tracks the car twisted sideways; the first time the brake cable tightened and held the car together; the second time the rear axel shifted enough to lock the wheels. Anyway, the car was scrap. I was able to buy an old Vauxhall from Brian Nadjiwon for $135. A long with the car came a toolbox full of mechanics tools worth about $500. I used the toolbox and tools for many years.

## Wild and Crazy Drivers

The year after I totaled the dealer car the same company refused to pay for Art's 650 BSA motorcycle when it was stolen. This was one time they were right. Art had arranged for a friend to steal it, who stripped many parts from it and then disposed of it in Lake Ramsey. He was loosing his nerve and decided to get rid of it while he was still alive. A long time ago he acquired a reputation for being a wild driver behind the wheel of a car. We knew when Art arrived at school. He couldn't resist, making his grand entrance with a four-wheel drift, skidding across the paved parking lot with tires screeching and dust flying. Marja was scared to death when we drove in the car with him. More than once she ended up on the floor of the back seat too afraid to look. On a bike he was able to do things he couldn't in a car. Doing 100 miles an hour down the white line with traffic going both ways was one stunt that gave him the excitement he craved.

One Friday night, we happened to be leaving town with Art behind the wheel. Traffic was a little heavy and Art forced his way into the slow moving traffic in front of a greaser driving a big 59 Buick. This apparently upset him and he began stepping on the gas, making the car jump up and ahead and then on the brake stopping just short of our back bumper. Art didn't like this kind of treatment and waited for the right opportunity. Just as soon as he saw an opening he put the brakes on rather quickly and unexpectedly, just for a second, causing a near rear-end collision. He then floored it to make a getaway, weaving from lane to lane between cars.

The near accident infuriated the already upset driver and he stepped on it also. The chase was on. We were hippies and not interested in fighting so running was the only other option. We had a slant-6 under the hood and the Buick behind had a monster V-8 but Art was driving. He rounded the corner on Brady Street heading towards the lights at Lorne Street rubber burning and the big Buick on our tail. Art put his right blinker on as if he was going to turn into the Esso bulk plant yard just south of Lorne St. Without slowing down he waited till the last second and then turned left instead, down Cross Street. The big Buick tried to follow but couldn't make the corner at the speed he was traveling and crashed through a white picket fence and skidded across the front lawn of the corner property and came to a rest up against the house. We obviously kept on driving, as if nothing unusual had happened, laughing all the way.

Of course this kind of attitude towards driving is a lot more serious problem when on a bike. For years Art had nerves of steel and had become a pretty good driver. He did things I wouldn't even consider but when he started losing his nerve, for whatever reason, he knew enough to get rid of the bike before it got rid of him.

Although, I never drove crazy like Art, I often drove stoned. One trip in particular stands out in my mind. Dennis and I had borrowed Art's 65 Ford to take a quick trip to Toronto to pick up some stuff. We hadn't planned on it but we ended up buying some keef. I had never even heard of keef but tried it and whoa; it was a potent. It was a concentrated, marijuana substance like hash but loose and powdery. Driving home that night in the rain I got hot as I often did so I rolled the windows down and took off my shirt. I can imagine what a policeman would have thought if he would have spotted this skinny, little, bare-back, hippie, boy driving in the rain, with all the windows open.

The glare of the oncoming headlights mirrored on the wet pavement was almost unbearable. My vision was so impaired; all I could make out was a steady stream of lights, light a string of moving Christmas lights coming at me; I knew if I could just stay to the right of them a few feet I would be alright. Finally, we stopped at a parking area at Lake Rasicot on Hwy 69 for a well needed rest. By the grace of God we made it home safely and when we shared the keef with friends the next few days they couldn't believe I actually drove home from Toronto high on this stuff. Every time I pass that spot traveling to and from the south I think of that crazy trip and whisper a prayer of thanksgiving to my merciful Father.

## Unexpected Visitors

Art made the odd trip with the Movers when I was not along. He was in Southern Ontario for some reason with a couple of the boys; just tripping maybe. Anyway, seeing they were relatively close to Mennonteville they decided to visit some relatives. It was early morning by the time they approached Millbank and figured Uncle Earl Wagler would be up and doing his chores. Sure enough, the barn lights were on. They walked in and found him milking the cows. They talked for a few minutes and Earl suggested if they go in the house they might get a cup of coffee; he would be in shortly for breakfast. So Art and his companions went to the house. Art knocked softly and walked into the old familiar farmhouse. They didn't see Aunt Edith so they made themselves at home at the kitchen table knowing she would be down shortly to get breakfast going.

As it turns out, a few neighbor farmers had been broken into, the last few days and when Edith walked into the kitchen and saw these 3 big, rough looking longhairs she freaked; the first thought that came to her mind was the recent "B and E's". She was startled, to say the least and quickly spouted out half in shock and half in fear, "What are you doing in here?" By the time Art could open his mouth she recognized him. It was a little embarrassing for all but it soon turned funny and they had a good laugh.

## Take This Job and Shove It

I continued my riotous lifestyle, while holding down a job for quite awhile. One beautiful fall morning, 1970 after partying all night, I decided I just couldn't keep going like this. I had thought about quitting my job many times but didn't want to cut the last thread that connected me with the world I used to be a part of.

This fine morning I was at Joe's girlfriend Shirley's house with Joe and he encouraged me to just do it. I took the phone and reluctantly called into work and told them I was not coming back, sorry. It is hard to explain my emotions after that call. I should have felt guilty and depressed but instead I felt free. The freedom reminded me of the first day of summer holidays when I was a kid; however, it would be short lived. The chains that were binding me were coming from within not from external forces.

## Back to Beautiful British Columbia

As the cold winter of 1970 - 71 set in; Sudbury's street activities began to cool down, once again, which I dreaded. Once again, Dave Ham was going west and invited me to go with him. As much as I hated winter I was torn between Marja and Vancouver and reluctantly agreed. He wasn't leaving until near the end of the January because Neil Young, my favorite musician, was playing Massey Hall in Toronto on January 19th.

I enjoyed tripping with Dave; we had visited Toronto in the past. Dave knew Toronto like the back of his hand. He seldom looked at a map. He knew the main streets running north - south and east – west. He just got an address and asked what main streets it was close to. Once in the general area, he just zipped in and out of lanes and back streets until he found it. I recall our first trip to "The Bohemina capital of Canada", so named because it was so unconventional, I imagine. This is where the flower children of that day hung out in coffee bars and clubs. Yorkville seemed to be the hub, a hippie haven; it was one cool place for sure. Our first visit there Dave recognized a wild and crazy hippie chick from Sudbury, Marcia. When he saw her, he leaned over, whispered in my ear, "She's a head". I had no idea what a head was; it sounded impressive. I found out later, a "head" refers to anyone who smokes up. I never figured that one out. I was sure everyone here did pot. I later spent a little time with Marcia and liked her a lot. She reminded me of Janis Joplin.

On another one of my early trips to "The Big Smoke" I was with Joe Lavigne. He was going down to cop some stuff and asked me to go along. I thought that was cool and happily agreed. He had a contact at Rochdale College and a deal was arranged. Rochdale, which opened in 1968, was an experiment in student-run "alternative education" and co-operative living. It was a free university of 840 students and teachers all living there together. The project finally failed for financial reasons and was closed in 1975. Neighbors had long complained that it was nothing more than a haven for drugs and crime; I soon found out why. As we approached the high-rise building I discovered one reason why I was asked to come. Joe handed me a wad of bills, $2300 worth, and told me to stick it deep in my pocket and forget it exists unless he asked for it; I knew what he meant. Inside the front doors we were stopped by a security guard carrying a sawed off shotgun. Joe convinced him we were not looking for any trouble, just wanted to see so and so in room such and such to buy hash. He said fine and let us through. We did our business and headed for home as quick and as casual as possible.

On January 19th, 1971, Dave, Billy and I were back in Toronto for the Neil Young concert, which was so good. It has been hailed as one of the top solo, acoustic, concerts ever. In 2007 someone realized how good it was and cut a CD. It reached #1 in Canada and sold 11,000 copies the first week. It debuted #9 in Ireland and #30 on the UK album charts.

A few days later we boarded the train and headed west again on the 3 night, 2-day ride. I was only there three weeks and decided to book a flight home. I missed Marja and was afraid I might lose her if I stayed too long. She confided in me much later she thought I would stay there and this would be the end of our relationship. I didn't know at the time but she had been let down a few times before by other "lovers".

The winter was long and hard. Some of the boys got jobs, others registered in college out of town and many downtown guys had gone west. The whole scene was losing its appeal. I got tired of sitting in the pool hall window, looking out onto Durham Street, all alone, with nothing to do but think, as I waited for Marja to get off work. Plus her group of friends didn't interest me at all.

Something was changing on the inside of me; my heart began to long for more. Many nights I fell asleep crying out to God to deliver me from this existence, now that I had a partner who I hoped would accompany me down that lonely road back home.

**Overnight Stay at 45 Maki**

Apparently one night I had enough sense not to drive home in a stupor and decided I would stay at Marja's parents place on Maki Avenue. I had met her parents a few times and her father especially didn't like my long hair. They were so disappointed with Marja's lifestyle that she had long stopped worrying about upsetting them, although her mother never gave up hoping, and praying for her as my mom did, also. When Marja was 17 she ran away from home and they had no clue where she was until they received a post card, days later, from California, informing them she was fine. They entirely disapproved with what she was doing; nothing could make it worse, so she thought.

We quietly snuck into the house in the middle of the night. She led me upstairs and pointed out where the bathroom was, her room and the guest room, where I was to sleep. I laid down for a few minutes and thought to myself, "What am doing here sleeping alone?" I got up and went across the hall and slipped into her bed. She must have been half asleep already or too out of it to notice. Some time before morning she realized I was beside her and was frantic. She told me that if her dad caught me in her bed he would kill me; he had a temper and would throw me over the railing in a fit of rage. At his funeral, 26 years later, I shared from the pulpit a near drowning experience while fishing with Mr. Laamanen. Later at reception, in the basement of the Finnish Church, the mike was open for anyone to share stories. Sitting there listening I remembered my first night at Marja's house and told the story as if it was another near death experience with Marja's dad. Everyone laughed except her brother Risto. He took the mike and said that if he had caught me he would have killed me too.

## My Mother's Failing Health

With all this trouble going on Mom was losing sleep and her health worrying about her children. She sat up late, night after night, at her living room window watching and praying for her children, pleading to God for mercy and to bring them home safely. Marja's mother was a praying woman also and Marja often heard her praying out loud, crying out to God to save her daughter. Mom's doctor arranged a meeting with us siblings, however only Gerry and Marilyn attended. His message was simple; if she didn't stop worrying herself sick about her kids a nervous breakdown was inevitable. She shared this with me one morning and I broke down and cried like a baby and promised her I would stop living the way I was.

I wanted so bad to please my parents but when it came down to making real change I was helpless. Over and over I asked God to forgive me for what I was doing to my mother. Many tears were shed falling to sleep as I vowed to change. The next day the reality of the night before vanished and I continued on my merry way but I was becoming more and more fragile and less confident. All through these crazy days and nights, I knew God had never left me. Even in a stoned stupor I was aware of His presence and love. This was most reassuring and haunting at the same time. Marja and I talked about taking the long, lonely road back home, away from this lifestyle, but we didn't know how to do it or where to start.

Marja continued to work at Flanagan's pub in the Holiday Inn until 1:00 am. I continued to wait for her and then take her home. My parents didn't approve of us sleeping together and they didn't like it that we smoked in the house but they allowed it and said nothing. Later that fall, sitting in Fred's Restaurant, only a few months after we had met, I proposed to Marja. To my delight she accepted. We would wait until next summer. She would be my birthday present. So July 10th date was set, 3 days after my 21st birthday.

## Tracy Parent is Born

In April 1971 Billy's wife, Sybil had a baby girl, Tracy Parent. This called for a celebration. When Billy came home from the hospital the party began. We had not prepared to party all night and soon ran out of booze, so it was off to the bootlegger. Eric, Sybil's brother agreed to drive me and Joe Lavigne came along. Eric was not that stoned or drunk but I think he was showing off and drove way too fast. We asked him to take it easy a couple of times but he didn't listen.

Traveling on Robinson Drive he got too far to the right, onto the shoulder and hit the side of a paved driveway. His little Toyota front wheel hit hard, the car flew 75 feet in the air, landed on the roof, in the ditch. Everything went black and quiet; it took me a few minutes to realize what had happened. I rolled down my window and crawled out of the car, now with a squashed roof. I sat down on a nearby stonewall, which still stands today, lit up a smoke and busted a gut laughing as the two big guys slowly squeezed out of their windows. Joe was about 5' 9" but well over 200 pounds; Eric was skinny but over 6 feet tall.

Eric had a sore leg and Joe seemed fine but was very upset at Eric and would have laid a beating on him if he hadn't been Billy's brother-in-law. Besides we were in a hurry to leave the scene before the police got there. We walked about 1/2 mile to Gloria's Confectionary to call for a ride. A few minutes later the police walked in. I guess we looked suspicious and they walked directly over to us. We had no choice; Joe and I told them what happened. Eric got charged with drunk driving. We felt bad for him but had warned him several times to slow down. We finally got back to Billy's with the goods and celebrated the birth of his first child. I didn't see Eric after that but heard he died a few years later in a drunken stupor. Apparently, he passed out lying on his back, threw up and choked on his own vomit. I must pause here for a minute's silence to sadly remember Eric.

The next morning Marja informed me that on her way home from work last night, they hit a patch of black ice, a short distance from the scene of our accident and a few hours later. Their car slid off the road, slammed into a pole and was totaled. The 3 passengers were not hurt. God was now turning up the volume, speaking loud and clear; slowly but surely getting our complete attention. It is hard to believe we were so dull of hearing and so reluctant to acknowledge His voice.

## One More Deal

It was obvious that a change was necessary; the writing was on the wall in bold letters. Billy and I discussed getting out this scene, moving west and finding a piece of property and settling down. Maybe we could learn to live off the land somewhat away from the action. If we could only do one more big deal, to make enough money for the trip west; we would be content. We joined up with Dave Ham, who was back in Sudbury. We decided to all throw in $1,000. For $3,000 we could cop four or five pounds of hash with a street value of over $15,000 if sold in grams. I was able to borrow the cash from my friend Barry Moxam who I had recently turned on to pot.

Rod Stewart was scheduled to play in Toronto; we decided that would be the time to go down. Dave had a friend named Roy that had a contact with good Lebanese hash. The plan was to meet on Saturday before the concert and check it out. Dave was taking his own car down on Friday so he carried the cash. Bill and I would catch a ride on Saturday with one of the boys.

When Dave got to Toronto he called Roy to confirm the meeting. Roy said his people were anxious to make a deal and get out of town so Dave reluctantly agreed to go alone and meet them that night. This was his first mistake. Roy was from Sudbury and Dave trusted him. What he didn't know was that Roy didn't know the other guys very well. As soon as Dave got in the room he sensed something fishy. He asked to see the hash; they asked to see the money and Dave turned to leave. He reached the door and had it half open when two guys jumped him and a third started hitting his knees with the butt end of a shotgun; Dave finally went down. I'm sure it took all three because Dave was tough and stubborn; he would have fought to the death. Unfortunately the $3000 was in his pocket; this was his second mistake. They finally got the cash from him and fled. Dave hobbled back to his car and drove directly to the police station. He told them the whole story and provided a name. They took his statement and did some checking. Within a couple hours they located their men. Three guys, all Americans had just crossed the border to Buffalo and to safety, with our money. So much for our last big deal. Art and his partner took advantage of the situation and let me sell a couple of kilos of weed they had just bought. I made enough money to barely pay back my debt.

## Back to Work

As our wedding day approached I tried hard to be good. I landed a job for $2.25 an hour, as a truck driver for Yolles Furniture. My helper was my good friend John Bell. He had never driven a vehicle with a standard transmission and wanted to learn. I showed him how to shift gears and let him drive around the parking lot behind the store. It was hilarious; I remember him bending right over, nose close to the stick shift trying in vain to find the right gear and steer the truck at the same time.

His girlfriend Louise had recently given birth to a baby girl and he was serious about changing his lifestyle, also. John had been a part of the Sudbury scene for a long time. In the mid 60's he was a lead singer for the rock band "The Inferno Five"; music was our main, common interest plus he was a fun guy to be with. He collected Marvel Comics and became very animated as he read parts aloud with his English accent. He was so comical.

We tried to reserve our partying for the weekends so we could get up in the morning for work. John was also a thinker and we had many good talks. God's word was burning in my heart and I couldn't hold it in. One night I passionately poured out my heart to him and shared the gospel of Jesus dying on the cross; he listened intently and was blown away. He was usually the one doing most of the talking. Something happened to John that night and he called me the next morning. The first thing he blurted out was, "Its still happening man".

Shortly after that John and Louise moved to west coast and I lost touch with him. He went back to school and eventually became a social worker. In the 80's he came back to Sudbury for a funeral and called me. He had heard about my dramatic conversion and we tried to connect but I was in such a different space; he couldn't relate to my new found, radical religion.

I only saw John once after that. It was in the 90's; John was the road manager for a hard rock, bar band. They were touring Northern Ontario and had a gig scheduled at the Brockdan on the south end of Sudbury. When he arrived in town he gave me a call and invited me to come hear the music. I didn't really want to spend the night in a bar but I wanted to see him and agreed to go and check out the gig one night. It was not my type of music at all. It was so loud it hurt my ears. I guess he could tell I was not impressed, especially when we left early. I haven't seen him since. I have looked for him but with such a common name as John Bell it is useless looking in phone directories etc.

## My Lonely Way Back Home

As the summer of 1971 and my wedding day approached, I pondered my life, what it had been and what it would be. I seemed to be in a state of limbo; lost in no man's land. I had to get out of the scene I was in. I was working and even started attending church again. I was desperate to do whatever I could to help Mom from having a breakdown. This is one thing I did not want to live with, the rest of my life.

I knew I was heading in the right direction but something basic was still missing. It seemed so close but always still just out of my reach. Deep down I knew God would have to show me the way and give me the power to change. I didn't expect it to be easy though. At least I now had a helpmate to hold my hand; together I hoped we could find our lonely way back home.

Some of the lyrics of the following Kris Kristofferson song may not apply but most of them speak volumes.

**Pilgrim**

See him wasted on the sidewalk in his jacket and his jeans'

Wearing yesterdays misfortunes like a smile

Once he had a future full of money, love, and dreams

Which he spent like they was goin' out of style

And he keeps right on a changin' for the better or the worse,

Searchin' for a shine he's never found

Never knowin' if believing is a blessing or a curse,

Or if goin' up is worth the comin' down

Chorus

He's a poet, he's a picker. He's a prophet, he's a pusher.

He's a pilgrim and a preacher, and a problem when he's stoned

He's a walkin' contradiction, partly truth and partly fiction'

Takin' ev'ry wrong direction on his lonely way back home.

The song ends with, "There's a lot of wrong directions on that lonely way back home", as I was about to find out. Marja and I both had a lot of growing up to do. We also had sown our wild oats and the seeds had grown deep roots and would surely sprout. It had nothing to do with God being angry with us. It was simply a matter of sowing and reaping.

## Things Got Bad and Things Got Worse

One lonely afternoon Marja happened into a bar to have a beer, alone, which was uncharacteristic of her. There happened to be two friendly men from Quebec at the next table. They were in town working for INCO at a nearby mine. When they ordered another round they bought one for Marja also and started chatting with her. Then they bought another round. Finally Marja said she had to leave; her fiancé was waiting for her. They asked where I lived and when she said, "Lively", they said that was the direction they were heading to go work the afternoon shift. They asked if she wanted a ride and she agreed. On the way out of town they took a back road detour and raped her and then dropped her off back in town. She immediately called me and I went in and drove her back to my home in Lively. She was distraught and broken; I was stunned and hurt for her. I called the police. They came and took Marja's statement. My parents were very understanding and supportive. We all shared her pain and tried to comfort her.

A few days later the police called Marja and drove with her to the mine, at shift change. Marja easily picked out the two men and the police questioned them; they didn't deny what happened but told a slightly different version. They were not charged. The whole issue has slowly improved for the victims of rape since 1971. In those days a woman was blamed unless she was practically dead from the abuse or at least showing obvious scars and bruises to prove she struggled for her life. The whole incident was shameful for Marja. She knows she should not have been drinking with strangers and especially she never should have gone into their car. Her judgment was obviously impaired. She sees now looking back that she was trying to fill the God shaped void in her life and drinking seemed to help, ever so temporarily though and with severe consequences.

Before that long hard winter was over Marja had another similar experience, this time, with so called friends. "Little Ron", as he was called; I don't even remember his last name and Dave Crossan told Marja they were having a little party; that I and a few others were on our way over to the Hotel room they had rented. Marja agreed and after several drinks began to get a little worried because I hadn't showed up yet; no one else showed either. Her concern was not unfounded; Dave soon started to aggressively fondle her. She was too weak physically and emotionally to do anything and wept as they both forced themselves on her. I'm quite sure Ron felt terrible about how this unfolded but reluctantly continued with Dave's plan to save face with his best friend.

I had known Ron for a few years and never expected this from him and strangely never saw him again after this incident. Dave, I didn't know well and was not impressed with the little I did know and he knew it. He carried a huge chip on his shoulder. I had seen him around but really only talked to him once. He approached me one day and asked for some stuff I was selling; he had no money but would pay me as soon as possible. He sounded desperate and sincere and I agreed, besides it was not worth a lot of money. He went to jail on a drug charge shortly after that for several months. When he got out I approached him on the street; he was angrier and harder than before. He just looked me in the eye and scowled, "Don't bug me, you got burned, ok?" I guess I shouldn't be surprised at how low people can go. Many have not had anything close to the healthy upbringing I had and look what I was doing.

Anyway, I couldn't believe this had happened to Marja again and I was in a state of shock, myself as the questions swirled in my head: what kind of man does these things? Why was this happening to my future bride? Life had lost its fun and I started to wonder how bad it had to get before there was a change.

After we were married, I would find out that Marja had actually been raped, for the first time, when she was 16 years old. One day a man, whom she had met through her brother Risto, appeared at her high school, while she waited for the bus. He offered her a ride home and she accepted. On the way home he took a detour and parked on a back road and forced himself on her. She said he was strong and she didn't know what to do; besides she was in a helpless state of shock. She felt ashamed and never told a soul. If Risto would have found out he would have beaten, this so called friend to a pulp, at least he would have tried. This guy was a boxer and tough.

Her introduction to sex was so different from mine and this tragic experience would have a profound effect on her and our relationship for years. Unless a girl has been trained by her parents to protect herself and that she has every right to just say "No", it is difficult for her to effectively resist a rape. A man not only often has power physically over a woman but also psychologically.

Over the years, Marja has several times, attempted to explain the overwhelming feeling of helplessness that accompanies the trauma of rape. The severe pain and shock, of this emotional experience, do not leave the victim for a long time, sometimes never. It is difficult for others to understand the paralyzing shame the victim bears and why they seldom find the courage to even speak of it.

She was a good looking young lady but saw herself as damaged goods. To me she was as beautiful as ever. I wanted to protect her and help her heal but I was in no shape to help anyone; I couldn't even help myself. Crisis piled upon crisis and after each one my attention turned to the heavens. I wondered what else would happen before I could get control of my life?

## Marilyn Busted

Gerry and Marilyn were also still involved in the drug scene. Marilyn went to Jamaica on a trip with her boyfriend, and brought back some stuff that he planned on selling. The goods were conveniently placed in Marilyn's suitcase where he said they would be safer. To make a long story short, the customs officials suspected foul play and searched their bags. They were both charged and sent to the Sudbury jail on an otherwise beautiful Friday morning in June 1971. My dad was out of town and didn't get back to post bail until Sunday, which happened to be Father's Day.

During these two days and nights in jail, as Marilyn pondered her life, God's spirit broke her and started a work in her heart that would last the rest of her life. To make the situation worse court was set for early in July, a few days before our wedding. Marilyn was so afraid she would be in prison and not able to attend. At their court case her boyfriend, who was an American, took the rap for trafficking and was sent back to the USA. Marilyn got charged with possession and was released with a fine and a criminal record.

## My Stag

On July 1st, Billy and Sybil rented a house together with us. Marja and I were to be married in 10 days and this would be our first home together. On Friday evening July 3rd, the week before our wedding date Hughie Doucette, a friend from Lo-Ellen who drove a new Dodge Road Runner with a 383 engine, 4-speed Hurst shift on the floor, stopped by with a couple other friends. They asked me if I wanted to go for a spin and I agreed. I had no idea that the boys had arranged a stag for me and I didn't want one. I thought we were just going to cruise around for an hour or so and then back home. We did cruise through town but then out towards the 4 corners and soon ended up at Hanninen's camp on Long Lake. I had been there before. The Movers often went there for a swim and a sauna and the odd little party.

When I got there I was surprised to see a big party had been arranged; my last chance to party with the boys as a single man. I don't how many were there but there was lots and some I didn't know very well. I soon realized there was also one girl there, Moe Moran. I knew her and Pentti had been dating but had no idea why she was there. I figured this must be awkward for her but took it as a sign that she had dealt with our break-up and was going on with her life. I spent most of the night outside in the warm summer air and never saw her at all that night.

Apparently an open invitation was announced downtown and at Lo-Ellen. I was pleased so many had gathered in my honor, although I didn't really want to get stoned, especially on LSD. Most of the guys felt the same way; they just wanted to have few beers, a few tokes and a few laughs. Gerry Burke had a different idea. He walked around with a 26er of Canadian Club Whiskey offering everyone a swig. This was not unusual but the fact that he put 50 hits of acid in it and told no one, was not only a little extravagant but dumb and took us all by surprise.

Within an hour or so the place was like a zoo. I had been to some wild parties but never before had I been with this many young people on acid, some no doubt for the first time, having no idea what to expect. This is not a recipe for a good time. After I started getting off I was aware of little of what happened on the rest of the property. I heard Joe had been drinking all afternoon in preparation for the big party and the couple hefty slugs of the acid laced C.C. was the last straw and he passed out in his van. A few hours later, to his surprise, he was suddenly awakened with LSD surging through his blood stream; He was now ready to go all night, full tilt.

Most of the night my full attention was centered around a small group of my closest friends that seemed to be drawn together like a magnet; it was my party but this was still a little unusual. What was not uncommon these days is I became preoccupied with the things of God and His call on my life, especially being on acid. I had long since realized that by doing drugs one opens themselves up to the spirit realm and in most cases not the "holy spirit". However, once again, God was merciful to me, and the conviction of His love for me, and my wayward heart was foremost in my mind. Once again, also I found myself preaching the gospel, the best way I could in my state. Several of the boys seemed keenly interested or at least they were fascinated by my passion. They stuck close by my side and listened intently. One of them suggested I was a messenger of God like "John the Baptist". I was "The voice of one crying in the wilderness". I'm not sure if the analogy goes any further than that.

I climbed up a big tree in the yard and stretched out on a large low branch and got comfortable and my comrades followed me and there we sat, grooved and talked. I have no idea how long we stayed in the tree. Time means little on LSD, but we stayed at the camp until daylight. I'm sure people came and went but I was absorbed in my immediate surroundings. I eventually got a ride home and climbed into bed around 10:00 am. I needed so badly to get some rest but my body was still literally vibrating. My head was swirling around and around and a strobe light was flashing off and on in front of my eyes. The chemicals in my blood steam and brain wouldn't let me sleep for some time. When I woke up Marja shared some news; Jim Morrison of The Doors had just died. They suspected an alcohol-induced overdose of heroin as the cause of his heart failure.

It wasn't until I began this writing and started conversing with Maureen, about our time together, that I found out why she was at my stag. She had been living there with Pentti for the summer and was informed, after the matter, that he agreed to let the party be held there. When she found out she was very upset and said she was not leaving but would just stay in the bedroom all night alone. This is what she did most of the night; several of the boys saw her and talked to her a bit. She decided not to party at all because she had to work in the morning. It was so loud and there was so much action going on she could not sleep. By 5:00 am she knew she was in no shape to go to work so agreed to finish off the last couple of ounces in the bottom of Gerry's whiskey bottle. Little did she know it was laced with LSD. She didn't get to sleep at all until the next night. Pentti's summer job was flying fire patrol for the Ministry of Natural Resources. So, Maureen joined him for the day flying high, over the great Northern Ontario bush land. She said it was actually a beautiful experience.

## "Be Married"

It is normal for the bride-to-be, to do much of the planning for her wedding and for the man to agree with her wishes, for the most part. The wedding day is the one big day that girls dream about for years; they want it to be special. So was the case for us. Our plans were made and the guest list was prepared, made up of friends and many of my relatives. Marja's kin are almost all in Finland. She has a large extended family there.

Marja picked out a beautiful white wedding dress with a hood. The bridesmaids, Elisa Miller (nee Laari) would wear a blue dress and Pierrette Homberg a red one. Beautiful white dresses were made for the two flower girls, Arlene Wagler and Leah Miller. Marja's Mom would weaved a crown of daisies for the bridesmaids. It seemed a little extravagant for my conservative Mennonite taste but she was footing much of the bill so I couldn't say much. When she informed me she wanted to go to Toronto a couple days before the wedding to get her hair done by a very special and expensive hairdresser, I disagreed. This was going too far and finally we came to an impasse.

Marja was adamant she was going even if I didn't approve. If I wouldn't drive her she would hitchhike, As if!! Well that was the limit for me and I told her, "If you go to Toronto I won't be here when you get back". She knew I was serious. She got angry and pouted about it for a while and then agreed not to go. She told me later that, although my decisiveness, at first upset her, it left a lasting impression on her. She admired me for my firmness and it gave her confidence in me, and in my ability to take the lead in establishing some parameters we both would need so badly in the coming years.

On July 10th 1971, on a beautiful sunny, summer day, Marja and I were married at Water's Mennonite Church. It was a multi-cultural celebration, to say the least. I was the first grandchild on my mother's side to be married and many of aunts and uncles were in attendance. It was also a mixture of classes, Conservative Mennonite men, in their long-sleeved white shirts and dark suits; women in their long pastel dresses and head coverings on one extreme and long haired hippies and girls with flowers in their hair on the other.

Art the groomsman and Billy the best man both had long thick hair. I had my hair cut and styled for the first time since I let it grow but it was still long. We were quite the site. I especially like the pictures taken of the wedding party with my Amish Mennonite grandparents.

Both of our mothers were so pleased with our union and were hopeful it was a good sign. I was so happy all day I couldn't get the silly grin off my face. By the time the reception was over my cheeks were aching from smiling. When we set our wedding date we didn't realize it was Mariposa Folk Festival weekend. All I knew was I wanted to be married on my birthday or as close as possible. What this meant was we didn't have a party after the reception in the church basement; all our close friends headed south to the festival. We heard of another party in town, hosted by people we knew and checked it out for a short time but soon decided this was no way to spend our wedding night and we headed for camp to be alone.

## Kukagami Lake

We had scheduled our honeymoon at Marja's parent's camp at Kukagami Lake. We had a lovely time there all alone and agreed we were finally on the right track. Together we felt confident that we could turn our lives around and leave the downtown scene behind. This, we would be able to do but not without a great deal of struggle and pain. We had survived years of reckless living, but not, unscathed.

Little did we know we would reap what we had sown. A harvest of grief was about to sprout. We had lived to testify to the fact, that even in our rebellion, we could not out-sin grace. Where our sin had increased, grace had super-exceeded, however, this did not do away with the consequences of our choices. We both had many personal problems to work through before we could begin a healthy relationship and start a family. We had no idea what the years ahead would unravel.

## Go West Young Man - Go West

I had determined in my heart to move to the west coast as soon as possible and Marja was in agreement. Billy and I talked about it many times and plans were made. Billy was eager to go with his new family and as well as George Parrett and Joe Lavigne. I wanted to work long enough to buy a decent car. We would follow the boys before winter, so we thought.

Early in August, Billy and the boys set out for the coast. After one month in our new house, we moved out. We didn't think we could afford the expense on our own. Time and again, I regretted not going west with them and tried hard to make the move a couple times later. Every fall for much of my adult life, as the cold of winter set in, I got a longing in my heart to leave and regularly talked to the boys on the coast over the phone.

Many days, through the long hard winters of Northern Ontario, I had an ache deep inside, an emotional and physical travailing. Cold, dry weather was hard on my skin, which affected my whole being. The longing to go west was also entwined with a hunger for spiritual reality, which has made it impossible for me to separate the two. For over 30 years I would struggle to comprehend this all-consuming craving inside.

George's parents were disappointed that he left. They had tried to keep him away from Billy and drugs. His father Bud, owned two dump trucks. George had been driving one and was set to take over the business some day but he couldn't resist the thrill of going west with the boys. He ended up in Northern B.C., got married and had a child. His new in-laws for obvious reasons did not like George. Perhaps his drinking and drug use was a factor. He told me years later that in their effort to get rid of him they falsely accused him to the police of bizarre behavior. George had character flaws, more visible than most; he was rough around the edges and liked to scrap. In any event, they got a restraining order and forced him out of their daughter's life. He was admitted to a psychiatric hospital for shock treatment and medication. The authorities shipped him back east, dejected and sedated. He spent the balance of his life on a disability pension using the prescribed meds and street drugs to keep himself going. He died a broken man at the age of 59. Over the years I saw him periodically and he visited our home several times and my heart ached for him. When he stayed clean except for the doctor's meds he was calm, polite and fun to be with. When he overindulged he was bold and sassy.

## A Real Job

Immediately after getting married, Marja's brother Risto got me a job with the construction company he worked for. My wages went from $2.25 an hour driving truck to $4.45. While I enjoyed working for Yolles Furniture, I needed a real job, now that I was married and wanted to save money to go west. I joined the Laborers Union and became a full time employee of Ray-Vor Construction. I heard most workers got laid off in winter, which was fine for me. Surely I could handle hard physical work for a few months until I made the trek west to join Billy and the boys.

The owner of the company, Ray Ward, changed from Wuorinen, was also Finn, who had a wayward son, by the same name. I knew of him, from the street. He owned an ultra-light plane and I heard he was a little wild, especially when flying stoned. Perhaps, disappointed in his son, Ray took Risto under his wing, as soon as he got out of college. He bought him a brand new red Corvette for a company car and treated him very well. Risto was a born leader, and seemed to excel at everything he did in life.

The expression "everything he touches turns to gold" was often applied to him. After high school he attended Cambrian College where he became captain of the hockey team. Apparently he was the College's first student to win the award as the top scholastic and top athletic student in the same year. He was enrolled in a 3-year Engineering course but after two years decided he was wasting his time there.

At Ray-Vor he did not "hit it off" with Fred Ferron, the French superintendent or with his 3 carpenter, foremen brothers. The carpenter union was made up mostly of Frenchmen and Finns. Mr. Ward soon realized it was a good idea to separate Risto and Fred and let them run their own jobs including hiring.

Risto's crew, which I joined, was naturally mostly Finn, including his father. Risto's jobs excelled and brought in better profits and his reputation with Inco blossomed, which would continue to be a big reason for his success in the years that followed. Risto soon realized he could run his own company. He went into partnership with John Dennis his friend and former professor at Cambrian. LaamDen Construction did well but didn't last long. Risto soon formed his own company Laamanen Construction, with his father as superintendent and most of his foremen and key workers Finns.

## Sow the Wind and Reap the Whirlwind

Meanwhile things at home were not quite as rosy. I had been given a hookah pipe as a wedding gift from Joe Lavigne who had tried it out to make sure it worked. It was stuck in the closet with all the other gifts and forgotten about, until our home was raided one afternoon while I was at work. I figured the RCMP was still watching me, especially with my best friend now on the west coast. However, I didn't care because I was working and not going selling drugs anymore. I thought I was home free but was mistaken. There were no drugs in our house but the police confiscated the pipe and I was charged with possession of a narcotic substance. The police charge read, "immeasurable amount of cannabis resin". What they found was so little it could not be measured but they had wanted me and this would do for now. I hired a lawyer, Guy Mahafee and went to court resulting in a $100 fine and a criminal record that would haunt me time and again in later years even though I applied for and received a pardon in 1977.

In August we moved into Marja's parents basement apartment on Maki Avenue on the south end of town. Rent was free and I was earning good money but this was no place for us to start a life together, for several reasons. Firstly we were not alone and secondly there was a bar in walking distance. By the time I got home from work Marja was eager to get out of the house. Many weeknights we walked to the Caswell Hotel, "CasBar" where there was live music, often Sam Lahti and his band. This made working for a living difficult and upset Marja's parents.

We continued to smoke pot and party on the weekends. Late one Friday night we decided to extend our party to a weekend bash by going to Barry Moxam's camp on Penage Lake. I snuck into the house and passed my stereo and large speakers out the window to Barry. There was no hydro at camp but Barry was sure his generator would work fine. The records played but way too slow. So much trouble for so little satisfaction. This seemed to be the order of the day.

Our honeymoon period didn't last long and settling into regular life was impossible. Marja was extremely unhappy; sitting in her parent's basement all day was more difficult than it was for me working. Often when I got home I realized she had been nipping that afternoon. When I expressed my anger at this habit she reverted to pills. We fought a lot, especially when drinking. Late one night, as we sat on the lawn behind the house, having a drink Marja, in a fit of anger, threw her beer bottle at me. Fortunately, she was not as good a shot as I was. We only lasted a couple of months there and moved to my parent's basement, which was a little better situation. At 49 Moxam we had more privacy and my parent's were so much more understanding but we had so much to work out with each other and with God.

I managed to keep working and we started attending church with my parents, which made them happy. I hoped it would help us adjust to every day normal living. We went through the motions but the emptiness was ever present. Drinking and the drugs were the only way we knew how to self medicate our ailment. We had a difficult time communicating effectively. I had no idea what she was thinking and was often tormented with jealous thoughts. She was such a beautiful young lady and attracted attention from the opposite sex wherever we went. She had thrived on attention over the years; not getting what she needed from me made it easier for her to still find it appealing. There is no pain that I have experienced in this life that compares to the ache of a jealous husband. A lost child comes close but is slightly more bearable.

## An Unexpected Visitor

That winter we spent an evening with Ruth and Dennis, who was still out on bail waiting trial. They had recently married and were living in an apartment in town. I had overindulged and was in no shape to drive but we were determined to get home. It was snowing hard and windy. I could only see a few feet in front of the car. As I slowed down for the lights in Copper Cliff, the car stalled; I turned the key but there was nothing. I put my 4-way flashers on and contemplated my next move; there was little I could do. I wouldn't even know what to look for under the hood. As we sat there I started praying out loud for help.

A few minutes later a man appeared out of nowhere and lifted the hood of our car. He did something under the hood and motioned for me to try it and sure enough it started. He shut the hood and disappeared as quick as he had appeared. We saw no car, no lights, nothing. We drove home with thankful hearts, not knowing what to make of our unexpected visitor. I guess it could have been an angel. Whoever it was, we were encouraged and determined to continue looking up for help. Sure enough help was on the way; it would come soon and sudden.

PHOTOGRAPH OF BEARER
PHOTOGRAPHIE DU TITULAIRE

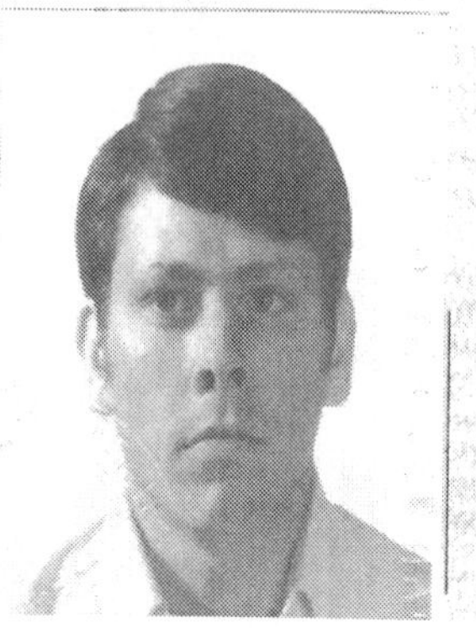

Benjie in Hopeville

1975 Passport Picture

Tel. Pager 245-5544 #9156

DON BAST
Sales Representative

1979

# CHAPTER 4

# The Cult Years (1972 – 1979)

## Revival Begins

Like the children of Israel who crossed through the Red Sea to freedom, I was about to receive a great deliverance, also. My joy would be similar to theirs as they watched in amazement as their enemies drown, giving chase. But also like them, when the initial celebration ended, a 40-year journey began towards the Promised Land. I was about to experience many twists and turns, sideways, forward and backwards, up and down, divinely being led along God's direct route through the wilderness.

In January of 1972 a group of young people from the Mennonite Bible College in Winnipeg toured Ontario and came to Water's Mennonite Church. A few names I remember are Abe Bueller, John Taves and a girl named Maryanne, who later became John's wife. Their simple, happy testimonies touched us all but especially Marilyn and Marja. After the service a group of kids came over to my parent's house. It was there, in the basement, sitting in a circle on the floor praying, that God moved quietly and powerfully in Marja's heart. She knew this was her time. Grace overwhelmed her with the faith to see that God had not rejected her because of her rebellion. She arose that night with a cleansed and peace filled, heart. By the end of the month Marilyn was off to Winnipeg to join her new friends in Bible School.

I was deeply touched and under great conviction. Thus began the battle of my life raging in my mind and heart, but I was not ready to give in, not yet. I was sincerely happy for Marja and the others. Although I knew their joy and deliverance was real it made me feel worse. Deep down I knew it was near. The strong pull from two opposing directions began tearing my insides apart. I was in torment but couldn't make the leap of faith.

The next few months were unsettling, to say the least. The downtown scene had lost its appeal; it seemed dead, like me. Cigarettes tasted bad so I switched to cigars and rolled pipe tobacco. I knew the crazy ride I was on was coming to an end and I was afraid of the unknown that lay ahead. Church became boring and awkward. I had grown up on the front pew of this church and knew how to talk the talk. The thought of "playing the game", pretending to walk the walk, was repulsive. All my life I had observed "luke warm" Christians going through the motions in order to please a spouse and hopefully win God's favor. This prospect had absolutely no appeal to me. On the other hand I felt responsible to somehow fix the problems, heal the pain and bridge the gap I had created in my family and church. They deserved better than what I had been dumping on them for far too long.

Gerry who had been living in Toronto, with his partner in crime, Willy Byers, was also on the move but not to Bible School. They had purchased some stuff and brought it back to Sudbury to sell. Unknown to them, a couple of their customers were RCMP undercover agents who had been stationed in Sudbury to do a major cleanup. They bought drugs from more than 30 dealers, including both my brothers. Gerry and Willy were charged with trafficking. They received 9 + 3 months and the same month Marilyn went to Bible School in Winnipeg, Gerry went to the Monteith Correctional Complex, a medium / maximum security prison in Northern Ontario.

Rick Ahola, another one of the Movers, was quietly and secretly fighting his own demons. He had broken one of the boy's unwritten rules and also found himself in the battle of his life. Unknown to us, he had been struggling with severe depression, trying to find purpose in life; he stepped over the line the rest of us dared not. In a moment of weakness he stuck a needle in his arm and found some immediate relief but when he came down he faced a reality worse than the one he had escaped.

There is something about speed or Meth, the street names for amphetamines that is so addicting that it is to be avoided at all cost. Many get hooked just shooting up once; Rick was one those victims and within weeks his life fell apart. He lost interest in eating properly, bathing or grooming. I was not with him when he made his initial stand to fight through the addiction but discovered him hanging onto a thread of hope shortly after. He was a mess like his unkempt, smoke filled apartment, a clear reflection of his broken and shambled life.

I visited him often in the coming weeks and hurt for him. We were fighting similar battles; mine was more concealed, raging inside not as visible as Rick's. For some reason, he was drawn to my parent's house, the home that had proved to be a place of refuge not only for the Bast kids but also for other Movers. My parents by their own admission were not qualified to offer us a solution. All they could give was love and acceptance, which proved to be exactly what the doctor ordered for Rick. God is love and the Great Physician, had poured His comfort into their hearts, over the years. Now they were able to comfort others with the same comfort they had received.

As the next few years unfolded Rick would also end up at the Bible College in Winnipeg and was eternally indebted to the Bast family, especially my parents for their help and he often talked about it openly. He was not ashamed to thank them publicly, for playing a key role in the success he was enjoying. At their special anniversaries, or whenever the opportunity arose, he humbly shared the help he received from them in his desperate time of need. Rick went on to have a successful career with the City of Greater Sudbury. He started out by driving the zamboni at the Walden arena and then became the arena manager. Eventually he became "Manager of Municipal Arenas, Community Centers and Parks Supervisor". He retired in 2011 with 30 years of service.

Soon all the Movers would disperse in different directions and go on with their lives; most of them would do very well. Out west, in the early days, Billy built homes and then got into the produce business. For years he owned and operate 4 fresh, produce, retail outlets in the Fraser Valley. Of late he has scaled down to just one store, one farm and a group of commercial customers, which he supplies. Like his father before him, he has a hard time slowing down. Greg had a career with Telus and retired young from his position "Associate Director in Service Management". Pentti became a commercial airline pilot, also retiring young with 28 years of service with Canadian Airlines and then Air Canada. Half way through his career he lost most of his right arm in a nut-picking machine. The union tried to get rid of him but he fought it and won. He is the only guy I know of who learned to fly 747's, with one arm. His itinerary for the last few years of his career was 3 trips to China a month. He now owns and operates 2 hazel nut farms in BC's Fraser Valley.

Back in Ontario, Murray became an electrician and had a long career with E.B.Eddy, now Domtar, in Espanola. He was the president of the Electrician's Union for many years. Dennis drove truck for 25 years for BFI Waste Systems in the City of Toronto. In the 70's he worked with Daniel who was head of security for CPI, Concert Productions Inc. When big rock bands came to town Danny often hired 200+ security guards. He took the responsibility of being the personal bodyguard for the stars such as Mick Jager and Neil Young. He has many stories to tell, of what goes on behind the scenes, most of which are not suitable for this writing. A few short ones are worth sharing. When Grateful Dead played in Hamilton, Danny had very long and curly, graying hair, similar to that of Jerry Garcia. They were also close in size and shape. At a distance, they looked like twins, walking down the street together; people weren't sure who was who.

On one occasion when Neil Young was in town he brought his big dog with him. Dennis, one of Danny's right hand men, was delegated one afternoon to baby-sit Neil's four-legged friend,. All Neil said was, "Don't let him get away from you because you will never catch him". He got away. Dennis chased and searched the streets of Toronto for several hours. Finally, exhausted and embarrassed he went back and found Neil. There was the dog with him. Neil informed him that he was kidding. He said this dog never gets lost and could find his way back from anywhere.

Randy went into the construction business and still operates his own construction company in Orillia. Larry also went into this same field like his father before him and held a number of different positions. One of his last jobs was for one of Canada's leading construction companies, Dufferin Concrete as Manager a redi-Mix plant. Early in his career he learned to operate drilling rigs used to make holes for blasting rock for Chisnel and Ganton the company his Dad owned. Later he graduated to a much bigger drill, "The Mole", a 13' diameter horizontal drill. One of his bigger jobs was the 15 km Scarborough Sewer Tunnell. The Bast boys had varied careers like their father, as you will discover as you read on.

## The Jesus People

I was impressed that Marja's and Marilyn's new found faith was solid and flourishing and I was also aware of God dealing with me. I took it seriously and was determined to at least be good, mainly for the sake of Mother. I am so thankful that God in His mercy began turning us around before she had a breakdown. She had been carrying such a heavy burden for too long; now there was hope. Even though Marilyn and Marja had both been busted for possession of narcotics and now had a criminal record their lives had made a total about turn. Finally there was a light at the end of the tunnel for Mom, which provided some comfort, as she considered what her family and friends must be thinking regarding her sons who had been busted for trafficking. Her youngest was already in jail and her oldest was waiting sentencing. Her middle son, yours truly, would keep his nose clean from now on. That was the least I could do.

The girls reveled in their new joy. However, their excitement wore on me day and night for several months. In March another group of young people came to Sudbury. This time they came from Naples Florida and held meetings at the independent Pentecostal Church in New Sudbury. The pastor of the church was Reverend John Murray. Marja, who grew up in the Finnish Pentecostal Church was familiar with this church and some of the members and so we decided to attend. End time prophecy and especially the rapture seemed to be the buzz of the day. Their message was simple; "Jesus is coming soon".

We went to a couple services that were being held nightly. The music was loud and the singing, led by Bill Brown, an ex-hippie and ex-druggie, was full of life. They had incredible testimonies and the conviction of my heart increased with every service. The war in me was peaking and something had to give. However, it was not as I had assumed. God was drawing me by

His love rather than by a sense of fear so I was caught off guard. On the third or fourth night we got a flat tire just as we arrived at the church. I was relieved. I now had an excuse to stay outside a little longer and sent the others in, so I could change my tire while it was still light out. My heart was heavy. I knew the shape I was in and I knew there was no use running away and there was no time left to stay, not where I was, anyway.

I took my time finishing the tire change and cleaned my hands. I went in and stood at the back of the church beside Marja's brother Risto. We listened there as Bill preached and when he gave the altar call that night I knew it was my time. I looked at Risto and said, "You going up?" He just shook his head. Without hesitation, as if being carried along, my legs started moving, carrying me up to the front. Several others were there and with my head swirling, I got down on my knees and joined them. I don't know how it happened but I exploded and completely lost control. The long hard struggle was over. I began praying and God broke my whole being wide open. I cried buckets of tears as I poured out my heart to the only One I knew Who could help me. I stayed there for a long time not knowing what to do next.

My conversion and deliverance were instant and powerful. God immediately took away my craving for drugs and alcohol. When I got up off my knees I put my pack of smokes on the platform and left them there. 40+ years later, I have never had another puff from a cigarette or joint since. A few weeks later I had 3 beers at a friends house, named "Lucky", which did nothing for me. After that I didn't have a drop of alcohol for over 7 years. The habits were gone but the memory lived on. Over the next 20 years I would have 2 reoccurring nightmares. The one was from grade 9. In it, I relived getting lost in the halls of Lo-Ellen Park Secondary and the embarrassment of being late for class. I still hate being late and I hate getting lost!

In my other dream I was smoking again. In dreamland I was able to smoke one cigar a day for awhile and then quit for a week or two and then have another. I enjoyed this control and every puff. The dreams were so real that I had to stop and think it through; did I really start smoking again? It doesn't take long to figure out that I can't recall any details like the brand of cigar or the time and place where I bought them or smoked them. This is the way I reassure myself that I have never had a smoke since 1972; other than that the smoking in my dreams was as real as life. I can see in the lives of loved ones around me how addicting cigarettes are and frankly I am scared to death to take that first puff, although I have thought about it a many times, especially when the black flies were bad.

The next night the revival meeting was so different and most enjoyable, especially the singing. At the end of the night Bill asked all to come up who needed prayer. Art was scheduled to appear in court for sentencing the next morning. He figured there was nothing to lose and up he went. Bill and the others laid hands on him and we all prayed for him. Bill assured him he was not going to jail; Bill was wrong.  I didn't make a big deal about it. That was a side issue, in my mind. God's love had been pursuing me and haunting me for years. Bill Brown was just the messenger God used to deliver the message that set me free from my bondage and imminent destruction.

## Art Off to Jail

Art showed up in court the next day to receive his sentence. He got 6 months definite and another 6 indefinite and was sent to The Guelph Correctional Center a.k.a. Guelph Reformatory. He was given time off for good behavior and was released after 4 months on July 22, 1972. Gerry was shipped back to Sudbury on day parole in June of 1972. He was able to work at my parent's produce store during the day and spend the night at the district jail, the local "Crowbar Hotel". This lasted a couple weeks and he was released. My parents were slowly getting their children back one by one. I find it so amazing how all 4 of the Bast children were led down the same road, almost to the point of no return, and then God began dealing with each of us, one by one, drawing us back into His arms of love.

## Probe 72

I enjoyed the rest of the meetings, and returned home, rejoicing in the Lord and finding favor with my family and neighbors. The news of our conversion spread fast. The Movers and old friends were not impressed; they couldn't comprehend what had happened to us. When they heard I took a hammer to my collection of 300 record albums they knew I had gone crazy. It wouldn't be long that I would regret this but at the time, I thought I needed to make a clean break; burning the bridges of influence behind me would surely prevent me from returning. If this was what it would take to follow the Lord I was willing to pay the price. I just didn't realize it would hurt so bad. Several of the boys, in particular, meant so much to me. They had taken me to their side when I was lost and alone. We had formed close bonds and now I was breaking away. I knew they didn't understand and the pain cut deep.

I knew Jesus had walked alone and He warned all who would follow Him of the same. I had known this all along and thought I had counted the cost. At least He gave me a wife and a sister who were willing to travel this lonely road with me. All the time I had been running from God I knew I was different and was called to walk a different path. All my life I had been listening to the beat of a different drum and now I prayed for courage to start walking to that beat instead of running from it.

Marilyn, Marja and I began getting involved in the Mennonite Church again. We attended all the services, prayer meetings and the youth group discussions. We were on fire for God and after several years of getting high on illegal substances we had found a brand new and exciting high. My parents in particular and a few church members were elated; others predicted we would soon cool down and fit into regular church life. They were mistaken. We would not cool down; we would continue to get hotter and hotter.

In April there was a worldwide conference of Mennonites scheduled for Minnesota Minneapolis. Dick and Anna Neufeldt agreed to go to represent our church and invited Marja and I to join them. Young Mennonites, especially attended from all over the globe. We sensed revival in the air. The excitement of the soon return of the Lord seemed to be the main focus. We came back home eager to preach the good news of the impending revival, and the Lord's soon return. I was asked to give a report of the convention the next Sunday morning and gladly agreed.

I stood behind the pulpit that morning and told them a wave of revival was moving across our land and they better wake up or they would miss out. I guess I had a burr under my saddle. All my life I had sat in one of those, not so comfortable pews, and took the heat, now I made the most of my opportunity to give a little of it back. It had little effect and I soon realized why I had left this church in the first place. It was a boring place filled with boring people. I figured a few sincerely longed for a renewal in their lives but they were confined and restricted to the system and helpless to change anything, even themselves. We quickly began seeking out other places more alive to fellowship.

## Reverend Murray

The first place we attended was the Pentecostal Church where the Jesus People had held the meetings that changed my life. Services in the Pentecostal Church were more alive, for sure and we enjoyed the singing and the worship emphasis. The speaking in tongues and prophecy were not new to Marja, although I observed these activities with cautious curiosity. I sensed God's love, His joy and acceptance; this was most important to me. There were several things, however that did bother me. Pastor Murray stood out as being a little strange, even in this setting, which was not easy. When he got excited, "in the spirit", he shouted in tongues, always repeating a combination of the same syllables that sounded like "a-hun-da-la-ba-si-a". He would close his eyes and wave his arms and his bottom jaw would quiver faster than windshield wipers on high. I tried not to look at him but it was so bizarre, quite comical actually, which made it difficult to concentrate on worship. His wife was not to be outdone by her preacher husband. She was normally reserved and soft-spoken but when "the spirit" hit, everything changed. Her head was thrown back and quickly brought forward. Her long hair, which was always worn in a bun, came loose, with the rest of her body and flew everywhere, as she seemed to take off madly in all directions, with eyes closed. She once commented that when she was in the spirit she never ran into anyone. I didn't take any chances and stayed clear of her.

We attended a few more "deliverance services", which only became more bizarre. Apparently, everyone's problems were directly linked to a demon that needed to be exorcised. Garbage cans were placed on the floor in front of the person kneeling, for prayer. They were encouraged to spit out the demons into the waste container as the Reverend or his helpers would slap them on the back to help loose the demonic hold. The prayer warriors stood over them, screamed in tongues and encouraged their victim to loosen their mouth and let it move freely so they could receive the gift of tongues and enjoy a new heavenly language, albeit with only a handful of meaningless words. We only lasted a few weeks in this setting and bravely moved on, with our faith only slightly shaken.

## Prayer Meetings

While we were at the Pentecostal Church we met Art Harper, a local man in his 40's. He invited us to a prayer meeting in his home in Val Caron, so we attended. Art was another large man like John Murray but much quieter. He was also soft spoken; to the point where he appeared quite timid and unsure of himself. You guessed it; when "the spirit" came on him while praying or prophesying he became as bold as a tiger. We spent long evenings sitting around his large living room, eyes closed, singing, praying and praising the Lord. We patiently "reached out" for whatever the Lord had and learned to wait for hours in expectant submission concentrating on His love and goodness for us. We prayed for each other with a desire to edify and encourage any who were feeling down. We gathered 3 nights a week, and were often up late. Especially those of us who had jobs, relied on our joy from the night before to compensate for our lack of sleep the next day. After one particularly exuberant meeting I sensed the Lord wanted us to pray for someone, for healing on our way home. So I drove downtown, parked the car and waited. Within a few minutes we saw a man in the distance coming our way on crutches and figured he must be the one and our excitement mounted. As he got closer we could see he only had one leg, oh oh! We sat quiet for a minute and I prayed, "Lord, I believe, but help my unbelief." I soon realized we didn't have this kind of faith, yet; it was time to go home.

Brother Harper was on the mailing list of several evangelists from the States and was planning on attending a meeting in Phoenix Arizona in August. Marja and I both were elated about this proposition and we started making plans. We would take our own vehicle and travel with Art, his wife and daughter. I set up a bed in the back of my 1970 Ford pick-up so someone could sleep while another kept driving. My sister Marilyn came along and so did my cousin David Bast, who had recently moved to Sudbury and was a regular visitor at my parents house. Although Dave didn't share the same spiritual fervor as we did he was eager to make the 5000 mile round trip. He was a truck driver by trade and loved traveling and I needed another driver. I found out many years later that he had been struggling with his own substance abuse, at the time, and welcomed the chance to get away from the local scene for awhile.

Marja was 7 months pregnant and when we arrived in Arizona the temperature was 104 degrees Fahrenheit and my truck had no air conditioner. It was hot for all of us but almost unbearable for Marja. The preacher we were going to see was Neil Frisbey the "Pyramid Prophet". His pyramid shaped temple was outside of town, in the dessert. We had heard reports of special sightings of spiritual beings and lights in the sky above and in the temple during the meetings. We were curious and a little suspicious, especially as we approached the large, fancy building. I noticed many Cadillac's, Lincolns and other expensive cars as we walked across the huge parking lot. The fact that women were dressed to the hilt in nightgowns, jewelry and make-up also bothered me but we reluctantly continued in. What concerned me the most, as we entered the sanctuary, were the many cameras I witnessed instead of the Bibles, I expected to see. To make it worse, I smelled alcohol on the gentleman next to me in the bathroom but I had driven 2500 miles and had to at least check it out.

The service was formal and professionally executed. There was very little scripture reading, if any, or preaching before the prayer line started. People were told to stand precisely at the right spot marked on the floor when receiving prayer from the prophet. Some seemed to be touched and blessed, although this was not the emphasis; not sure what it was. It was obvious people came looking for something extraordinary and had their cameras ready. We went back to our motel rooms heartbroken and sorely disappointed. Had we driven so far to see this cheap show? As we gathered in Art's hotel room later, he was his usual quiet, confident self as he shared about another meeting, kind of on our way home, in Little Rock Arkansas. This was a Tent Meeting and the preacher / prophet was David Terrell; he called himself "The End-time Messenger".

We were obviously a little leery as we entered the huge tent a few days later. Brother Terrell was one of the few preachers left traveling back and forth across the "Sawdust Trail" of the south. It was so called because of the fine wood chips spread down the isles of the tent to keep the dust down. Clinging to the coat tails of the "healing revival" he moved tirelessly from city to city. Thousands of people had already gathered and sat quiet. We were a little late but I didn't mind sitting at the back in case we decided to make an early exit.

Mr. Terrell, who apparently only had a grade 2-education, wore all black, suit, shirt, socks and shoes with no tie. He sat on the platform steps with his guitar in hand, where he talked and sang. His message was simple, "Behold the Lamb of God". He told us that when he was 9 years old and bed-ridden, with bone cancer, Jesus stood in his bedroom with this same message. Jesus told him to get up and walk; as he obeyed he was instantly healed. He was now lugging around an ex Barnum and Bailey tent, apparently the world's largest, telling his story of the saving, healing power of the lonely man from Nazareth.

I had never heard a preacher with such a bold authority and simplicity all combined in one package. As he continued I felt goose bumps all over my body and I started weeping. I looked around and noticed Marja and Marilyn wiping tears also. We were hooked; whatever this preacher man had, we wanted.

That night we came back for more and this time sat at the front, bibles open soaking in every word. His tent meetings lasted for 9 days, one 3-hour service in the morning and another in the evening. It wasn't just the simple message and the healings weren't that impressive; it was more the awesome presence under the tent that captivated me. We attended a couple more days and then floated home rejoicing and praising the Lord for His goodness and power.

Prayer meetings now escalated to a new level of excitement. I began reading Brother Terrell's material and searching the Bible daily. I wanted more of God; all He would give me. Sometime later we brought a young believer along to one of the tent meetings. He was a university Arts and Theatre student and was eager to meet Brother Terrell after hearing our stories. After sitting through a couple meetings, he was amazed and called "this preacher" the best one-man show he had ever seen. We thought that was cool and gave God the glory, well part of the glory, anyway; we were very proud of "The Prophet".

On Brother Terrell's posters and news ads his pet slogan was prominent, "Behold the Lamb of God", taken from John 1:29. Over the coming months we gradually discovered, beholding Jesus, meant hearing what He said and strictly obeying. The message was simple enough to understand but not easy to do. "If any one will come after me, let him disown himself, and take up his cross, and follow me" (Matthew 16:24, Mark 8:34). Terrell warned us that this was God's message for His people.

We were encouraged "to sell whatever we had and give to the prophet like the first century church did. Only those who would "sell out" could be assured the power of God in their life and the ability to endure to the end and be saved (Matthew 10:22). Enduring was clearly defined by Brother Terrell; taking up your cross daily meant living a holy life of fasting and prayer.

## A Son is born

On October 1st 1972 Marja and I rented a cottage off Penage Lake Road 10 miles west of my parent's house. We set up our humble furniture and got ready to start a new family. On the evening of October 8th, Marja went into labor and I took her into the Sudbury General Hospital. Shortly after she got settled the labor pains began to lessen but her contractions continued all through the night and into the next day. Even though she was exhausted, she was only able to catch a few winks sleep between her contractions as I walked the floor patiently waiting the arrival of our first child.

Around 8:30, the evening of October 9th, I went for another coffee, in preparation of another late night. Almost immediately after leaving the room, she went into hard labor, and before I returned our son was born, a few hours before Marja's 23rd birthday. I had waited by her side for 24 hours so I could be there for the big moment and only left for a few minutes and missed it. We were ecstatic; the long hard labor was over and our son was healthy and beautiful. We thanked God with hearts full of joy. We named him Benjamin after the patriarch Jacob's youngest son. His middle name would be Carl the same as my dad. The next day we took him to our new home in Whitefish.

Marilyn moved in to help Marja with her new responsibility. The next night as we prepared for bed Marja's spotting turned to bleeding and we began to pray for healing. As the night wore on the bleeding increased and our prayers took on a new level of concern and intensity. We called Gerry and he came over to join Marilyn and I in prayer. We tried hard to stay awake and pray but as fatigue set in we seemed to take turns dozing off and then reviving to continue praying. In the middle of the night Marja started passing more blood clots, a few as big as oranges. We all were awake now and became frantic.

Marja, who was completely limp, appeared to be quickly losing consciousness, due to loss of blood. It was now too late to consider making the long drive to the hospital. Instead we began crying out in earnest to the Lord, to have mercy on us and heal Marja. Amazingly, shortly before dawn, just when we thought we could not continue any longer, Marja suddenly received a surge of life. To our surprise and great joy, she got up on her own strength and went to the washroom. 1-day old Benjie who had slept peacefully at her side through the 8-hour ordeal, woke up and Marja sat up in bed and breast-fed him.

She was very weak for a few days but the bleeding had stopped and she seemed to have no other ill effects. We were so relieved and so thankful. The next day, Marja told us that it felt like there was a ton of bricks on her chest, everything was dark and she could faintly hear our cries in the distance, as if we were at the other end of a long tunnel. We later shared our story with our doctor friend Paul Martin; he said it sure sounds like Marja was approaching heart failure. We had learned a lesson that night but not one in line with common sense. Instead of teaching us, not to take these kinds of chances but rather to err on the side of caution, it had the opposite effect. We were young zealous believers; we considered this near tragedy a test from God, which we passed; now our faith was stronger than ever. Now we were ready to trust Him more.

## The Fasting Life

I began reading David Terrell's material and listening to his tapes. Meetings with Art Harper became less frequent because of the greater distance to travel, now that we had moved. We also now had an extra little passenger that needed constant attention. I was still working for Ray-Vor Construction but spent all my spare time studying and making copious notes, which I shared with Marja and my siblings. We were so eager to learn and the material was inspiring; we couldn't get enough.

Brother Terrell spoke much about fasting; he said this was the key to unlocking God's secrets and power in our life. I read a book called "The Spiritual Fast" and with little planning I began a fast, not knowing how long I could go, because it was winter and I was working outside. The book claimed that a real fast was to drink water only, so water it was. After 3 days my stomach seemed to go to sleep and the physical hunger cravings stop; my emotional hunger or mental appetite never went away.

I was 135 pounds when I started and immediately started losing weight. It was torture but I wanted to know God and believed this was the way. Brother Terrell taught that 40 days was a complete fast, although few are called or able to go that long. I hoped I could some day endure this accomplishment but not this time. I was so weak and cold; it became more difficult to do the job I was getting paid to do.

My father-in-law, who was my foreman at work, stood at the bottom of my ladder, one day, shaking his head in disbelief and disgust. He knew I was fasting because I didn't bring a lunch and had enquired from Marja the reason, which he obviously didn't understand or approve of. He impatiently held the ladder so his, 120 pound, son-in-law wouldn't blow away. I managed to go 16 days and reluctantly gave into my hunger pangs. Whether the pangs were physical or mental, I didn't know. All I knew was that I was hungry and weak and needed to eat.

Obviously, I hadn't read enough and when I broke my fast, I overate, and with the wrong kind of food also. I had stomach pains and was constipated for several days. However, this was merely a minor inconvenience compared to the new joy and energy I was experiencing. I had a hard time sleeping and my spirit seemed to soar. My mind was sharper to grasp God's word. All I wanted to do was to study and hated going to work. Around Christmas I got laid off, which was normal and fine with me. Through the winter I collected unemployment insurance and dedicated myself to study and organized regular prayer meetings. Fasting became a part of our life and we learned how to properly prepare. Our last meal was comprised of fruit and vegetables and possibly fruit juices for a day and then strictly water. To break the fast the process was reversed. Regardless how short a fast was it was difficult not to over-eat after and then suffer the consequences.

## Massey Days

Early the spring of 1973 we began looking for a bigger house so we could all live together and have more room for meetings and not have to worry about traveling to gather. We were sure the time was short, therefore "seeking God" was our number one priority in life.

We found an old rundown farmhouse south of Massey that we could rent cheaply but it needed a lot of work. Carl Brohart the owner agreed to buy the material if we provided the labor. So Gerry and I rolled up our sleeves and began renovating. We tore the old plaster and wood lathe off the walls, put up paneling and installed flooring. We cleaned and painted to get it respectable enough for women and children to inhabit. Marilyn volunteered to move in to help clean and cook for us. Marja and Benjie soon followed and thus our communal lifestyle began. Here I studied the Bible daily and listened to tape after tape of Brother Terrell and other preachers. Most evenings we gathered to pray, sing and share God's word.

All over the US the prophet was establishing special areas where his followers gathered and began preparing for the "Great Tribulation" soon to come. We hoped and prayed that this house would be the beginning of a Northern Ontario "Blessed Area". Every time we were able we traveled to Brother Terrell's 9-day tent meetings in various cities south of the border. When I got called back to work I advised them that I was not available, which upset my father-in-law a great deal. My parents and Marja's were so happy and relieved that we had survived the drug scene. Both our mothers, in particular had continually prayed for us through those hard years. I guess they felt the urgency was finally over but now by the way we were beginning to behave they were not so sure.

Over the next two years we went to many tent meetings in the southern States as far away as Mobile Alabama and San Antonio Texas. We were so hungry for reality and someone to lead us. The tent meetings were so powerful and pulsated with life. Every now and then a young man would get so excited he would jump out of his seat and run around the perimeter of the tent behind the seats. This usually brought a smile to Brother Terrell's face; he periodically initiated this practice. When the crowd was particularly exuberant he would shout, "Somebody run around the tent". Without hesitation a young men would take off like a bullet, dust flying, happy to accommodate the Prophet and release his pent up energy.

Don Clowers who appeared to be Terrell's right hand man and fellow preacher was married to a Canadian and began coming to Canada for regular meetings. I became his contact here and was honored to eventually become the vice-president of the Don Clowers Evangelistic Association of Canada. He had a large church in Fort Payne Alabama, which I attended as often as I could. I got to sit on the platform with the visiting preachers and was always introduced as his main man in Canada.

Besides fasting and praying, giving was a part of the price one had to pay to acquire God's blessing and anointing. We heard story after story of the faithful ones who sold their houses and lands, like the first century church and laid the money at the prophet's feet. Offerings were an important part of the meetings. God usually showed the Prophet what kind of offering to expect. He would say things like, "God showed me there are 50 people here today that He wants to give $1,000 each". If they obeyed a special blessing was coming to them personally and the city where the tent happened to be located, might be spared at least some of God's judgments. He would ask them to stand up and he patiently waited until he had 50. This often took an hour.

We didn't own property but literally gave all we had including the clothes off our back. We sold the bedroom suite we had been given as a wedding gift from Marja's parents and put the money in the offering. When they found out they were hurt. Her father was visibly angry and who could blame him. We never considered their feelings because we were so consumed with pleasing God. It was obvious His servants were blessed spiritually and physically; the faithful few were promised the same blessings. Believe it or not, we took our wedding bands off and put them in the offering bucket.

During a special offering for a missionary venture in Guatemala I took off my favorite dress boots off, the ones I was married in. I loved those two-tone brown and black boots but I loved the Lord more and would do anything to please Him. However, I was a little confused and disturbed a few days later when I saw the song leader wearing them on stage. This was one of the first red flags that popped up. At the time, we brushed it off thinking the prophet would not approve and knew nothing about it.

## My Parents 25th

On May 25th, 1973 my parents celebrated their 25th anniversary in the fellowship hall of the Mennonite Church where our wedding reception had been less than 2 years prior, with many of the same friends and relatives present. Uncles and Aunts from down south, most of the congregation and some neighbor friends all attended to honor my parents; it was a packed house.

When the microphone was opened for anyone to speak, a common message prevailed. Many praised my parents for their faithfulness over the years. They mentioned the fact that they had recently been tested severely and had remained steadfast in the faith. It was obvious they were referring to the hell their children had put them through. Everyone present knew about the drugs, the jail sentences and now "the cult".

As I listened my self-righteous pride and fervor burned inside. Before I knew it, I was on my feet with microphone in hand. I could not pass up this opportunity to testify to the real truth, especially with a house full of backslid, lukewarm Christians. I acknowledged my parents pain but was quick to add that their children also carried a heavy burden. We had deep sorrow watching our parents wasting their time "playing church". I ended my short rebuke with one of my favorite verses, "If the blind lead the blind they will all fall into the ditch". My parents had been through so much already and I never even considered that this was their anniversary celebration. I had more sense then this and love when I was stoned. I was totally oblivious to my bad attitude and their sensitive feelings.

Obviously, everyone present was shocked and I am sure none were impressed. My performance confirmed the rumors they had heard about us. John Zacharius, the pastor and master of ceremonies, quickly said, "let us sing another hymn of joy and hope." It is hard for me to imagine the kind of bold arrogance I displayed, although at the time something seemed to just come over me. Almost like outside of my body, I observed myself get up, walk to the front, and start talking.

Like the early apostles, I thought I was being carried along by what I was sure was the anointing of holy spirit. Ironically, years later the pastor confided in me, that although I was a young, arrogant and self-righteous "Christian", the short message I delivered was a wake up call for him. Not long after this he got involved in the "Charismatic Renewal Movement" that swept through many Mennonite churches, which is another whole ball of wax, I am not going to touch. I am pleased that I got a second chance to redeem myself. 15 years later, at my parents 40th I was the Master of Ceremonies and openly apologized for what I had said at their 25$^{th}$ anniversary, to largely the same crowd.

## Judgments Were Coming

David Terrell taught God was going to judge America for their sin. This meant hard times like famine were ahead. He warned, only those who fast several days a week and prayed 3 – 4 hours a day would be able to handle the great tribulations. I began to wake up at 4:00 am so I could get my prayer time in before the others got up.

Many of Terrell's followers were "preparing for famine". Large gardens were planted and many jars of food were canned. God showed Brother Terrell that by the end of the 70's a great destruction would hit the world, especially backslid America. He regularly prophesied about disasters like plane crashes, earthquakes and tornados. These things happened regularly somewhere around the world and the Prophet was given credit for being able to see these things and even cause them. Like many others we planted a garden and began canning.

Some of the "Terrellites" took it very serious. Marja and I visited a wealthy rancher, Marvin Williams, who owned 4000 acres in Florida and was in full production, preparing for famine. He had his own slaughterhouse and workers. They could and did often slaughter a couple cows, several large hogs or 100 chickens in a day. He lived in the middle of one of the "Blessed Areas" approved by God and endorsed by His End-Time Messenger.

Brother Terrell announced these locations and introduced the leaders who attended the meetings and sat on the platform behind the Prophet. Their churches in the heart of the Blessed Area began to grow substantially. There was one in Dothan, Alabama where Brother Cross had a large church, another in Springfield, Tennessee where brother Ellis was the pastor and Fort Payne Alabama where Don Clowers' was. Brownsville Texas was home to Brother Terrell; Bother Dawson pastored when the Prophet was on the road. Thousands flocked to these areas and others. The Prophet made the rounds regularly and held meetings. God also showed him there was to be, at least one area in each province of Canada. We were determined to do all we could to be an integral part of a blessed area in Ontario.

While preaching brother Terrell would continually wipe his perspiration with a white handkerchief. He had boxes full of them all neatly folded. These he collected to mail out to the faithful supporters who needed a miracle. Often, to the delight of those in the front rows, he would throw a handkerchief into the crowd and people would scramble for it. I heard that one hanky was to be buried in the ground in each Canadian province as a mark of faith, with the promise that near this location a blessed area would be established. I asked Brother Clowers to talk to the Prophet to see if I could be in charge of the making sure they were distributed and buried in Canada. He did and I was given the awesome responsibility of carrying it out. I knew of a brother on the east coast who would take care of the Maritime Provinces; contacts were made out west and blessed hankies were mailed. I buried one between Barrie and Toronto and one in Massey were we lived.

I realize this is all so bizarre and may be difficult for some to understand how reasonably normal and otherwise sane people can get so wrapped up in a movement and convinced of things that are so stupid. There are several reasons why, which really don't answer the question adequately, but this is all I have to offer at the time. Firstly, we were young believers with little understanding of God's word. Secondly, the meetings were so powerful and we got caught up in the energy under the tent; call it mass hysteria if you will. Watchman Nee calls it the latent power of the soul. Whatever it was it was real. Besides the Bible is full of remarkable stories no less astonishing than what we believed. To be honest though, each time we arrived at a new tent meeting we had a hard time getting into "the spirit" of the meeting. We concluded that we must be "backslid" for not being faithful enough in fasting and prayer. So we started praying in earnest and submitted to "the spirit" in the meetings. Soon we were back on track, once again.

Obviously I was also more prone to extremes than the average Joe. I had just recently escaped from a drug-induced reality that had influenced my thinking and habits profoundly. For several years I had smoked pot daily and rubbed shoulders with bikers, speed freaks and drug dealers. As I look back at those years I am amazed at how quickly I accepted this lifestyle and the business dealings we were involved in, as "normal". I am not sure which one was more abnormal, the cult years or the hippie years.

Let me attempt to put things into perspective. Is what we believed, at this time, any more incredible than the delusion that swept over Germany in the 30's and 40's. Millions of good living, sane, German people eagerly endorsed Hitler's plan to rule the world, which included the extermination of millions of Jews. Is what we believed any worse than this or for that matter the doctrine of eternal torment, that I was taught at an early age by "sincere, sane, Christians". I was told **God is love,** His mercy endures forever and He also **knows all** and can see all **from the end to the beginning**. Therefore God knew before He formed Adam that He would end up throwing the great majority of mankind into a lake of fire to be tortured forever and ever.

I will be the first to admit; in the 70's we were a part of a wholesale brainwashing. However my brainwashing had started years before that day I walked under David Terrell's revival tent. Now in my 60's as I look back at my life and consider the many things I have believed; the teaching of an eternal hell is the pinnacle of all that is stupid, sick and utterly repugnant. The person I was when I believed that, I scarcely know anymore.

I am sincerely thankful that I was born in a country where I am free to pursue the "American dream" to be happy; to get a good education and to pursue a meaningful occupation. However much of what is supposed to bring happiness is simply vanity. There is something more we all want and need out of life than to "be successful". There is a deeper reality that evades us because we get so caught up in the "cares of life". Some of us find it easier to admit this than others. I was never satisfied long with the status quo. School was boring for me. I tried but could not get motivated to do good work and please the teacher in order to get good marks; in order to get a diploma; in order to get a good job; in order to be successful; in order to be happy. I just couldn't buy into the program although I tried hard.

In church I had the same problem. I was not content being a faithful member, giver, and worker; something was missing and I was not about to sit there week after week listening to same old sermons, looking at the backs of the same old heads. I knew there was more to it than what we were being told and I was willing to trade anything the church or the world had to offer to discover what that "more" was. Obviously my craving for reality and my reckless abandonment opened the door to much trouble and grief but the price I had to pay to discover what little truth, I now have, has been worth it all. In my heart, deep at the core of my spiritual being I knew only the truth would make me free. If I end my life unknown and penniless but find the truth I am looking for I will be of all men most happy.

## Narrow is The Gate

I was convinced, the price I had to pay, to please God was "separation from the world", which included my old friends. They were part of the culture I had escaped. I didn't really avoid them but didn't want to see them either. I had told them about Jesus, heaven and hell. They didn't get it at the time and they wouldn't get it now. I was built with different parts and had known it from my youth.

Randy Howard was one of the boys that did see the light. He had recently come to a dramatic, turning point in his own life. While in Europe with Greg McGuigan he took some bad drugs and his trip ended up being the worst nightmare of his life. Randy thought God told him to jump into an empty well as a test of his faith. He came home with a back injury and a broken spirit. Sometime later, he came to visit us in Massey with his wife Barb, baby girl Favian, and his sister Jill. When they heard the stories about the Prophet and witnessed our joy and zeal for the Lord, they quickly submitted to the move of the spirit in our midst and soon moved into our big house with us. Gerry and Marilyn were still there; they had never left; Art was on the road driving truck and joined us when he could.

All those living in the house submitted to following the rules without questioning. Fasting in particular, was an important part of our spiritual growth so we decided that everyone, even breast-feeding women could at least fast one day a week. Like many "Terrellites" we chose the Sabbath to be that special day. Before sunset on Friday we had a big meal and then would not eat until Saturday evening. Naturally, we tended to overeat on Friday knowing it would be a long 24 hours until the next meal. There was always a sense of accomplishment after the long day was over and we found such joy in refreshing the old body we were desperately attempting to kill.

Of course we didn't realize it but our efforts backfired and the more we tried to crucify the flesh the harder it fought back to stay alive. Instead of dying it became the focal point demanding attention. We became preoccupied with self-examination. We rejoiced when we thought we were doing well and wallowed in the mire of guilt and shame when we couldn't measure up to the high standard we had set for ourselves. It is now obvious to me that self-righteousness and self-condemnation are flip sides of the same coin.

What accompanied this problem was a continual comparing of one another, also. We were plagued with thoughts about who fasted the most and who was willing to pay the price and follow God to the end. Questions like this surfaced continually. We knew this was wrong but we were helpless to block them from our minds. This only added to the feeling of dread and defeat that pervaded much of the time.

It was not all lows, though; there were times of great rejoicing and worship. We really did love the Lord and each other but were caught in a mess of religion and deception thinking we could be righteous by works of law. I am convinced that, especially when fasting, we were open targets to the spirit world with little understanding of what we were fighting. Our inability to exercise common sense was directly related to the unseen forces at work.

During a meeting Brother Clowers' came to me and said God had a message for me. He laid his hands on my head and began to prophesy. He predicted many good things to come but also told me I would  be tested. He said I would soon go through a time of depression. He called it my "dark day of the soul". He encouraged me to be strong and added that if I was faithful God would bless our group and me abundantly. I was so "hungry for God" and was deeply touched but had no idea what to expect.

Time went on and I gave it little thought until midway through the long winter of 1973, I discovered for the first time in my life deep depression. I am the type of person that needs to be busy, slaying my dragons daily. I easily get bored and restless but this was different. A dark cloud came over me for several weeks. I didn't have the energy to talk much let alone lead Bible studies or prayer meetings. I continued to go through the motions remembering the entreaty to be faithful. Then one day, as sudden as the darkness had come, it seemed to lift and with spring in the air I was back to my old self. The joy of the Lord returned and was so welcome and our prayer meetings and Bible studies were once again alive and exciting. Even at the best of times though, we were up and down, on a spiritual roller coaster ride, tossed to and fro, from a mix of mountain top experiences and the doom and gloom we believed.

## Lost in The Bush

One day, I took the mile or so trek to the back bush, as I often did. Here I had a snare line for rabbits in winter and hunted partridge in the fall. On this particular November afternoon I went a little further than usual and was still hunting close to dusk. Normally this is not a problem but to my surprise it suddenly started snowing very heavily. So thick was the blowing snow I could not see more than a few yards in front of me. I quickly started heading the direction I thought was home, walking rather fast. I was well aware of my pace and knew it was not uncommon for in-experienced hunters to panic and walk in circles for hours. I hoped my awareness of the fact that I was in a slight panic mode and was concerned about doing this very thing, would help. The longer I headed hard in the direction I sensed must be the right way, without seeing anything familiar the more worried I got. I could not see any direction far enough to get my bearings so I continued walking and praying. After what seemed a long time, too long for the distance I thought I needed to go, I came out of the bush into the open field and could dimly see the beautiful, warm lights of home. Once again I was reassured that God was taking care of me.

## We Were Poor

Sometime that year my Unemployment Insurance ran out and although Art had a fulltime job and helped with the rent we were very poor. This also was a matter of faith and we took it in stride. That fall we noticed the remains of a local farmer's potato and squash crop scattered about the field and inquired about all the vegetables left behind. He said we were welcome to help ourselves; he had picked up all he wanted. We collected hundreds of pounds of squash and potatoes. We placed them on large racks so we could inspect them daily. Some had cuts and bruises and needed to be used first. I never imagined there was so many different ways to eat these vegetables. This was our main diet through the fall and well into the winter.

Every once in awhile when funds appeared we would splurge and buy things like flour, sugar, coffee, molasses and beans. Paul and John Martin paid an unexpected visit one afternoon, I suspected to check up on us. The stories of our cult commune had spread quickly and folks were naturally concerned. We had just recently bought a big bag of beans and were delighted to share a meal of home baked beans and home made bread fresh out of the oven. Our excitement over eating so well was hard to hide. After our visitors left, while collecting dishes, we found a twenty-dollar bill under one of their plates. We were a little embarrassed but most happy for the cash.

## Benjie's Accident

We quickly realized our communal house was too small, so Randy and Barb found a house to rent a couple miles away, although they were back for every meeting, which was often.

The Howard's were just as poor as we were and without a vehicle. I sensed the Lord telling me to give my truck to Randy who needed it worse than I did. Without questioning I obeyed.

There were aspects of this lifestyle that were so good and I enjoyed them thoroughly. It was during these days I started hunting, gardening and cutting firewood. I was home all day either working or studying. I spent a lot of my time with my beautiful young son who was eager to help in the garden or piling firewood. I adored him and took him with me wherever I could. Some days I would put him on my shoulders and walked to the back pasture and bush while I prayed. The two of us made trips together. On one occasion we took uncle Art's school bus to Southern Ontario. Hanging out with him was all the recreation I needed in life.

By today's standards we were a little strict with Benjie and overly protective but we wanted the best for him and he was a very happy child. He received a lot of attention, especially being an only child with an aunt and uncles around. Every couple months though he seemed to get increasingly restless and strong willed. If he got too defiant he got a spanking with the belt. I know this is frowned upon today but it worked wonders with Benjie. A few swats on the bum instantly changed his attitude. He cried for a short time and was visibly remorseful. After a short explanation and a few minutes of comforting hugs he was off again his old happy self. 20 years later, I twice tried this type of discipline on Star with exactly the opposite results.

One afternoon while I was out, Randy came over. Backing out of our driveway he thought he ran over something with the back wheel. He got out and was shocked to see our infant son lying on the ground. He frantically checked him over and didn't see any broken limbs but could clearly see the tire marks on his back. He picked him up and carried him into the house and broke the sad news. When I got home Benjie lay still and listless on the couch with no apparent pain or interest in getting up; we began praying. He never moved that evening, through the night and the next day. We continued to pray believing the Lord didn't want us to "rush" to the hospital.

Recently I received a deep gash in my chin, splitting firewood. It bled quite profusely but I never even considered the long trip to town to get stitches. I put a tight band-aid on and eventually the bleeding stopped. I still wear a scar to this day, however it has been covered for many years by my beard. Believing God for myself was one thing but for my only son, it was more difficult but I wanted to be faithful, so we waited. On the 3rd morning Benjie got out of his bed and began walking as usual. Everyone was quickly informed and praises unto God ascended from every corner of the house. This was another confirmation we must be on the right track. We became convinced that this is what the Bible meant by, "the just shall live by faith".

## Spring Thaw on Lake Penage

On one trip to Sudbury I visited Barry and Lorraine Moxam at their 45 unit, Wellington Heights Apartments. It was on the south end of town and here they had an ideal arrangement. Barry, who was a jack of all trades, did most of his own maintenance, plumbing, drywall and painting etc. Lorraine did the books and collected the rent and paid the bills. Barry's mom lived in one apartment with his sister Vivian and a couple other family members also rented apartments from them.

On this particular visit I brought along a David Terrell preaching tape on "The Anointing of the Holy Spirit". They had recently become interested in spiritual matters and were attending the Mennonite church. They were a little leery of my grand stories about the prophet but agreed to listen to the tape with me. Barry, in particular, was very moved. He had never heard a message like this and he couldn't sit still. He said he could feel goose bumps running up and down his legs and back. He was immediately sold. I left him some material and we kept in touch.

The communal house in Massey was a busy place most days; I needed to be alone to hear from God and gravitated to my closet daily but preferred the back forty when weather was good. Barry and Lorraine once mentioned that I could go to their camp, on Lake Penage, if I ever wanted to get all alone for awhile. It was on an island, miles from the marina, and all civilization. I took them up on their offer several times usually just for a day or so at a time. I do remember being there alone once, in the heart of the winter, for about 4 days. During the day it was a beautiful, quiet getaway and I was able to get completely absorbed into the silence only experienced in total isolation. I have to admit, the nights were long though and it was a little scary being on an island in winter so far away from everyone. But I knew, after being there alone for a few days, I would enter into a different space. This realm is where I thought I had to be to hear from God and to receive His anointing to preach the hard gospel we believed.

Marja and I decided to go to Moxam's camp over that spring thaw of 1974. We packed our supplies into Barry's truck and he drove the 3 of us, across the ice, as late as he was sure it was safe. I had already gone through the ice on this lake once, in 1955. We didn't know exactly how long we would stay but knew once it started to thaw there was no way in or out until the ice was gone and we could be retrieved by boat. We had no phone or any other means of contacting the outside world. This was the kind of seclusion I wanted to share with my wife and son.

Between our times of reading and praying, we thoroughly enjoyed playing with Benjie and gave him a lot of attention those days. He was at such a cute age. We spent a lot of time outside exploring the island looking for signs of nature waking up after the long winter. I have been reminded about this time on penage over and over again, the last 40+ years for several reasons. Every time I hear the wind blowing through pine trees I think of the hours we sat out on the rock under the big, beautiful, pines on the island of Penage. Also every time a dry brown leaf catches my peripheral vision, being tossed by I gust of wind, I think of Barry and Lorraine's camp. One day out romping around with Benjie that is exactly what he saw. It took him by surprise and he was sure it was a squirrel or another little critter scooting past him, way too close for comfort. He screamed and ran into Mommy's arms. He shook for a long time, shedding big tears and was slow to be comforted.

Our goal had been to quickly faze into a fast and so we didn't pack as much food as we normally would. For whatever reason, we found it difficult to fast and decided instead to ration our food. For 3 weeks we had a lovely time and thought we were on track with our daily quotas; most of the ice was gone and we still had a few days food left, plenty for our son, at least. We were wrong and the last few days were difficult. We found out later, there was still a few icebergs floating near the marina so Barry decided to wait a little longer then really necessary before coming to get us. This we did not anticipate. I had observed a lone duck swimming close to shore for several days. I found a shotgun and believe it or not, one shell. I knew it was better to shoot ducks as they flew overhead with their soft underside exposed but what was the chance of that? I kept an eye on it for a couple days hoping it would come closer. Finally, with no apparent choice I pulled the trigger; I saw pellets splash on the water in front, beside and behind but the duck flew away.

We had a few cookies left for Benjie the last couple of days and on what turned out to be our last day he got a sucker for lunch. There was nothing to prepare for supper. We had set up a little child's table and chair in front of the window were he enjoyed eating. Several times that day he sat down at the table and looked at Marja and waited; there was no food to give him. It broke our hearts watching him. I can't imagine what it is like for parents to see their children slowly starve to death but this has been the fate of millions. What a relief it was later that day to hear the sound of a motorboat off in the distance. It was early evening and we had resolved to spend one more hungry night at camp. After briefly telling Barry our story, we quickly and joyfully packed up and headed out. Back home we shared our experience and encouraged all to continue in the faith.

### The Moxam's Long Weekend Visit

The news about "The Prophet" spread quickly to the rest of the Moxam family. Barry's brother Calvin, who now went by his first name John, was particularly interested. I had lost contact with Him since he left home to join the army about 13 years prior. He had married Carol Dixon, from Lively, and had three children, Bobby-Joe, Cindy and Jon-John. That same spring of 1974, they decided to join Barry on a trip to Massey to meet us and hear about the message more fully. They came with the intention of spending the weekend but as it turns out, they never did go back home to live in Whitefish. Instead, early the next week, they went back only long enough to pack up their belongings, load their furniture on a truck and then headed back to the Massey commune to live. We were crowded once again but happy to share our house and hearts with our new converts.

## Revival Meetings in Canada

Because of the increasing Canadian interest at Brother Terrell's meetings, Don Clowers began holding "Miracle Services" in Toronto. We met some folks there who quickly became close friends. Among them were two black families from Toronto, Clement and Shiela Duff and Ernie and Joyce Clarke who had 4 beautiful children, Janet, Sandra, Kevin and Jeff. They had recently heard about brother Terrell on the radio and were so excited about his ministry. They soon left the Baptist church they had been attending to follow the prophet. We also befriended Helen Gangur and her two children Danny and Diane who where from Proton Station 40 miles west of Barrie.

We convinced Brother Clowers to come to Sudbury for a 4-day meeting. We rented the Fraser Auditorium from July 11-14 and started spreading the word. One afternoon Johnny and I were hitchhiking to Sudbury and Doug Alkenbrach picked us up. Doug had grown up in the Mennonite Church where his parents were members. Johnny asked him if he would like to come hear a good preacher. His reply was "I've been listening to a good preacher every day of my life." He was referring to his mother. We were disappointed that few people were interested in what God was doing but were also thankful that we were among the chosen few and eagerly prepared for the big crusade.

Brother Clowers was a young man in his 30's but had been preaching since he was 15. He was bold and direct and had a "gift of knowledge". During one of the services, as his custom was, he walked the isles calling out certain individuals that God led him to. He asked them to stand and began sharing personal information, like where they were born, circumstances that led them there that day and secrets they had not shared with anyone. He would say things like God has showed me you are struggling with smoking and you have a package of cigarettes, naming the brand, in your purse. He continued by informing them that God was delivering them from the habit at this hour.

This was an impressive gift. Although, I also all longed for a personal word from the Lord, I was caught off guard when he came over to me with a special message. This time it was not predicting another dark day of the soul. Sister Jill, who knows shorthand, wrote down his message as he spoke. The following is the highlights. "As I was praying in my room this afternoon your face came before me. God is going to grant you your heart's desire; He is going to give you the revelation that you have long desired. He is going to give you wisdom. He is going to make a man of God out of you. It is going to take time, prayer and patience and I am telling you that you have touched the Lord." He went on to say that "this young man is part of the reason I am here" and told of my many travels to the States etc. Tears ran down my cheeks as he spoke and for months to come I pondered in my heart what he said.

## Let the Dead Bury the Dead

On July 31st my grandpa David Bast died at the age of 79, the same day his eldest son had died 11 years earlier. My response to the news and the question of attending the funeral was, "let the dead bury the dead". We had burned all our bridges, which meant separation from Christendom and our extended family. We sensed no need to be involved with funerals or weddings. This I would regret and later attempted to make up for my long absence and unconcern.

Over the next couple years we continued going south to 9-day meetings under Terrell's big tent whenever we could, with little money and no place to stay when we arrived. For one meeting

Johnny and I set out in his old Vauxhall Viva. We had $27.00 between us. With gas prices at 29 cents / US gallon in the States we would be fine going down and would worry about money to come home after the meetings were over. Later that summer, with a little persuasion we convinced Barry and Lorraine to take their new Ford Club Van with a group of us. On another occasion Barry and Johnny and I went in Barry's pick-up truck. Later Art bought an old school bus, which he converted it into a make shift camper with bunk beds. Now we were equipped to travel further and more often. One trip 7 of us headed for Texas, a 4000 mile round trip. On the highway we were quite a site. Once at the tent meeting we seemed to fit right in.

Border crossing was always tense and we were refused entry on several occasions because we looked so poor and we were. We went to Niagara Falls first; if turned back we headed to the Fort Erie, Buffalo crossing. A couple times we had to cross at the Windsor, Detroit and once we made the trek to Sault Ste. Marie before we got in. We were determined to get to the meetings and never once did we turn around and go home. There were times the border guard didn't know what to do with us and sent us inside to talk to someone with more authority. Our vehicles were periodically searched and there were always many specific questions. It always seemed to be a judgment call on the part of the one questioning us. If they liked the idea of a bunch of kids going to a religious tent meeting in the sunny south, we were in, if not, if was off to the next closest border town.

One of the most bizarre crossings we made was with a huge box full of brand new shoes. Gerry had acquired them from the shoe store he was working for. They needed to get rid of hundreds of pairs of old stock and liked Gerry's idea enough to just give them all to him, no money, no invoice, nothing. We timed our trip to arrive at the border in the middle of the night. The huge box in the back of our truck was by far the most prominent and interesting item on board. To start with, the guard had to take a look in the box to confirm our bizarre story. It is not every day that someone wants to travel all that distance to take hundreds of pairs of shoes to a holy man of God, so he could transport them to Guatemala to distribute to the poor, especially with no paperwork. It was a gift, there was no money spent and there was no documentation. After scratching his head a few times he dug to the bottom of the box and was convinced we were telling the truth; he smiled broadly and told us to have a nice trip as he waved us on. I don't think things would have gone that smoothly during the day or with most other guards. Events like this increased our faith; this was all the confirmation we needed that we were pleasing God, which was our all-consuming passion in life.

What little money we had we put in the offering pail and did odd jobs, like cleaning restaurant garbage cans, on the way home for gas money. An American friend told us where we could sell our blood for extra money, so we did. Unfortunately the next time we tried, our blood was rejected; it was too low in iron, probably from not eating properly. This did not deter us; getting to the tent meetings was greatest thrill life had to offer.

After getting known as Brother Clowers' man in Canada I was asked to sit on the platform behind brother Terrell with the other preachers from all over the States. This was an honor, however it did have a downside. One night, when the prophet was preaching on his favorite topic, about how God was going to "whup" (whip) America he took off his shirt and commanded every preacher, on the platform, to whip him with his own belt across his bare back. I was glad to be a part of this move of God but hadn't bargained for this. I reluctantly and half-heartedly obeyed. As strange as it seemed, who was I to question God. Besides, hadn't His prophets of old been a little strange, also?

## Dundalk Days

On our way home from a meeting that summer we visited Helen Gangur at her farm in Proton Station, where she lived with her children, Danny and Diane. Her husband had an apartment in Toronto where he worked and periodically joined his family on the weekends. It had been a working farm at one time but was quite run down. There were goats and chickens running around and a large garden that needed attention. Helen was frantically trying to keep things running and her children helped as much as can be expected from two teens that grew up in the city. It was obvious the place needed a full time hired hand.

Helen's primary goal was to can as much food as possible before famine came; according to "The Prophet" it was not long to wait. The kitchen looked like a storm had hit it; canning jars and supplies and food were scattered and piled everywhere. During our visit Helen asked if Marja and I would consider moving there to help her. We talked briefly and readily accepted. I could see beyond the clutter to the potential. Art also saw the possibilities here but his sights were squarely centered on one thing, Helen's beautiful 16-year-old daughter, Dianne. Even though Art was 9 years older than her, they hit it off superbly and quickly.

With Johnny and Carol in Massey I knew the place would keep running without us. Johnny was working for Carl Brohart the owner of the farm and another one next door where he lived. Johnny was a big strong man with years of experience on heavy equipment and enjoyed operating the farm tractor and other equipment. Like Carl, he also enjoyed hard work and was a great asset to him.

In September 1974 we packed our personal belongings and headed south to the Dundalk area with the hope this would also become one of Canada's first "Blessed Areas". Helen had the vision and was delighted to find eager young people, on the same page. The spacious front room, which had been a living room at one time, now seldom used, was set up as a little apartment for the 3 of us. Marja and I rolled up our sleeves eager to help turn this confusion into a productive enterprise. Benjie was almost 2 and a busy little boy; he enjoyed exploring the barnyard and playing with the animals. Watching him interact with the baby goats or chase the chickens was all the entertainment we needed. He was adored by all and continued to get the kind of attention he was used to.

As we worked we shared stories, back and forth, with Helen about our past and the many experiences that brought us all together. Things moved along for a short time quite well until the day the Lord gave me a revelation regarding our dear sister. Both Marja and I almost immediately noticed many of Helen's life stories had to do with the shameful way her relatives had treated her over the years. We also struggled with not being accepted by our family but realized these separation issues were mainly because of our extreme move to the religious right. We believed a hard gospel and were taught we would suffer persecution and just accepted it as the norm.

For a couple of weeks, day after day, Helen went on and on about how she lived in constant fear because her family was out to get her. She was convinced they were plotting against her, which we found hard to believe. During my quiet time the Lord showed me the root of her paranoia was a "spirit of bitterness". I felt with the laying on of hands and prayer she could be set free from the tormenting influence. Without thinking about it too long, I called her aside, and confided in her what the Lord had showed me. I assumed she would be happy to have us support her through the process of finally being delivered from the force that haunted her day and night. I was mistaken.

She was not only older than I, but she considered herself more mature as far as spiritual matters went. There never was any discussion about the validity of my revelation, in fact there was no discussion at all; we were to pack our bags and leave ASAP. This should have taught me that a more subtle approach might have accomplished better results but it didn't register at the time. Her reaction did confirm to Marja and I that she was a deeply troubled lady; we could now see her problem was more serious then being unable to forgive relatives. We also realized our partnership would not have lasted or accomplished much.

Besides, I felt strongly about what God had showed me; I never considered I could be wrong. I was doing the Lord's work; the outcome was in His hands and I was willing to suffer reproach for His name. Actually, I expected this treatment because of the prophetic gift and calling on my life. I took great comfort in the fact that God's reward would some day out weigh the suffering I had to endure now. This was not the only time that God gave me this kind of specific insight. I frequently saw beyond people's words and actions to the root of a deeper problem. It took me a long time to realize that immediately confronting someone may not be the best way to help them. 13 years later, in another communal setting, we encountered a similar situation. This time I approached the brother in question, in much the same way I did Helen and interestingly, received the exact same response.

## Art Caught in the Middle

Helen's brother-in-law had an old, rough farmhouse nearby we could rent immediately and cheap until we figured out what we were going to do. So we were out of there as quick as we had moved in. This didn't faze me at all. Initially, I was a little disappointed at the abrupt end to my dream to build a shelter from the coming storm, together with the Gangurs. The Lord quickly assured me He had something better in mind. I didn't give much thought to the dilemma this created for Art. I had always been the "spiritual leader" of our little flock; Art was content to be working full time; to come and go as he could and support the group in other ways. So I was taken aback when he approached me and gave me the sad news that he could no longer "follow me"; this was the end of the road for us.

Art, my older brother, had been my closest companion since our childhood. We grew up together, even spent summers away from home together at a very early age; we had stayed close all through school, the whole drug scene and now following the prophet. His decision was final! He was in love and he knew that either his wife to be or his closest friend and brother had to go; I understood his predicament and decision. I had been married 3 short years and would have left 100 brothers or best friends behind to cling to my precious wife.

As strange as it may sound, the pain of his words didn't really register because a sensation of pleasure flooded over my whole being. The reality of the Lord's presence was so evident and I was honored to suffer this way for Him. Now, as I write about this crossroad in my life, and rehearse others in my mind, I can't help wonder why I seemed to be drawn into one crisis after another. In a strange way, it was like I craved the reality and excitement of a "zero hour". I get bored easy and it is at these times I seem to be most alive.

I don't know if the extreme highs of the drugs I took created in me a dire need or if I was drawn to drugs in the first place out of a lack, already part of my makeup. Either way, it has been difficult for my wife and children to understand my actions during these times of crisis in my life. I am thankful for the love and the support they gave me over the years. It has not been easy and I am sorry for the pain and grief I have caused them, although at the time I was unable to seriously consider their well being.

In this case, as in others, I sensed no remorse for the dilemma I had caused. It never occurred to me to say I was sorry, hoping I could take it back and try again; instead I felt euphoric. Art's words instantly transported me into a surreal state of shock. It is not that I didn't grasp the serious ramifications involved but in a "spiritual" sense maybe, in a weird way, I thoroughly enjoyed the moment. I compared it to the persecutions of first century believers, or those of my ancestors, who also went away rejoicing that they worthy to suffer for His name's sake.

## Herdsman

Art and the Gangurs went on with their lives and we went on with ours. Soon after the split we heard about a local farmer looking for a "herdsman". His name was Filippo Caradonna. He lived in Toronto but owned a farm nearby. He had 40 head of red, white faced, Herford cattle and 3 milking cows. He was offering free rent, heat and hydro for someone to feed his cattle and milk his cows. We met with him and he immediately liked us, especially Marja and Benjie. We quickly moved into his old but well-kept, farmhouse. He kept his bedroom off the kitchen beside his wine cellar and a pantry full of treats like Italian meats and pastry, which he generously shared with us. He showed up the odd weekend without notice and almost without exception had a special treat for Benjie, whom he quickly adopted as his own grandson. This was such a delight after our limited diet in Massey, although fasting became more difficult.

Around this time I made the worst decision of my life. I decided to get a vasectomy. As much as I loved my son, "my only son", I thought it best not to bring more children into a world that soon was going to be plagued with God's judgments. When I consulted Brother Clowers on the matter he agreed it was a good idea; he had 4 children. It wouldn't be long before this operation would begin to haunt me and the pain of what I had done would never leave. As a child, I had a great admiration for the large families close by. As I got older, I dreamed of having 7 children; they would learn to play musical instruments and we would sing and play together for hours on end. What was I now thinking?

Having said this, I must add that I wouldn't change a thing even if I could because of the good that resulted from this otherwise disastrous decision. Later I would adopt 2 girls that I never would have if I already had 7 children of my own. One of adopted daughters also gave me a granddaughter who has brought me so much joy and I love them both dearly. I could never trade them for any number of more children. Also, I can now, to some degree at least, understand how people get into the dumb predicaments they do. I am a little more tolerant and gracious because of how stupid I have been. 12 years later I had a vasectomy reversal. Apparently it was partially successful but no children would be forthcoming.

I kept in touch with Art on a personal level but we didn't have meetings together and we have never talked about our falling out. On March 16, 1975 Art and Dianne were married in Don Clowers church in Fort Payne Alabama. We were invited and Marja was asked to a bridesmaid; so we made the trek south to our favorite place away from home. A few months later, I heard Danny and Helen were in a terrible car crash, driving Art's van; it was a total wreck and Helen was left a cripple with years of rehab therapy ahead of her.

Others from Sudbury began to gravitate our way. Jill, Randy's sister and Linda Mackie who we knew from high school joined the group in the Dundalk area. They found jobs in a restaurant and rented an apartment in nearby Shelbourne. That year, after Christmas I made, what would be, my last trip to Fort Payne Alabama. Don Clowers was holding a 9-day winter meeting in his big church and Danny Gangur wanted to drive down in his Mustang by himself. Although, there was a permanent wedge between Helen and I, she still preferred someone, even me, accompany her teenage son on the trip. Danny did all the driving and the trip only took 21 hours. We arrived at the church before sun up the next morning. Danny parked in the huge parking lot as far away from the church as possible so as not be in the way or to be disturbed. He put his seat back and quickly fell asleep.

I was very tired and may have dozed off for awhile. I am not sure if I was half asleep or in a stupor when I had a strange experience. I know I was awake somewhat because I distinctly remember gripping the handle on the dash securely with both hands. It was dark and I couldn't see anything but was keenly aware of a presence outside, in front of the car. Whatever it was, it was applying a tremendous pull on my body like a huge magnet. My natural inclination was to hold on for dear life. The sensation was like a large elastic band around me trying to pull me out of the car. As the force moved away from me the band got tighter and pulled harder and I hung on. After what seemed a long time the pulling force started to lesson and I began to relax ever so slightly. I sensed the battle was over and whatever it was, was going to continue leaving.

As crazy as it may sound, I started to second guess myself. I thought, "What if it was an angel that had a special blessing for me?" I totally stopped resisting and actually made an effort to release myself to leave with it. I have no idea how one could do that sitting in a car seat in a trance but that is what I tried to do. In any event, it was too late; the pull was not strong enough and soon dissipated all together. Danny continued to sleep oblivious to the trip his strange passenger almost went on.

Danny stayed around for a day or so but had more interesting adventures in mind than a revival meeting. Not me; I was in my glory here. By this time, I was the Vice-President of The Don Clowers Evangelical Association of Canada. I not only sat on the platform behind Brother Clowers; I once had the honor of handling the microphone cord. I had observed men with years of experience perform this duty. In this huge building as in the big tents hundreds of feet of cord is required because these preachers didn't stand still. They were all over the stage and often walked down the isles to minister to individuals. If they went too far 2 or 3 men were required to keep the cord from getting caught or tangled, which may distract the preacher and disturb the move of the spirit. The cord had to be smoothly released as he walked away and neatly and quickly coiled back up as he came closer.

Don Clowers introduced me at most meetings. He was so proud to have the support of a Canadian, just like his wife, Sharon. He had arranged for me to stay with Greg Staub his organist. He was a young single man who lived alone in a house trailer on the outskirts of town. One night after the meeting Greg dropped me off at the trailer and went out with friends. As I lay down on his couch, which was my bed for two weeks. Here I had another, strange visitation.

Whether I was in the body or out of the body I don't know; it was so real. It was not a dream; not like any other dream I ever had before, anyway. I can't recall how long it lasted but I was up at the ceiling looking down on myself lying on the couch. Unlike the first experience in the church parking lot this one spooked me a little. I have no idea what the purpose of it was. I received no inspiration or insight. 40 years later I have come to only one conclusion; I was messing around with spiritual, forces that I never should have been.

All the time I was gone Marja had to do the chores alone. This meant going upstairs in the barn and throwing down enough bails of hay to feed 43 head of cattle. Besides distributing the hay she had serve them "chop", ground up grain, which was piled in 100lb bags in a nearby storeroom. She had to pull the bags down off the pile and drag them across the floor before opening. There were also the 3 cows to milk twice a day, by hand. She enjoyed the fresh, organic milk and made a lot of cheese but worked hard for it and let me know when I got home. Phillipo admired her all the more when he found out.

At the end of the meetings, with my ride home long gone, I had no choice but to take a bus. It was a little scary traveling in the Deep South late at night. The back of the bus was full of blacks, who were a little rowdy while the quiet whites sat at the front. The only empty seats were in the middle, between them. I sat quietly and minded my own business. I was not able to sleep much. My mind was full of what I had learned and how I would share it with the small flock back home. I also wanted to keep one eye open not sure how safe I was. I have no problem with black people in particular. I had several good black friends but I felt uneasy, as I often do, south of the border.

It was not a pleasant trip but I arrived safe and sound in Buffalo NY the next afternoon. I had a couple hours to kill until I caught my connecting bus to Toronto. I was loafing around, minding my own business, when two plain clothed policemen approached me. I wasn't sure who they were but was about to find out real quick. The one gentleman asked me if I was a Canadian. I said I was. He continued by asking me if I ever had a criminal record. This was a little odd, seeing I was as straight looking as I could be, so I thought. Now when I look back at my passport picture from those days I see a hard, serious man with cold eyes.

I knew there was no point lying, which is seldom a consideration for me, in any situation. Since I was a child, I have always taken pride in the fact that I tell the truth, and replied, "Yes I am". Now I had their full attention; the one doing the questioning quickly blurted out, "What for?" Without hesitation I calmly said, "For the possession of a narcotic". Wrong answer! Well, it was the truth, but not the right answer to get me out of the quicksand I was sinking into. As slick and as quick as could be, one of them forcefully grabbed me, spun me around and threw me against the wall that I had been leaning on. It seems to me he had practiced this maneuver several times before.

At this point I was still not overly concerned. I was no longer a criminal; I was a man of God on my way home from a Holy Ghost Revival Meeting. I had no idea of the seriousness of a foreigner treading on the blessed soil of the mighty U. S. of A. while at the same time possessing a criminal record. Criminals were seldom afforded the honor and privilege of visiting the greatest country in the world. I was about to get a crash course in foreign affairs, as it applied to our Sister Nation, Big Sister, that is; more like Big Brother or schoolyard bully. These guys were now outraged at my cool audacity. Maybe they viewed me as a sassy, little, smart ass. They firmly escorted me away, one on each arm, to their nearby office. Here I would go through several hours of interrogation. One officer fired one question after another, while other went through my suitcase looking for, hoping for, something, anything, to incriminate me. I found it amusing; all he could find was my Bible, religious books, tracts and tapes. I was the only one amused.

The officers made it quite clear that even though they found nothing illegal, they had every right to *deport* me. This was not a new word to me, although I had previously not understood its meaning. If deported from the USA, under no circumstance could I ever, for the rest of my life, set one foot on their holy ground. Even though they decided not to deport me and seal my fate, this altercation would be recorded. They informed me, if I ever had a very, good reason to come back to their country, I would have to get an approval, first. This meant filling out an application and paying a non-refundable fee, regardless of their decision. The process could take months; I was to keep this in mind when making plans. They also made it very clear that I was a fortunate, young man, being allowed to walk out of their office with only this, albeit harsh warning. This was the good news, the bad news was I had missed my bus. I had to wait several more hours for the next one and so did my brother waiting at the bus station in Toronto.

Soon after this incident I completed an application for a pardon from the Canadian Government and in 1977 I received one. I realize this pardon probably means little to a US border official. Today, I still feel uneasy entering the States, although I have done it quite a few times since. Several times we have been harassed and more than once been asked the same question, "Have you ever had a criminal record?" A couple of these I document in later chapters. I always wonder what the border guard is reading on his computer screen and why he phrased the question the way he did. Was it normal procedure to ask specifically, *"Have you ever had ever a criminal record"*? Or was this prompted by my history in their records? I have no idea. After that, I didn't attempt to cross the border again until November 1983 when Marja and I drove to Florida with Kel and Mary Lynn Honsinger. They knew my dilemma but agreed to go for it and at the border  we had no problem crossing.

Back home we got the news of a tragic accident. On December 18th 1975, Don and Aldene's middle son Kenny John was run down and killed by an impaired driver. He was only 17 years old. He had been walking on the Highway going into Lively, with his friend Robin Eastwood and another boy, in the dark. Apparently he ran across the road just as the car driven by a 31 year old man from Lively was passing another vehicle. The driver had been drinking and was charged with impaired driving. Again we never considered going to the funeral, even though the Forbeck family had been very close to ours. The fact that Don was my namesake never even crossed my mind at that time.

Gerry and Jill who had been courting for some time set a wedding date for January 30th 1976. They also went south to Alabama to Brother Clowers' church for their wedding. I could not consider trying to cross the border. Hard to believe I missed my own brother's wedding but these were strange times.

## My Ongoing Affliction

My eczema, which I was told I would grow out of in my teens was as bad as ever. I discovered, the less I ate, especially sweets and carbs the better my skin was. This was a confirmation I was chosen to live the fasting life, just like the holy men of old and the few real ones today. I continually asked God for healing and continued to stand in prayer lines at the healing services. I had observed many folks take off their glasses and throw them away or their medicine as an act of faith and apparently some were healed. So it was with me; I decided to stop using the cortisone ointment I had used for many years. This caused my skin to break out bad, real bad. I remember filling the bathtub with hot salt water to soak and massage the puss filled hive type sores, all over my body, especially my legs, until they broke. The tub was a mess; blood and body fluids ran down my legs for hours after. I would dab them until they dried and then be tormented for days with an incredible itch as they scabbed to heal.

I heard a story of a sister who had broken her glasses as an act of faith but couldn't see properly and was having a problem functioning her daily tasks. Somehow the story got to Brother Clowers and he informed them, "If you can't see, God has not healed you. Get yourself a pair of glasses until God actually heals you". I found this advice rather peculiar from a man of God who held regular healing services and was actually a real eye opener for several reasons. Firstly, it showed me that the prophet and Brother Clowers, his #1 preacher could actually differ on some points. This was one of many red flags that went up but it would take years for us to realize how naive we were and how profound was the influence these men were having on our lives. The second thing it showed me was that certain aspects of "living by faith" could actually be practical and in accord with common sense.

After hearing about Brother Clowers advice to the near blind sister I decided to talk to Him about my skin problem. He had no idea how bad my skin was and was shocked when I showed him my sores from head to toe. He told me to go to the doctor and get a cortisone shot and a prescription for ointment; I did, as soon as possible, and it was like a miracle. In a few days it was like I was totally healed. Although the cortisone shot provided a rather temporary relief, it was much appreciated at the time. I continued to be plagued with my affliction and also kept using cortisone in an attempt to keep it under control. However, I would eventually discover that after years of constant use, cortisone stops working effectively.

## So Long Massey

Gerry and Jill rented an old farmhouse outside of Dundalk. So our focus for a blessed area was definitely shifting. Now that the majority of our small group was settled in the Dundalk area, it made it easy for the others in Massey to start thinking about moving also. In the spring of 1976 we found a farm for rent just outside of Dundalk for John and Carol and their 3 children. John immediately bought a tractor and started ploughing a field to plant wheat and beans. Some we would save for famine; the rest we would sell. Randy and Barb soon followed to the new blessed area to be and Massey became a memory. We rented an old church in Cedarville a small town nearby, where we held our meetings. From an early age I had sensed the call of God on my life to preach the gospel and I took it serious. I studied and prayed for hours in preparation for each meeting. In spite of the fact that I was convinced I had a word from the Lord, I was terrified of the prospect of an "outsider" paying a visit to one of our services. I instinctively knew that  what we believed would appear very strange to a "normal carnal Christian".

Rain, sleet or snow we did our best to gather; it was not always easy because we were living in the middle of the "snow belt". Some winters we could have touched the hydro wires standing from the top of the high banks if there was a way to climb up. There were times when there was not enough room in the vehicles available for everyone to fit so 1 or 2 would actually ride in the trunk. Johnny usually volunteered himself and his son John Jon. Of course Benjie thought that was fun and did not have to be coaxed into joining them. We held our meetings in Cedarville for almost a year when we got an invitation to join a small group of Terrellites in Alliston. They were old and their church was old but they needed a preacher. So our little group doubled in size and I kept studying and preaching.

Nothing brought me more satisfaction then preaching from God's word. Gerry also jumped at the chance to share his thoughts from the pulpit when given the opportunity; the others were happy to be one of the chosen few. I especially loved pointing out how Jesus spoke to the hypocritical, religious leaders of His day. I guess I still had a bur under my saddle regarding organized religion and particularly those in authority. We were not like them. We were not merely "playing church" to appease God or to feel good; we took it serious. We were the real believers in Jesus who had left all to follow Him.

I was continually torn between getting a full-time job or not. Although, most of our group had jobs and clearly understood their responsibility to support those who labored in the word, their love offerings were not enough. They did what they could financially and often sent me thank you cards and letters, especially the girls. I have saved some of these because they are a fond reminder of the love we shared that was a healing balm and eased the pain of the condemnation, that always lingered between the lines of the truth we cherished and tried to live.

The letters from Jill, Linda and Marilyn, in particular, contained words of love and encouragement that kept me praying and studying for the will of God. I appreciated them so much but they only made the struggle to decide what to do more difficult. They referred to me as the "Man of God" and their "Shepherd". They wrote me messages like "I don't know what I would do without your ministry that gives me the courage to live for the Lord." In one letter Linda even acknowledged my struggle over getting a full-time job and encouraged me not to. She said she was willing to work and support me so I could continue to give myself to the Word. She went on to say that if I worked full-time we would miss out on what God desires to bring forth in us and none of us would make it; she meant, endure to the end.

On the other hand, the needs of my wife and son were ever before me. It was easier for me to be content with having the bare necessities of food and shelter but more difficult for Marja who was doing her best to run a household with so little. During that summer I worked a couple months as a flagman for Arnott Construction. I also received the odd call from George Barnett, a local carpenter, when he needed a helper. Doing my 1975 tax return I discovered my total income that year was $3,000.

## Filter Queen Days

Early in 1976, at Marja's pleading I started searching the local paper to find a job. The first ad that caught my eye was from a company looking for workers to demonstrate home sanitation - air purification systems. This kind of work did not sound overly appealing but I wanted to be faithful to God and to please my worried wife. Besides it might be something that would help my chronic allergies and skin condition.

Although I had never sold anything before, anything legal that is, I called the phone number and made an appointment for an interview. Their office was located at the Rockford Plaza, a few miles south of Owen Sound. As I sat in the waiting room I realized the product this company sold was vacuum cleaners. I did not consider this prospect very promising but now that I was here I would listen to the sales pitch. As I walked into the manager's office I was met by a tall, good looking man, about my age. He was frantically brushing fresh ashes off his desk with his suit coat sleeve. The room was full of smoke and he had a silly grin on his face. I am sure, by my appearance, he never suspected I could recognize the smell and knew exactly what he had just been smoking. My immediate thought was, "Oh God, what am I doing here?"

To my surprise Mr. Randy Brooks was not only a very likeable, young man but also a very convincing salesman. He informed me that there was no knocking on doors; all the appointments were set up in advance and the commission sounded enticing. With no obligation on either side he persuaded me to come back tomorrow and just spend the day with a salesman.

So on Feb. 24, 1976, I arrived back at the office ready to go on the 9:00 am demonstration. I met Morad El-Jourbagy the Sales Manager, a well-dressed Egyptian man in his 30's, and the other staff. I would be riding with Rod Duench a man about my size and age; he even had short, dark hair like mine. I was not very hopeful but had nothing to lose and thought I may get a free restaurant lunch, which was a treat those days. Besides, my wife was so happy to see I was making the effort to find a job.

To my surprise, the "Filter Queen" was a rather impressive machine; after Rod's convincing 45-minute demonstration the people wanted to buy it. They had little in the way of carpets and didn't need a power nozzle. The basic machine sold for around $300. The commission for this sale was $75.00; not bad for less than two hours on the job. To my delight Rod sold 2 more that afternoon and earned $250 that day. This was the average love offerings I received in a month. In construction I earned $5 an hour. Rod just earned $30 an hour for the day. I was sold. I didn't even own a vehicle but Johnny, who was a good mechanic, always had his eye open for a good deal on old clunkers. One 4-door Chevy he bought was not that old but had been used by the previous owner to transport pigs to and from the market. It was filthy with about 4 inches of hard packed manure on the floor of the back seat. I worked for hours digging it out, trying to clean it good enough to use for work. All these things we took in stride realizing they were a small price to pay to know the truth.

The normal procedure called for 3 days training but before I headed home that evening, with some coaxing, I convinced Randy I was ready to go. Although he was reluctant, he saw I was determined and said, "Okay, see you in the morning". So with Johnny's cleaned up Chevy sedan I showed up at 8:00am for the sales meeting and instructions for my first appointment. About 15 men, of all ages, had gathered for the upbeat morning session. Yesterdays success were shared and there was a loud round of applause for Rod, for selling 3, in one day.

Direct selling was big in the 70's and Filter Queen was thriving. Randy and Morad were obviously running a very successful franchise. They openly talked about the money they earned. This little branch alone, sold 1600 machines the previous year. Even at an average selling price of $350 x 1600 that is $560,000 in sales. Not bad for the 70's. In the days that followed I would hear lots of grand stories. One of Randy's favorite was the time he moved here and was looking for a house to rent. The real estate agent asked him what his income was and he replied $10,000. She said "per year?" and he said "no per month." As I would find out, sometime later, Randy was slightly embellishing. He also bragged that the Ontario Sales Manager, Jack Johnston earned more last year than Gerald Ford, the President of the United States.

Randy boasted he could go into any house in town to do a demonstration and after being there one hour he would have made himself at home; so much so, that he felt comfortable going to the fridge, without asking, to help himself to a beer. I took all this big talk with a grain of salt but after I got to know him better, I wouldn't be surprised if he had tried. I had to admit there was something very appealing about it all. Randy in particular, was very convincing; I could believe this guy was bold enough to try almost anything. Apparently he had the sales records to back up a lot of his boasting, also.

I heard it said, in direct selling, regardless of the product, 15% of the sales force earns 80% of the commissions. As I looked around the room it was fairly obvious to me who the 15% were. Some of the older guys were just looking for a reason to get up in the morning, get out of the house, socialize and maybe get an easy sale and earn a little extra cash. There were those also, like Randy, Morad and Rod who saw the potential to earn some lucrative earnings. I made up my mind that if this is where God wanted me, then I would also join the 15% club.

My first Filter Queen demonstration appointment was in the little town of Tobermory. I had heard of it. It was at the top of highway 6 where the Ferry to and from Manitoulin Island launched from May to October. In February, as I would soon find out, the town is literally closed for business; there is no town. I drove to the end of the road and saw nothing that even resembled one. I managed to find a phone booth and called the office. The secretary assured me there were a few people who lived there in the winter and put me on hold while she called the folks. She came back on the phone and gave me specific directions. The driveway was not plowed but I eventually found the path, through the snow, to their door.

I was greeted by a young couple who offered me coffee and we settled in for a cozy time together. I don't think they had many visitors through the long winter and were happy to have me drop in. I figured they were not in the market for an expensive vacuum cleaner but I was here now and I needed the practice demonstrating the machine. I went through the book, I had rehearsed the night before, slowly and methodically, page-by-page and then through the demonstration attachment by attachment. An hour later I started neatly packing up all the pieces. To my surprise the man of the house asked if we had a finance plan. He said he had a good job working on the docks and would be back to work in a few months. I said, "Well yes, we do!" I filled out the application and phoned the office and gave Morad the details. He told me to leave the machine. I took their trade-in, congratulated them on being the proud owners of the best vacuum cleaner made, and we said our goodbyes. I rejoiced as I drove away anticipating my next appointment. I had just earned $75.00. I couldn't help but wonder if this was the channel the Lord had chosen to bless our little group.

To my delight, I sold 5 Filter Queens my first week on the job, which was beyond my wildest expectation. I now was excited about the prospect of what this could mean. The possibilities seemed to fit with the hard gospel we believed, albeit in a strange way. We were taught God was going to have a special people; He was going to bless the faithful abundantly, in every way, but only those willing to pay the price to follow Him. The others in the group quickly shared my enthusiasm. Johnny and Gerry would come on board soon to cash in on this opportunity. Word got to Art and when he got laid off from his winter job of delivering home-heat fuel that summer he also joined the team.

That spring of 1976 Ernie and Joyce Clarke bought a new car and kindly offered me their red, 1966 Dynamic 88, Oldsmobile. I gladly accepted and gave Johnny his car back. This big boat had a 460 cubic inch motor and would literally fly, almost. There was one long, straight stretch of road I took coming home after my last demonstration each night and I couldn't resist the temptation to put the pedal to the metal. The back fenders were rusted enough that at 115 mph (185 km/hr) I noticed they were flapping up and down like wings. I never forgot the Clarke's kindness and mailed them $1200, in the 80's as payment for the car. We also visited them years later on their small farm near Dundalk. They moved there shortly after we left and are still "following the prophet" today, as far as I know.

Now with a steady income we rented a house in the nearby town of Hopeville and said goodbye to Fillippo; our herdsmen days were over and I sensed it was time to move on to bigger and better things. Being the dreamer and visionary that I am, I began praying earnestly that God would bless our little group and prosper our business dealings and our crops. I specifically pleaded with Him that this area would become an official "Blessed Area" and He would grant us our own Filter Queen franchise so we could work and worship together. Whatever God had for us I wanted. Failure to acquire His best meant a failure to please Him and this would mean to be a failure in life.

## Marilyn and Paul Are Married

The summer of 1976, wedding bells were ringing again, this time for my sister Marilyn and Paul Reimer. Marilyn knew traveling to Alabama, like her brothers had done, was out of the question but she wanted Don Clowers, the man of God, to marry them. Paul's family would not take kindly to traveling south to watch a flashy American evangelist marry them, besides Paul's dad was a man of the cloth and would have to be involved in the ceremony. Don Clowers was scheduled to be in Toronto for a meeting in the middle of July so arrangements were made and the date of July 18 was announced.

It wasn't until the morning of the wedding, backstage, that they found out Mr. Clowers, being an American, could not legally marry them. So, it was left to Reverend John, Jacob Reimer and Don Clowers, a few minutes before the wedding was to begin, to work out the details. As Marilyn walked down the isle, she didn't know who was doing officiating. To her dismay it was Paul's dad, she quickly became an emotional wreck.

Four year-old Benjie was the ring bearer. He was cute, no doubt, but had a hard time concentrating on his duties at hand. Instead he found amusement in throwing the pillow up in the air, with the ring, thankfully, well secured. This of course delighted his best friend, 6-year-old John-Jon and amused many others but gave his mother a near nervous breakdown who was standing close by, as the Maid of Honor, but too far away to reach him. Marja and Marilyn stood facing the front beside each other both silently weeping.

After the dread awful, long, boring, Mennonite-style, wedding message from Mr. Reimer, finally, Brother Clowers bounded on stage took the microphone and saved the day with a booming, inspiring message. Apparently, Marilyn is hoping to write her own life-story some day so I will say no more about this momentous event. That fall Paul also joined the Filter Queen team as the service manager.

## Sales Manager

In the 5 months that followed I became one of the top sales people and was finally able to provide for the needs of my wife and son, although my initial enthusiasm was waning. It was hard to keep motivated day after day. Some folks were happy to look at the Filter Queen but simply could not afford it. Others were just not that interested in having a clean house. I saw filth and poverty on the back roads of Grey Bruce County I had no idea existed in our country. Some places I literally followed a path winding through junk and garbage across what used to be a lawn and continued into the living room to chairs so dirty I really didn't want to sit on wearing my new, polyester 3-pc suit.

I quickly purchased several new suits at Kornblums Men's Wear in Owen Sound. The store was owned and operated by an elderly Jewish man. We became friends and he took me golfing with him and his friends on occasion. I immediately fell in love with the game that would eventually become a passion of mine. I jumped at the opportunity to purchase a set of new clubs from the finance company we dealt with. They had just completed a nation wide promotion and were selling leftovers for $50. What a turn around our lives were taking in just a few short months.

Outwardly things looked great but I was getting tired of the constant, daily, direct selling life style. I could tell story after story of those days but will only share a couple. One lady screamed and ran out of the room as soon as I pulled the hose out of the box. She was terrified of snakes and would not let me continue. Another elderly lady happily bought the machine and then the next morning changed her mind and instead of calling our office, she called the police with the story that I had pressured her into buying it. I had no choice but to go back with her cheque and pick up the machine. While there I made a point of sharing with her that God will judge all liars. This prompted another phone call from the constable.

On paper I had an excellent sales record but was getting increasingly weary by the hour. I wanted to quit every day but Johnny and Gerry were now on staff and it looked like they would be just as good at selling, if not better than I was. By July I was near the end. I did not want to do another demonstration. To my surprise and delight Randy got promoted to District Manager out west. Several of the best salesmen, including Rod, were going with him. They were all promised their own sub-branches as soon as possible. Morad bought the franchise and his first and most important task was to hire a Sales-Manager. When the dust settled I was the obvious choice for the position. I was elated and so relieved; my days of direct selling were over; no more late nights driving all over the country.

Doing demonstration after demonstration had become boring. The highlight of the day had been meeting Johnny, Gerry and others for lunch to share our sales stories. We ate well, too well; I usually had a hamburger and fries and a piece of pie with ice cream and within a short time I couldn't keep my eyes open. I had to pull over on the side of the road and I literally passed out on the front seat of my car. Anyway, those days were over, I had been faithful and survived. I would now be recruiting, hiring and training, which I was more suited to. I would be paid $15 on every sale in the office, which was often 100 or more a month.

With the promise of extra income we rented a nearby farm. I purchased 10 heifers, a young bull and 4 pregnant sows. I was not only a successful businessman now but also a farmer. One night shortly after we moved into our new place there was a thunder storm with high winds. I had gone to bed and Marja went for a bath. She had dried herself and had just left the room when a bolt of lightning stuck a tree in our yard. There was a loud thunder clap immediately followed by a second loud crash, from the bathroom, which awoke me, and then darkness and quiet, except for the wind we could hear blowing through the house. We found a candle and made our way to the bathroom and discovered the complete window pane shattered and hundreds of pieces of glass in the bathtub and all over the floor. We closed the bathroom door and went to bed and eventually fell asleep. Marja in particular took a long time to settle. She couldn't help but think about what would have happened to her had she still been in the tub when the lightning struck. Laying in bed she sensed a strange feeling, as if an angel was in the room, and had goose bumps all over.

Outside the next morning we discovered a large tree down in the back yard. Under the tree was our hydro wires. The tree had pulled the wooden frame, holding the electrical insulators, out of the wall on its way down, demolishing the window.

The Owen Sound Filter Queen franchise continued to flourish for the rest of the year. To keep the momentum going, in June we attended a high power Sales Conference in Toronto. It was a very expensive one-day gathering with one session after another. Many big names were there like J. Douglas Edwards, Zig Ziglar, Art Linkletter, Murray Banks and Joe Gandolfo. These guys had made a fistful of dollars selling and now traveled full time sharing how they did it.

Every March and September were nation wide contest months that ran a full 5 weeks. Following the contest was a weekend celebration in a posh Hotel. The distributor took the Sales Manager along and any salesman that sold at least 25 units in the contest month and paid the complete tab. It was here awards were handed out to the top salesmen and managers in the country. The top brass attended decked out to the nines. The conference officially started with a complete demonstration on stage by the top salesman in the country. It was a lot of hype and partying but I knew there were more than a few people here earning large sums of money and they didn't mind flaunting the fact. By the end of the year I had earned $15,000. This wasn't great riches by any stretch but it was the beginning, I hoped. For now it was a lot better than the $3,000 I had earned in 1975 but more importantly I knew God was blessing us as we worked together and continued to fellowship together, although not near as frequent as we once did.

On September the 13th my grandmother Bast (nee Steinman) died at the age of 83. The funeral was only a two-hour drive away but we were in the middle of a contest month and had to keep our priorities in order. As I look back, I see this lack of concern for family as one of the blatant signs of the depth of our deception.

## Dad's Education and Career Change

Dad was also making his own career change. He had been getting increasingly restless sitting behind the wheel of a truck contemplating his life. He wanted to accomplish something more than just making a living, albeit a good one. Because of his interest in Native issues and the influence of a friend Art Solomon he decided to go back to school. He had been traveling for some time with Art to Ontario Penitentiaries, who was teaching Native Study courses to inmates in jail. Art was aging and would eventually need a replacement. Obviously a qualified Indian was his first choice but possibly a Mennonite with the right attitude, the right training and a degree would do.

My Dad had not been in school since the age of 14. In 1942 when he showed up for grade 8, the teacher informed him there was nothing more she could teach him and sent him directly to Wellesley High School. Unfortunately he was not there long when he got caught smoking in the schoolyard with a couple older boys and they were all expelled. 34 years later a keen interest in issues such as "War and Peace" and the problems with our Native Indians began awakening in him. In the fall of 1976 at the age of 48 he enrolled in a graduate course at the University of Manitoba in Winnipeg.

For the next several years he would continue his education while working with Art. In the spring of 1982 he earned a Bachelor of Arts degree in "Law and Justice" and "Native Studies" from Laurentian University in Sudbury. His final was an oral exam in Ojibwa. A few years later he enrolled at the University of Waterloo as a full-time student. On Friday afternoon, after a full week of school, he drove to Toronto and jumped into a Wilson's truck and spent the weekend hauling a 40' trailer to Thunder Bay and back, grabbing a few hours sleep here and there. In June 1990, at the age of 61, he received the degree of "Master of Theological Studies" from the University of Waterloo. His graduate thesis was "The Environmental Crisis: A Spiritual Crisis". He soon began teaching Native Study correspondent courses part-time for Sudbury University. While teaching, he also worked for the family business and continued there until August 2008, the month before he turned 80.

Meanwhile back in Grey – Bruce county when the dust settled at the end of the contest in September of 1976 Johnny had sold 29 units and Gerry 25. So it was off to Toronto to a fancy Hotel for a taste of the rich life. What a contrast it was to the Massey days we had experienced only a few short years prior. This was a costly trip for the company but the contest had brought in extra sales and it was time to celebrate. We recorded 101 sales for the month, which means Gerry and Johnny sold over half. I still have my original sales record sheet. Dave Bumstead a young local man I hired was 3rd with 15 sales. He only worked part-time on weekends and after school during the week. When he finished school he would join the team full time and would also marry Sister Linda who was working in the office booking demonstrations. Behind David was Art with 11 sales. Sales continued strong for the rest of the year.

## A Gift to The Prophet

That fall Barry and Lorraine sold their apartment building and moved to the Dundalk area to be part of the potential "Blessed Area" and also joined the Filter Queen team. They needed a change in lifestyle and also wanted to bless the prophet. No one came right out and said it but we all believed by blessing God's servant we may influence God to smile on our group and area. There is no point in lying about it; this is what we were thinking.

Anyway, they struggled with how much to give and how much to keep for their own livelihood. As far as I know, they did not tell anyone, what they had decided, at least they didn't tell me, Brother Clowers or Brother Terrell. Somehow word got to the Prophet that the time was right for him to make his first visit ever, to Canada. A meeting was scheduled in Toronto and a cheque for $16,000 was written and dropped in the offering bucket. They also gave their slightly used 10 passenger Ford Club Wagon to the ministry. We heard later Terrell was quite upset that he had to come all that way for this small amount. By this time he must have been very wealthy and had been led to believe he could expect a much larger amount. A few years later he was busted for tax evasion and apparently served time in jail. Too bad for him.

## Moving Again

Early the spring of 1977 I realized my workload at the office was too heavy to keep doing the farm chores also. Paul and Marilyn were happy to move in and take over. Marja, Benjie and I rented a little chalet at the bottom of the Talisman Ski Resort hill near Creemore during the off-season; before winter we would once again be on the move.

The beginning of March 1977 marked the start of another Filter Queen contest month, we broke records, having a ball doing it. Johnny, Art and Gerry all sold 25; this time it was off to Montreal's posh Chateau Laurier Hotel to be wined and dined, well dined, we didn't drink. In fact, things were going so well in Grey Bruce County, Morad got promoted to District Manager in British Columbia. I was first in line to buy the franchise from him. I was elated. This is what we all had been praying for, but I needed $20,000. Where could I find that kind of money?

I told Mom and Dad about my situation and they volunteered to re-mortgage their house, which was almost paid off. They knew this was a good opportunity for all 4 of their children. They had observed us working and prospering together and were so happy that not only the drug days were over but also the cult days also appeared to be coming to an end. I would simply take over their mortgage payments. I was so sure this was "of God" that I cheerfully accepted. So, at 26 yrs old I became the proud owner and operator of a thriving small business with 15 sales people and an office staff of 5. Like the Movers used to say, I was now "The Big Dea - Ler".

My first choice for a corporate name was "Living Clean" [with Filter Queen] and although it cleared the Ontario Government search for available names, head office rejected it. They said we were inferring people were not "clean living people" if they didn't own a filter Queen. This was just smoke and mirrors. They had, no doubt, heard about our religious zeal and although they wanted us to do well they wanted no part of appearing religious. We decided on "Sunny Side Distributors", instead. Our theme song became "Keep on the Sunny Side". We began every morning sales meetings singing it with enthusiasm.

I promoted Art to Sales Manager, which understandably upset Johnny; he had been there first and was our best salesman. This was the main reason why I didn't want him as manager; I didn't want to lose his sales. He expressed his disappointment and I decided to compromise and had them share the management duties. This way they could both still sell part-time and train part-time. After Dave Bumstead finished high school he came on board fulltime. His younger brother Doug also joined the team. They had grown up on a nearby farm and knew how to work and also had many contacts in the area. They would both eventually go on to have successful careers with Prudential Life,

Dave became a District Manager and Doug one of the top 10 salesmen in the country. As far as I know they are still there.

We now had a solid sales core of hard working, honest guys and continued to do well. Roberta Boucher, a 16-yr old girl from Chapleau, who we met in Toronto at a crusade, also joined us in the office booking appointments. Kate Howe, a local lady took care of the book keeping. She became a good friend and we still keep in touch with Christmas cards 35 years later. These girls were a key part of the business. It took a special mix of friendliness and persistence to get folks to agree to open their home to receive a gift for spending the time to watch a free demonstration. There was absolutely no obligation on their part but a good salesman could find enough dirt in their house with this great vacuum cleaner that many would want to buy it. It was said, "The machine sold itself" but a good salesman knew he had to also sell himself, also. It was a total package. He had one hour to win the customers trust and affection if he was going to make the sale.

Although I personally could not go south to the tent revivals any more, it seems all of us were so busy being successful we were slowly losing the need to go. So, Brother Clowers came to us and held meetings in the office sales room. I enjoyed slipping him a crisp $100 bill whenever he made the trip to minister to us. Several times at the close of his service I asked for the microphone and took up a second offering, for the man of God, for his personal needs. Brother Clowers ginned sheepishly while I collected the money for him.

Around this time, it started to register that Brother Clowers was slowly distancing himself from the prophet but I didn't know to what extent. He talked about being associated with other preachers such as Kenneth Hagen and Ken Copeland, two of the forerunners in the "Prosperity Gospel" movement. This shift to the left seemed to fit better into our present lifestyle. We were enjoying our success and gave Brother Clowers a lot of the credit. He did an article on me in his monthly magazine. The heading was "From Drugs to Success". It featured "before and after" pictures of me. One with long hair and denim jacket; the other in my fancy suit sitting at my desk.

## Back to Lotus Land

The next contest month was Sept. 1977 and the conference was in Vancouver. Johnny and Dave both sold 25 machines and we were off to beautiful British Columbia. From our Hotel room on the waterfront of Burrard Inlet we could see the mountains in the background. It brought back memories of the winter of 1969 when I lived here with Dave Ham. It reminded me of how bad I wanted to leave Sudbury, in 1971, and move here, when Billy and the boys made their exit.

I called Billy and we spent a day together after the conference was over. We took the Ferry to Vancouver Island and found Rainer Funk and Dave Ham in the little town of Sooke. The whole experience was surreal. I loved Billy dearly and had such good memories of our hippie years together. The bond was still there but I had changed so much and found relating to him awkward. However, I left BC with a new appreciation for the west coast and deep down hoped I could somehow, someway make this my home.

Late in 1977 I ordered a new Chrysler Lebaron from the local car dealer. Hard to believe but it slipped off the icy ramp while it was being unloaded; it was damaged too bad to fix quickly. The dealer found a slightly used one with only 6000 kms. It was charcoal gray with red leather interior and power everything. I also bought a half-ton truck, which came in handy on the farm and also at the business. Seeing Paul was taking care of my livestock and was also the serviceman he got to drive the truck. A few months later I bought a 1975 Ford LTD so Marja could drive the Le Baron. Money came in and money went out.

Before the skiing season began we moved out of our chalet and rented a  newer, bigger house that backed onto Balmy Beach in Owen Sound. Benjie began attending kindergarten and I started playing shinny hockey with a group of locals. We were now settling into normal urban living. I even bought a color television and started watching hockey. It wasn't long ago that I thought those days were over forever but alas they were back, just like that. At playoff time I soon got hooked almost as bad as when I was young. To make things worse I was so busy at the office and so preoccupied enjoying our prosperity I had little time or need to study and pray, not to mention spending quality time with my beautiful wife and son. A nagging guilt surfaced periodically but was ignored and soon forgotten. God was blessing us and that is what mattered.

Ironically, something good seemed to come out of the fact that we were too busy for spiritual matters; we were slowly being released from the grip of the prophet and his religious bondage. I had been aware of this for some time but had no idea where we headed. It was uncharted waters for us. As long as God was leading and blessing I wanted to hang on and enjoy the ride. Our new freedom and joy was so uplifting and yet it was a little scary because the change was happening so fast.

There was another problem that I was well aware of with this much success and talent in one small office. It was the fact that some of these guys would eventually want their own office and franchise. It happened sooner than I anticipated. In the spring of

1978 Johnny was offered a franchise in Goderich; he accepted. Dave and Linda were going with him. Also Barry and Lorraine would gravitate that direction and scraped together what little money they had left and bought the Laundromat in nearby Clinton. Paul had already found another job and a friend of Barry, Reg Hunka had taken over as the new service man. To make things worse, not long after Gerry and Jill decided to head back to Sudbury and Randy and Barb would follow them. I was about to loose my top three salespeople and the best part of my office staff. I knew we could not survive without them and I did not have the desire or the energy to start rebuilding from scratch. The dream was over as quick as it had begun.

My main purpose in buying the franchise was not to establish a career for myself but that we as a group, could work together and follow the Lord together. If we would have sat down and seriously talked about it and prayed about these decisions, we may have realized, "united we stand and divided we fall", but we didn't. With the group heading off madly in all directions it became apparent it was time to pull the plug. If this was the end of God's work here there was nothing I could do about it.

Interestingly, before everyone dispersed Brother Clowers called me and said he wanted to visit and have a special meeting with the group. I picked him up at the airport and he carefully told me he was parting ways with David Terrell. He confided that he had increasing concerns about things and when he shared them with the prophet they were not received well, although he had no idea how bad it was. When he arrived home from his last trip to Canada he was faced with complete mutiny; he didn't even have a church anymore. In his absence, David Terrell held a special meeting in Fort Payne and announced, "Brother Clowers has been taken over by a seducing spirit". The majority of the large congregation accepted this explanation. If there was those who had their doubts, they had no recourse against "The Prophet". Their pastor was no longer welcome, although he had labored there for years. Another pastor was already set in place. I didn't know any details about the ownership of the church and property. All I knew was that the prophet held a lot of clout.

As Brother Clowers shared his story tears ran down my cheeks. Several different emotions simultaneously overwhelmed me. First of all it was shocking, but it was also sad. How could two brothers who had worked so long and so close have this kind of falling out? To my surprise I also felt a great sense of relief. I instantly realized that I had been ignoring a secret fear that something was amiss. I had brushed aside the stories of the prophet's riches, about his 100's of suits and pairs of shoes, his secret mansions in other countries and a secret wife. There were things he had said from the pulpit that also bothered me, but I had ignored them. I remember one time after he prophesied of calamities to come; he added, "This is what the Lord has showed me but even if He didn't He will bring it to pass because I am His prophet and my words will not fall to the ground." I now shudder at such arrogant boldness. It also bothered me when I heard some of his followers talking about Ezekiel 34:23 and other places that mentioned, "My servant David". They claimed the servant mentioned was David Terrell. I couldn't see how this was possible but just pushed the thought to the back burner.

One vision the prophet had, in particular, I now find extremely interesting. In his vision he was climbing a very high mountain. About ¾ of the way up he discovered a pot of gold. The Lord spoke to him and said he could take the gold or leave it and continue to the top where few men had gone before. He could not take the gold with him. Of course he claimed nothing would hinder him from going all the way to the top. Later when we heard of his private jet and enormous riches we knew better.

We had experienced a great liberty the last few years. I now knew it was because we had not been able to go to Terrell's meetings. To Brother Clowers' great relief, I bought his story hook line and sinker. It was like he was telling me something I had known for a long time but wasn't able to face it. There were others in our group who were not so happy about this development. Barry and Lorraine felt sick when they heard the news. They had given the prophet a large sum of money and a near new van. They knew they had been deceived and were understandably angry. They took it hard and as far as I know they credit the contention over this issue a factor in their eventual divorce.

Brother Clowers assured me he would now have more time to spend in Canada. Being the Vice-President of his association and his key contact he wanted me more involved in the ministry. He even invited me to come south to work with him. He was going to start a new church in Chatanooga Tennessee and needed an assistant pastor, I could hardly believe my ears. What an honor this was and what timing. I knew his church would grow and prosper; this was my opportunity to be in the ministry.

I, immediately let my district manager know I wanted out as long as I got my $20,000 back. I knew he would have no problem selling the franchise solely on the sales reports for the last 5 years. He could not believe his ears. He had people lined up who would jump at this opportunity but questioned me out of curiosity. He could not understand how I had worked so hard for 2-½ years and would let it all slip away. I couldn't explain all the circumstances and especially the spiritual aspect and didn't try. Things happened very quickly after that. I soon received a cheque for $10,000, which I gave to my dad. The balance would follow in several installments over the next few months.

I knew getting a visa to work in the US would not be a simple process and may not even be possible but I had to try. If this was God's will no man could stop it. Brother Clowers said his lawyer would be available to help any way he could and he told me to find out how to get the process started. I made a few calls and found out that application would have to be made through the office of the Consulate General of the USA, in Toronto. There would be a series of interviews once my application was received. So, necessary documentation was quickly submitted.

On May 31st Marja's parents were off to Finland for 5 weeks and Marja and Benjie went with them. June was my last month at Filter Queen; the new owner took over July the 1st, 1978 . I also moved our furniture out of our house on Balmy Beach Road and stored it in the barn where Reimer's were living in Kilsythe. I moved in with Paul, Marilyn and 1-yr old Heidi and looked forward to a much needed rest. I cleaned up the loose business ends, did some golfing and enjoyed time with my sister and little niece.

For some reason the oil ran dry in my big Ford LTD while Paul was driving it and either the oil light didn't come or he didn't notice and fried the engine. I got rid of it cheap; easy come, easy go. Reg who was going back home to Sudbury wanted to buy my truck. He didn't have the cash to pay me so I arranged for him to take over the payments. This is one of many decisions I made quickly without much thought or prayer. A few months later the bank notified me; Reg's truck payments were behind and they would repossess it if I didn't make the payments ASAP.

I heard he was back to drinking and it looked like he was not going to get a job real soon so I decided to take the truck back. When I called him he refused to give it to me. The bank told me to go see a bailiff. This was my introduction to Nicky Dellelce, the oldest son of the prominent and infamous business lady,

Mama Dellelce. He told me there was no problem getting the truck back but it would cost me $50. I knew where Reg lived, so he said, "Let's go". The truck was in the yard and Mr. Dellelce knocked on the door and showed Reg his badge. It took a few minutes but he convinced him the truck would be impounded; until he could pay the bank the late payments. I watched in silence as Reg reluctantly handed Mr. Dellelce the keys.

Back at his office, we sat down and Nicky said, "That will be a $100, son". I reminded him he had previously told me $50. He said, "Do you want the truck or not?" I didn't argue with this big, tough looking, businessman. It didn't really come as a surprise when I later heard he had made the front page news. Apparently he paid someone to burn down his Silver Beach Tavern so he could collect the insurance. After the job was done Nicky refused to pay what he promised. The man went to the police and Nicky was charged and made the front lines of the Sudbury Star and went to jail. I heard he was treated like a prince and actually enjoyed his holiday. Justice was served.

## The Worst Year of My Life

Marja was not keen to move to Toronto and a little uneasy about even trying to move to the States. I was determined to at least begin the process, even though there was only a slight chance of ever getting approval and she reluctantly submitted. The decision to proceed without her "sincere blessing" put a further strain on our already up and down relationship. I needed to be close to Toronto and I also needed to work during the application process. We rented an apartment in nearby Mississauga, registered Benjie in school and in hockey. He was 5 years old when his hockey career began. Today at 43 he is still very involved in "Canada's game", coaching both his son's teams. Once we were settled I started reading help wanted ads.

The first job I applied for was selling "Sun Guard", a product installed on windows to keep the heat of the sun out to cut air-conditioning costs. Marja came along to the interview. The man across the desk was 6' tall and weighed 515 pounds. He reminded me of the Humpty Dumpty pictures I had seen. He claimed high-rise buildings have so many lights and business machines that a heating system is not necessary, however air-conditioning costs were enormous. I was in no position to argue. He also confided, he had been an "All American" university basketball player. When his wife died he gave up on life and began eating insensibly. Not sure why but I agreed to take the straight commission job.

We decided to go out for lunch to celebrate. He literally had to turn sideways to walk through the doorway. At the restaurant he needed two chairs to sit on and ordered soup and bread and a lot of butter. He almost emptied the salt and pepper shakers in his bowl. I'm sure this activity was the most exercise he would get all day. He ate half a cantaloupe for desert. We parted and I showed up for work the next day.

Taking this job was another bad decision I made but would be far from the last one during this dark period of my life. I quit working for Sunguard after 3 weeks and registered in a Real Estate course. I found Real Estate interesting and did well. I decided to go to work for Polzler Real Estate on Mississauga Road. Apparently almost any office would hire new licensed sales people. They joked that there was only one prerequisite to getting hired, "you had to be breathing". Frank Polzler, the owner, had put together a winning team with Greg Gilmour as the Sales Manager, who had done extremely well selling. I liked Greg and he was impressed with my resume.

The first week after I joined Polzler, Greg's new Lincoln Towncar came in, actually both his Lincolns came in. He thought it was only fair to buy his wife one too, a new Mark V. Within a short time he assured me I was the best new agent on board and I would do well in this business.

Townhouses were selling cheap and with little down. I found one that needed work and I thought it would be a good starter home and investment. We were in no position to invest money because we had none. We prayed about it and decided to make an offer with nothing down. If they accepted we would go for it; nothing ventured nothing gained. They signed it back for $500 down. We really couldn't afford even this small down payment but decided to go ahead anyway.

To make things worse, instead of giving my dad the balance of the Filter Queen money as it came in I used it to pay living expenses and to fix up our new home, all the time hoping I would soon be earning enough to pay Dad back. We painted and had new carpets installed. It looked great. Unfortunately it cost a lot more than I had anticipated and I was using borrowed money that I shouldn't have been spending.

I quickly tried to resell it cheap and we would be content to live in our 2nd floor apartment until I was better established in real estate. It did not sell and we had no choice but to move in and hope for the best. We made a feeble attempt to change the lifestyle we were now used to but failed miserably. As our credit card debt escalated, all I could do was hope and pray that God would bless my new career and that sales would start coming in to bail me out of the mess I now found myself in.

## Thomas W. Martin

Back home, on November 15, 1978, at the age of 63, Thomas Martin was tragically killed at his home next door to where I was born. Eddie Young had been digging a trench for him with his backhoe. Thomas was in the trench digging by hand and according to one of the Martin's, "Eddie never should have dug such a deep, narrow trench; it was obviously unsafe." According to one of the Young's, "Thomas was warned not to go down in the hole;" but he did and the walls caved in and he was buried alive." They were probably both right. This was the main man my dad had worked with for over 30 years establishing Water's Mennonite Church. It was a tragedy for the congregation, the community and especially his family. I was so consumed with my own problems I didn't consider going home for the funeral.

To make a long story short, we lived in the Toronto area for a year, from August 1978 to August 1979. It was the most difficult year of our lives, in many ways. Reading through the copious notes in my diary about this time was most depressing. I lived from day to day in a state of shock not knowing what to do. I managed to get a 2nd mortgage from a loan shark for one year at 30% interest. I borrowed another $2,000 from my Uncle Mervin and Aunt Mary. I found myself pushing people for a sale and I hated myself for it. I started to regret much of my life; the drug years, the cult years, not to mention, the stupidest mistake I ever made, which was getting a vasectomy. We put our names on the list to adopt a child, a playmate for our son. I wanted to fix at least one problem I had created. We were told it would take years to get a healthy, white child. We said we would consider any child.

Finally in January 1979, after nigh 6 months with very little pay, I started averaging one sale a week. Things finally appeared to be falling into place; Greg and Mr. Polzler were very happy as was

Marja. The early estimation that I was the most promising new agent was appearing to be right. In a morning sales meeting, Mr. Polzler bragged "Don does everything in his power to put a deal together". I had mixed feelings about those accolades. Amazingly, at precisely the right time Johnny sold his Filter Queen franchise and came to visit us looking for a career change. He was instantly eager to get into Real Estate and I sold him a cheap town house close to ours

By March I was on target to earn $50,000 and was flying high. I couldn't help but look at new cars as I passed the car lots and dream about living in a house like the ones I was selling. I enjoyed being constantly on the run, working 7 days a week but my personal life was suffering more than ever. I didn't have time to eat properly and seldom spent much time with my wife or played with my 7-yr old son but things were finally going well for me, so I thought. For no known reason, as fast as the sales began they stopped. It was like someone shut off the tap; I wonder Who? For many weeks I recorded no sales and was behind the eight ball again. I was told this was common for new agents and all I could do was keep plugging away. I soon fell into the worst depression ever, with no energy or vision to continue. For the first time in life I could relate to why people are driven to drink, drugs and even suicide.

By contrast Johnny had just finished Real Estate school, joined the  Polzler team and was dreaming of big things. We created a partnership thinking it may spark something in me but it didn't help. By now I was flat broke and over $20,000 in debt. Our credit cards were to the limit and we didn't know where grocery money was going to come from. Now over 30 years later as I write about the state I was in, I am overwhelmed with emotion. I was caught off guard to discover that the dread of what I went through had been safely tucked away in my memory.

## Caroleen-Ella

In the middle of our financial crisis Children's Aid called; they had a five-year old Cree Indian girl from Saskatchewan who needed a home. She had been in a foster home for two years and had twice started the adoption process and had been rejected by the prospective parents, both times. We needed to be very interested before we could see her. This was one thing we decided to pray together about. We received a picture and a record of her long medical history. She was one of 50 people in Canada with "Kartagener's Syndrome", which meant all of her organs, including her heart were on the opposite side. Along with this condition came a weakness in the lungs, which made her susceptible to colds etc. She also was the victim of Fetal Alcohol Syndrome. The profound affects of this condition we would learn about, first hand, later. Worst of all, at the age of 3, she had been taken out of her family's home with severe head injuries. The medical report said that even after 3 operations, she still had a 6" scar on her skull made from a sharp object, probably a screw driver.

In spite of all her problems we quickly concluded she was meant to be in our family. Children's Aid paid for our flights and my dad gave me his credit card for expenses and the 3 of us were off to bring home a little sister for Benjie. We flew to Saskatoon and rented a car. We met the worker in Nepawin and she took us to the foster home to meet Caroleen. She was living with a quiet, elderly women whose husband was a trapper and gone much of the time. Mrs. Ogren had taken in many foster children over the years Caroleen being the most recent.

Caroleen was extremely shy with a limited English vocabulary; the worker figured maybe 50 words. Her native tongue was Cree but hadn't spoken it for the last 2 years. Benjie played with her on the living room floor as we observed and talked. After a few hours I asked her if she would like to come and live with us. Without hesitation she got up, grabbed her coat and headed for the door. Approaching Toronto, standing looking out the window of the plane at all the city lights she began squealing with excitement, "Ooo Eee, Ooo Eee" over and over again.

We arrived home safe and sound, now with another mouth to feed. We figured, regardless of our state of affairs, Caroleen was better off in our home than in a foster home and possibly more rejection. We soon realized the extent of the constant medical attention she would need. Tubes were installed in both her ears to drain fluids. Every evening Marja would have her lie face down on a slanted coffee table and pat her back to drain her lungs. Whenever we visited the hospital with her, doctors gathered around and got a kick out of putting their stethoscope on her chest to confirm her heart was indeed on her right side.

Caroleen seemed to adjust into our family well but it was hard to tell because she was so quiet. Soon after she came to us we discovered she had a high threshold for pain. Apparently this is something one can develop through training. We noticed cigarette burns on different parts of her body, especially her arms. Besides this we realized, even when she was visibly hurt, she did not cry. One day she fell off a swing and landed hard, square on her head. We rushed to her aid expecting her to scream. Instead she quickly got up and didn't utter a peep even though the fear and pain was clearly visible in her eyes. I knew she was hurting bad but she seemed incapable of crying. It was like she had never learned how or along the way she was trained not to cry. Neither was she interested in our sympathy.

I was reminded of the rough night I had in the hospital at 10 years old when I broke my arm. Even though I been painfully sick all night I never cried either. Not until my mom walked into the room did the flood-gates burst wide open. I had needed comforting all through the night but because there was no one there to comfort me it was easy to hold it in but when I saw Mom that was it. I wondered if Caroleen had trained herself to hold her pain inside because there never was anyone there for her, to give her the comfort she craved. We wanted to reach her heart with our love but felt so inadequate.

## Days Numbered at Polzler

Things at the office by now were real bad; I hated to go in but forced myself. On Sundays, especially, I felt terrible being there and little was happening, anyway. A couple we befriended in our complex, invited us to church one Sunday, a Pentecostal church called Mississauga Gospel Temple; so went along with them. Fred Fulford was the senior pastor and his message, to my surprise, was quite inspiring. It was not at all what we had experienced in Reverend Murry's church. Up until that time I had not reconsidered darkening the door of another "Plenty Crosstal" gathering, as David Terrell had referred to them.

I began seriously reading the Bible again and other books and crying out to God for help. I also did a lot of soul searching, knowing I needed answers and soon. I was getting ready to hear the still small voice of God, I had once been so familiar with. Deep down it had been softly shouting to me for a long time.

God came to my rescue early one morning in June. For no apparent reason I was suddenly awakened around 4:00 am, the same time I used to get up to pray. I was restless and agitated, scratching frantically; I knew I should get up and didn't hesitate; I was desperate for the Lord to speak to me. I made coffee and sat down in my chair beside our bookshelf.

My attention was drawn to one book, "All Things are Possible". In this writing, the author covers the Healing Revival that began in the late 40's with William Branham and Oral Roberts through to the early 70's. He took an objective approach and simply documented the life and ministry of many prominent preachers of the last 25 years. There was a section on Jack Coe, A. A. Allen and others I knew. Even David Terrell's ministry was covered. Most of them enjoyed years of success, which was followed by subsequent failure, such as alcoholism, deception and even tragic death in some cases. A new determination rose up in me that morning; I would not allow the enemy to destroy me, like he had these men. From that hour I began to walk softly before the Lord. I opened my heart and allowed my spirit to freely cry out, like it had been longing to. My ear was now attuned to hear the still small voice I had ignored for too long. I went to work that day with a new outlook on life.

In June and July I sold enough houses to keep going but sensed my days in the big city were numbered. I realized by then, to get a working visa to the USA was a very long and tedious process, nigh impossible. I could not stay here that long and I concluded that God never planned for me to do so. I didn't know what He wanted but I knew it would unfold.

On August 15$^{th}$ a cassette tape came in the mail; it was a message by Ken Copeland called "Our Covenant With God". Although, it is not difficult, for me now, to find gross error in his Prosperity Gospel message, there was one point he made that God used to speak to my heart, loud and clear. As I listened to the message God lovingly exposed how I had fallen into the mess I was in. He gently but forcefully reminded me of the many specific warnings I ignored and I recalled being uneasy about decisions I had made in the last few years. He showed me how loose I had been with my finances and how foolish I had been to go in debt. I had become greedy and in my search for success, I had emulated the preachers I followed. I had been the leader of our little flock and I had been led astray. To make things worse others had followed me. We had been tricked into going after the pot of gold on our way up the mountain. In doing so, I had failed my wife and family and most serious, I had sinned against God. It hurt deep to realize what I had done but at least I now had my answer and a starting point to work from.

In church next Sunday the pastor preached on Mary and Martha and their devastation at the death of their brother Lazarus. Why didn't Jesus come to them sooner? Why did he wait till Lazarus died? I thought of the last 6 months and the tears I had shed pleading with the Lord to come to my rescue. I now knew why He never came; I had not been ready. I was now eager to follow Him and allow new life to come out of my dead kernel of hollow dreams. I immediately listed our house. Marja and I agreed we had to go back home to Sudbury for a time at least, to get our bearings and decide what we wanted to do for the rest of our lives. Or as John-Jon had recently and innocently asked me, "What do you want to do when you grow up"; good question. I had just turned 29 and I didn't have a clue.

Interestingly my eczema got better over the next few weeks. Stress was not good for my skin ailment; when the peace of God renewed my mind, my body also reacted favorably. While still in Mississauga we heard David Terrell was coming to nearby Brampton on a Friday night and so we decided to check it out. Apparently, he now had a burden for Canada. He was still loud and bold like I remembered him. As before, he boasted how he was the one God talks to but now it sounded hollow and rather boring actually. I was amazed at how much he had changed in such a short time? I now know all the change had not been on his part. Not sure who changed more him or me.

It was a rather small crowd but I saw a few old friends; they were happy to see us. Joyce Clarke let us know she was praying that God would restore us but there was no allure at all. The Clarke's had bought a farm near proton Station a few miles from where we had been. They were still hoping this was going to be a Blessed Area. We visited them there about 10 years later; they were still "following the prophet". It was a happy / sad visit. We heard later that David Terrell didn't show up for the Saturday evening show in Brampton; his son Randall took the service; I guess he lost his burden for Canada that afternoon.

We began spending time with Johnny and Carol renewing the closeness of our old friendship. Johnny was also talking about moving back to Sudbury. In the days that followed we traveled to Sudbury and spent time with Gerry, Jill and Randy. We also met with Barry and Lorraine. We had been through so much together and it was good to talk about it. I loved them all and felt responsible for introducing them to David Terrell and the religious bondage we endured. A few of them were very angry and it would take a long time for them to sort it all out and find healing. We were all embarrassed at how we had been so gullible for so long. Most of us took it in stride, realizing it was a necessary step toward spiritual maturity. We were thankful for being delivered and thankful for the education the whole experience had provided and amazed we were all still friends.

On August 27th I went into Polzler's office and cleaned out my desk. I shook a few hands and received a few hugs and kisses from the ladies and said, "Goodbye". Around 10:00 pm that night we hit the road heading home. I was tired but I had a song in my heart as I drove through the night. I sensed I was leaving not only the big city behind but with it my worst nightmare also. This was hopefully a new beginning for us.

Many years later and after many hours of soul searching and studying I would come to some satisfactory understanding of these days. David Terrell was not really the root cause of our bondage; he had also been a victim, like us. God is not tempted by evil and He did not tempt us either. Each one of us, including Terrell, had been tempted by our own desires and together we had been led astray and enticed. Although it had been a long painful period, we had learned a valuable lesson.

This chapter began in the spring of 1972 with a homecoming of sorts and a turning back to the Lord. 7½ years later, I was once again heading back home, eager to start a new chapter in my life, which would cover approximately same length of time. In more ways than one I had gone full circle. After this time around,  I was no doubt a little wiser but unfortunately a lot deeper in debt.

Theodore Batten

Florida: November 1983

ANNOUNCEMENT

DON BAST

ICG Liquid Gas Limited is pleased to announce the appointment of Don Bast as Branch Manager. His responsibilities will entail the co-ordination of prompt fuel delivery to residential/commercial customers, construction sites and the sale and installation of the many propane appliances available at our 1040 Kelly Lake Road location. He brings with him 10 years sales experience, 5½ years with ICG.

LIQUID GAS
1040 Kelly Lake Road
Sudbury, Ontario

Ben' Grade 8 Graduation Night

# CHAPTER 5 - (1979-1986)

# Busy Working for the Lord

### Back Home in Sudbury

Without much difficulty, we found an ideal house for rent. It was a 3-bedroom bungalow in Walden, only a couple miles from my parent's place and a short walk from Jessie Hamilton Public School. It came with a big yard backing onto a ravine and acres of bush. My kids could now grow up in the same kind of setting I had enjoyed so much. Our landlords, Mr. and Mrs. Kantola, were Finn and lived next door. Olie was a carpenter and knew Marja's father and brother well. They were happy to get "good people" to rent their house, that is until our first month's rent cheque bounced. They were not impressed. There was a mix up in transferring the little bit of money we had from one account to another. We explained the situation and they accepted our story but asked for cash, from now on.

Although, we were broke with no job, still owning a house in Mississauga, which we desperately needed to sell, we were home, enjoying a peace we had lost somewhere along the way. I explored a few jobs at manpower; nothing seemed appealing. I was in the prime of life, with no idea what I should do. I wanted to work for the Lord full-time, but where? I considered staying in the Real Estate business; surely I could do better in my old stomping ground than I did in "The Big Smoke". I talked to a realtor; he would hire me immediately but I was not ready to commit myself to him; so I said no and decided to wait.

After supper on August 30th Marja and Caroleen went picking blueberries with my parents. Benjie and I tackled the task of painting an old brass bed. He was almost 7 yrs old and such a neat kid. I enjoyed spending time with him and never wanted to get so busy again and lose our connection. He was so open to spiritual things and often got excited when we prayed together, tucking him in at night. He seems very intelligent also. The other day he asked me about birth control. Do most 6 year olds think about these things? I tried to explain it in a way he could understand. I didn't want him discovering the facts of life from the other boys in the neighborhood the way I did.

On Sunday morning, we attended the Pentecostal church, Glad Tidings Tabernacle, known as GTT, with Gerry and Jill. We enjoyed the service, especially the worship time in song. We were not interested in joining a church, especially the largest one in Northern Ontario but craved fellowship. The folks we met were friendly and seemed sincere and most important, we sensed the joy of the Lord, so we decided to return again.

**Finding a Job**

Marja's brother Risto heard I was looking for a job and dropped in to talk to me. He said he had a few days work for me if I was interested. His construction company had plenty of work and he was doing very well for himself. We had kept in touch over the years and he knew I was used to wearing a three-piece suit to work but thought he would ask. It was humbling for me, to say the least, but this was no time for pride to rule the day. I needed money in the worst way and accepted. I would have to work 12-hour shifts from 8:00 pm to 8:00 am. What could I say? It was a dirty job at the Nickle Refinery but the pay was good. Laborer's hourly pay rate was over $9.00 and time and a half after 8 hrs and weekends. It was not much fun but I hung in for 3 days and earned $550. I was so thankful to be able to pay some bills and there was a joy in doing hard, physical labor for a change and to be paid well for it.

We continued attending Glad Tidings Sunday mornings and we were blessed. I never thought I could fit into a denominational church again but it felt right. There I met Dalton Fawcett a real estate broker who worked alone but was looking for someone to join his company. He offered me 80% commission. Most other companies only share 50%. We hit it off well and I liked Dalton, so Marja and I spent the next few days praying about it.

Before we could decide Risto called again and offered me a full time job. He needed 6 carpenters for a job in Elliot Lake and all but 3 of the 500 in the union were working. Construction was booming in Northern Ontario. He went on to explain that the union agreed to give 3 laborers their carpenter papers if they came in and paid their dues. Risto had never heard of such a thing. The union rep had told him he must have 3 old Finn's he can send in who are banging nails when we are not looking. Risto didn't have 3 old Finns but he had 2 young Finns and a brother-in-law. Instead of working for 5 years as an apprentice I could get my journeyman ticket over the counter, it was almost unbelievable. The pay was 12.96 / hr. plus 10% holiday pay.

Marja and I agreed this was a sign of what I should do. I could drive with a couple other workers and leave the car at home for Marja. I packed my tools in my old toolbox and on Monday morning at 5:30 we headed for Elliot Lake. We stayed in the bunkhouse 4 nights and headed home Friday after lunch. The food was incredible; a buffet was spread out for breakfast and supper with a selection of meat, pasta, vegetables, deserts and much more and a choice of bagged lunches. The fresh air and exercise was a healthy change and I sensed a new lease on life had begun. I could now easily pay my bills including my parent's mortgage payments, the debt I incurred to buy the Filter Queen franchise. For the next 10 years I would make their payments until the mortgage was paid off. This is a hard way to learn a lesson; I hoped I was learning it real good.

**Hectic Lives**

We saw a lot of my Mom and Dad these days and cultivated a new and close relationship with the two people who had done so much for me and the ones I had hurt the most. Our new place had a sauna in the basement; they came over regularly, especially Saturday evenings and we often stayed late to visit. Art was building a house on Fen Road near Whitefish, so I helped him on some Saturdays. He was also working in Elliot Lake, as was Paul Reimer. We saw a lot of each other and played pool in the evenings in the bunkhouse. It is great having family close again; it was not communal living but in some ways it was better.

On the weekends Benjie played hockey in the Walden arena and we took in the odd Sudbury Wolves game with Caroleen. On Sunday we all went to church at Glad Tidings. My heart was so full; I felt like I would burst and could barely hold back the tears of joy. We began to befriend some of the folks there and felt more comfortable, all the time. Our children liked the kid's activities, especially Crusaders, which was like Girl Guides and Boy scouts, with a Christian influence. Benji was doing well in school but Caroleen had a more difficult time. Communicating was a chore because of her limited vocabulary and her cleft pallet. Marja arranged for her to get special speech therapy classes at school, which seemed to help a little. Her and Benjie both loved living in the country close to the bush and also made friends easily. Caroleen could throw a baseball or football as good as the boys her age. During the summer holidays they both played organized baseball and Caroleen pitched one year.

Staying in Elliot Lake all week had its downside. I didn't sleep well partially because my skin is so dry in the winter but mainly because I was away from home. I missed my family, especially Marja. When I was home, life was so hectic and things became increasingly tense between us. She felt abandoned all week and I was tired when I got home. She wanted to go out and do something but weekends were so full already. We had little private time together and argued often late into the night. I found some comfort in watching sports, which only increased her resentment and loneliness.

One night that fall I had a terrible dream that she left me. I awoke realizing we had been drifting apart for some time, living in two different worlds. I was determined to do better "in the relationship" but I had no idea how bad things really were. Apparently, men seldom have a clue what "the wife" is going through. The long, lonely nights at home all week were wearing on Marja but she didn't tell me how serious it was and I wasn't tuned in enough to read between the lines. One night she finally shared with me her burden and the story of her lowest moment when she almost did something she would have regretted for the rest of her life. It got close enough to give her a good scare before the Lord intervened in dramatic fashion and rescued her.

The fact that she told me immediately impressed me deeply. Her openness and brokenness provided me a wake up call , also. I wanted to learn how to better meet her needs. I had not only failed to fill the void she had, I was unaware of it. I had been fighting my own demons. Long ago my jealous heart had been torn to pieces and had not healed, which left me incapable of helping her? The incredible pain of past experiences cut deep. I had forgiven her, for her past, but found it impossible to forget. Every time I thought about it the old wound opened again and tore at my insides. The woman I loved dearly and cherished above all else in this world held my fragile heart in the clutch of her hand to do with whatever she wanted. I was so vulnerable and it scared me.

What saved our marriage was that we both were convinced there was no excuse for 2 believers not to be able to work out any problem. There is an old saying, kind of a joke, I guess, regarding Mennonites I learned growing up. “I never considered divorce; suicide and murder a few times but never divorce.” The word did not appear in Mennonite’s unwritten dictionary. I knew this truth had been engrained, at the core of my being, early in life but it had more power than I had realized. I knew we would continue on together, somehow.

The outside job In Elliot Lake continued into the winter and I was pleasantly surprised that it seemed to get better as time went on. I got along with the workers, especially the Finns. They knew I was Risto’s brother-in-law and that helped. I started playing pool most nights and was getting a reputation as the poolroom shark. This is fun but I am getting restless to accomplish more in life. I longed to be in the ministry doing something with lasting value. The others seemed content to have good paying jobs and accept this as there lot in life. I reminded myself I had bills to pay and this is where God had placed me. I finally paid off all our credit card debt. Slowly we were making headway and I wanted to remain faithful but deep down I knew there was more for me to do. By December the job was winding down and most workers got laid off and I joined a small crew in Sudbury. Before Christmas all jobs ended and I was off for the rest of winter. It was a good change and rest.

We quickly became a novelty at church because of our zeal for the Lord and especially because we had just come out of a cult and easily made new friends. Friday nights I played hockey for the GTT team in Copper Cliff and periodically went out of town for Church tournaments. We started spending a lot of time with several couples in particular, close to our age. Rick and Sharon Stickles, Harry and Nancy Barc, (later Bartz) Ted and Carolyn Djaferis, Kirk and Anne Misenheimer and Pastor Paul Cassidy and his wife Judy became good friends.

In the spring I received a letter from the carpenter's union; our contract had expired, talks had stalled and we were on strike. My holidays would last longer than anticipated. I visited the picket line a few times but as little as possible. I am as busy as I want to be. I periodically helped Art building his house. I tilled Dad's and Gerry's gardens and planted much of Dad's.

## Young Peoples Ministry

That summer I got involved in organizing and playing baseball with the church team, which means attending meetings having parties, some at our house. I also became an assistant to Kelvin Honsinger, the youth pastor and began teaching a youth Sunday School class. Besides all this, I also became the World Vision Rep for the area and a regular usher in church. I was regularly being asked to come to the front to pray before the morning message and felt blessed and humbled to do so.

Jouko Merivirta, Risto's purchasing agent and youth leader at the Finn church invited me to speak to his youth group. They had a group of sincere, young people and we had a good meeting. I loved sharing God's word when someone was eager to listen. We saw a lot of Jouko over the next year. Marja and I both enjoyed his company and he knew he was welcome. He was single and new in town with few friends. He was also Finn and we had a sauna, which is convenient. He knew he could use it anytime he wanted.

We soon became a big hit with the large youth group, partially because of our colored past. I overheard a few boys sharing that they wanted to go out "into the world" and "acquire a testimony" before they settle down and serve the Lord, hmmm. As I read back through my day-timer for 1980 I was amazed at how busy our lives were. We had family and friends over for a sauna, dinner, lunch or coffee several times a week. Besides this we went to church at least 3 times a week. I was also involved in organizing sports tournaments. I played ball and golfed at least weekly, often with Pastor Cassidy. I often climbed into bed between 1:00-2:00am. I can't imagine attempting to live like this today and the idea holds little appeal but we were young and full of energy.

Besides all this activity I had two children who play baseball and I tried to spend personal time with then, also. Then there is "the relationship", although strangely we seemed to be close again, with no real tension It was hard work but I continued to make a conscious effort to spend quality time with Marja and keep short accounts. As good as things were, there was still an aching pain from the past ever lingering just below the surface.

Rick and Sharon Stickles came over for dinner and sauna one Saturday evening. As the custom was the men went first, in the buff. After being in the heat for awhile I started getting a dizzy. This happened periodically and as long as I got out of the steam fairly quickly and got some fresh air I was usually fine. On this occasion I lingered longer than I should have and it hit me harder and faster than usual and I started passing out. I managed to get out to the change room and collapsed on the bench, naked. There I stayed, on my back, motionless, in a semi-conscious state a half hour or so. I could hear poor Rick muttering to himself and talking to me but I was so weak I couldn't answer or even move. He frantically moved a cold, wet cloth back and forth from my neck and then to my forehead. Finally I came around and assured him I was fine; I was still as white as a ghost.

Rick and I continued to get together regularly to play catch or watch sports on TV. I don't remember us having another sauna, though. While on strike I continued to look for a full time career working for the Lord. I filled out applications with organizations like World Vision and Youth For Christ. Construction was good money but I wanted to accomplish more in life.

## Tragedy in Waters Township

I was not the only one getting restless and looking for a change in life. John Zacharias, the pastor of the Mennonite church and other members had joined the charismatic renewal movement. John helped organize a conference, which I attended and briefly met with John at the church office to apologize in person for my bad behavior at my parent's 25th anniversary. He was gracious and actually told me that my criticism that day was one more confirmation that spurred him to seek more from God.

George Elsasser attended the conference as a key speaker. After the Sunday night service we went to my parent's house. George and Ross Calford got out the guitars and George led us in a lively time of singing, just like the old days. He was as vibrant and loud as ever. Laurie James must have heard the music and wandered in. He had been drinking and was lamenting his broken life; he appeared at the end of his rope. George prayed with him and he was touched. The next day he told my parents he would never drink again. I am sure he meant well but he was powerless to do what he so desperately needed to do and didn't stay dry long.

The following day, a family friend and Waters church member, Walter Salo was tragically killed. According to some accounts he committed suicide. He had been severely depressed of late. The newspaper said he was sitting on the train tracks and probably never heard the train. That was hard to believe. Others said he jumped in front of the train.

Laurie's story is not any better. In September of 1983, at the age of 40, in a drunken state he fell down a flight of stairs and died. The unofficial story is that he may have been given a nudge. I pondered the purpose and meaning of these lives. I knew what the typical Christian explanation was, especially in Laurie's case; he messed up his life along the way and hardened his heart to the degree God's love couldn't reach him. Now he would burn in hell forever. Neither Laurie's helpless life story nor this Orthodox doctrine sat well with me. I sensed a deep sorrow over the loss of this man who had lived next door and I longed for understanding.

Apparently my Dad struggled with understanding these same issues. At Walter's funeral he said from the pulpit that he didn't think a God of love would harshly judge someone who struggled so long and hard with depression. What he was referring to was the popular teaching that claims committing suicide seals ones fate eternally. It was not common for anyone to question things like this openly, especially from the pulpit and at a funeral, much less. I guess the Bast children come by it honestly. My Dad continued to challenge any theory that didn't make sense to him, for the balance of his long life.

**Life at 30**

The youth of the 60's considered anyone over 30 as being old and not to be trusted. It seems many people got depressed about turning that page on the calendar, also. I didn't know what the big deal was about turning 30. For me July 7, 1980 was just another birthday, albeit a special day. Risto took me to the private Idlewylde Golf and Country Club for a round of golf and a fine dinner after. I believe this was the only time I ever golfed with him. Fred Seal the sales rep for Wavy Concrete joined us. He was a nice guy who could hit the ball a mile but not often straight. It was a gorgeous day and I had great time. The strike ended the next day and I went back to work with a good raise.

That summer Johnny joined the Labourer's Union and started working for Risto's company, Laamanen Construction. In August Gerry also got hired as the truck driver / gofer. Here we were, the three of us, working at the same place again. Over the years I have been accused of meddling and trying to control the family; that hurt. I was only trying to help and couldn't shake the dream of working together. This same year, Marja and I began going out for dinner with Risto and his wife Aino on a regular basis. He always paid the bill and good red wine was always a part of the meal, which I slowly acquired a taste for.

The summer was busy and went by quickly. In August, I decided to go to the Gascho reunion after being absent for so long. We stayed at Mary and Merv's. It was good to be with my extended family that had meant so much to me growing up. The older I would get the more I would appreciate my heritage and relatives. Sports remained a big part of my life and now that I had several other Christian guys with the same interests, it was a lot easier to be continually involved in one game or another, which was a constant point of contention in our marriage. I tried to involve my children in these sports as much as possible and even got Marja out for a game of tennis once in awhile and the odd golf tournament. Somehow getting others involved made it feel less selfish and made it easier on my conscience. I even got Paul Cassidy and John Zacharius out for a round of golf. I figured to get a Pentecostal and a Mennonite pastor together for a game of golf must be something that pleased God. With the pastor's blessing, I organized my first annual GTT golf tournament. It was a good way to bring church people together with non-believing spouses and friends. That made it a very spiritual exercise, aye?

**Kelvin Honsinger**

That fall, Pastor Kel asked me to accompany him to the 200th anniversary of Sunday school in Detroit. Gerry Falwell was the first evening's speaker but I don't remember anything he said. John Macarthur was also there and I bought his book called Kingdom Living, which I am sure became a best seller. We left Detroit at 6:00 pm for home. We got the Montreal Expo's playoff baseball game on the radio. They were winning 2-0. To have a Canadian baseball team in the post season was to make history; we found a sports bar, ordered Ginger Ale and watched the game. The waiter came by every ½ hour or so and teased us with, "You alchi's want another drink?" We arrived at Kel's in-laws in London at 11:00 pm and slept on the floor. I liked Kel a lot; he was a natural leader and determined to do what he could with his life to make a difference. His Dad was a career pastor and served as the District Superintendent for P.A.O.C. I also quickly befriended his 1-year old daughter, Meredith. After church while everyone visited I often carried her to a window to see if we could see any birds. When we spotted one she squealed with delight "birdie, birdie".

## Hockey, Hockey, Hockey

Like many boys in Canada, especially Northern Ontario, hockey seized my attention young and held it. I don't know if it is the speed of the game of just because its "Our game". For a few years, during the cult days, I was able to block hockey out of my mind and life as I did many other things. After I was set free from the religious bondage, the attraction returned. I didn't mind having visitors on Saturday evenings as long as they didn't mind watching Hockey Night in Canada. Like in my early teens, the playoffs once again, became the highlight of my year.

Friday night hockey with the guys from church was also a highlight of the week. This was not enough; Harry Barc decided to form a team to play in an industrial league and asked me to be the manager. He put together a team of the best players from our church and the Finnish Pentecostal Church, plus a few other good players he knew from work. All of the games were late, some as late as 11:00 pm. It took me 2 – 3 hours after the game to unwind, which meant getting to sleep between 2:00 and 3:00 am; little wonder I was sleep deprived and often got a cold and a sore throat.

I thoroughly enjoyed thinking about different hockey lines and defense combinations in an attempt to optimize talent. I had spent many hours as a child doing this with hockey coins. I proudly wore the "C" on the front of my jersey and number "7" on my back. As soon as the puck dropped I was transported into a different zone, a brave new world. When I was on the ice, and especially when I had the puck, I experienced a high that only competitive athletes can probably appreciate. There were four teams and we were easily the best. At the end of the season I was tied for second place in scoring. We also traveled south to play in tournaments. I never seemed to get too much hockey.

On November 27th there was another tragic death in my home neighborhood. Bobby Jarvi started walking home drunk the night before as he often did, not unlike his father before him. They found him in the ditch in the morning frozen to death. I thought about how unfair life was for some people. What chance did he have growing up in an alcoholic's home? Why did I grow up in a Christian home and more importantly, what was I doing with this fortunate life I had been given?

## Time for a Change

At work that winter every week seemed to get colder and I began sending out resumes, again. In November we began a large siding and roofing job at INCO's Iron Ore Plant. The building was 110' high and we were there most of the winter. December 1980 was an exceptionally cold one. I think every night went down to below –30 Celsius and even hit –40 several times. The days didn't warm up much and I was literally freezing every day at work. I couldn't seem to dress warm enough and still be able to move around in order to work. My goal each morning was to survive until 10:00am coffee break when we got to go inside and warm up. I was usually one of the last to go back out again because I knew it was a matter of survival.

Although my father-in-law was the company's superintendent and my bother-in-law was the owner I didn't want to get caught the last man in the coffee room so I followed close behind the others even though my small frame of skin and bones had not sufficiently warmed up. Not that the others were obese by today's standards but they were built different. They had been doing this kind of work all there lives and were tough. They used to do chin-ups or see who carry 2-100lb cement bags the furthest at lunchtime while I kept bundled and had a power nap. One of the foremen Saccu seldom wore gloves while working outside unless it was colder than -20. I prayed that the Lord would find me some other kind of employment in the off-season. I did not want to do this again next winter. Even though the money was good and there was the potential of an inside job, albeit probably a long way into the future; I knew I could not wait and was delighted to get 2 weeks off for Christmas.

1981 started out just as hectic as 1980 ended. The whole year would be a time of hustle and bustle, always on the go, with people coming and going from our house. During the first few days of January I started looking for a job seriously. I visited several Life Insurance companies and wrote the tests. I knew the answers they wanted. They were looking for people with an ambition to succeed and earn big money. Something didn't fit and I walked away from that idea. Before anything materialized I got called back to Elliot Lake for another job. So on January 6th it was back to being away from home and bunkhouse life.

My roommate, Reijo Martikkala had a serious snoring problem; a problem for me, that is. This guy could snore louder in his sleep than I could awake. I don't know how anyone can make a noise so loud by simply breathing, and not wake up. Several times through the night I would slip my leg out from under the covers and kick his nearby bed hard enough to wake him so he would roll over on his side. The snoring would stop for awhile as I attempted to go back to sleep. This went on for several weeks, finally I made arrangements to bunk with Johnny who was now working here also.

On the weekends I made an effort to spend more time with my kids, especially Ben. I felt so close to him. I still tucked him in at night and prayed with him. He is so loveable, warm and open to spiritual things. He has made several good friends from the neighborhood. Among them are two Finn boys, Paul Rintala and Eric Jarvi. Caroleen is a real tomboy and would rather tag along with Benjie and the boys rather than spend time with the girls. She is as rough and tough as they are and loves the bush.

To my surprise and regret Kel announced his resignation in February. He had been offered a position in the Burlington church where his dad was the senior Pastor. He would leave early in April and I knew I would miss him. We seemed to have a bond I have experienced with few others in life. I would miss him but was thankful for the time we had together and would cherish the memories all my life.

One Friday night at hockey the opposing center's stick came up during a face-off and cut my lip. The ref didn't see it so there was no penalty. When I looked the guilty player in the eye he shrugged his shoulders, as if to say, "No big deal, get over it". Kel who was playing defense slowly skated forward to check out the damage and get involved if need be. He glided too me and kept going and took us all by surprise when he almost effortlessly bumped shoulders with the other center knocking him flat on his ass. Kel was muscular and solid on his skates. This little gesture and the stern look on his face made a statement that everyone present understood on some level. I am sure this incident meant more to me though; the others would probably soon forgot about it. I didn't forget about it and we continued to be friends after he left Sudbury; a week doesn't go by that I don't pray for him and his family. We visited him a few times over the years that followed, usually when one of us had tickets to a Leaf's game.

Before Kel left, Paul Cassidy, the senior pastor asked him to talk to me about my belief system and specifically the doctrine of the trinity. Apparently Al Chevrier, husband of Connie, nee Cantelon, daughter of the former District Superintendant of the

P.O.A.C., alerted Paul to the fact there may be a problem with me accepting one of the Pentecostals sacred cows. I guess it became an issue now that I was involved with the youth group and especially, now that Kel was leaving soon.

Kel arranged a meeting with me, which ended up being a two-hour discussion about the trinity and a few related issues. After I shared my understanding of the scriptures he was satisfied that I was not a heretic and there was no need to worry. Dave Beasley, Paul Cassidy's brother in law was hired as the new youth pastor and was scheduled to arrive a month after Kel left. I was asked to fill in as the interim youth pastor.

I phoned Marja every night from my room and she seemed to be doing well. A growing appreciation of her filled my heart when we were separated. I wanted to stay close, but I am torn, continually aware of her ability to hurt me. My love for her made me so vulnerable. No one else could fill me like she did and no one else could kill me like she did. It is true, "love hurts" and when the pain cut deep I found myself turning to sports for comfort. This she resented, which made things worse. Around and around the vicious circle of life continued.

While working in Elliot Lake I read two books, "Kingdom Living" and "Not Regina" They are vastly different but both captivated my interest. Deep down I had a hunger for more truth. I learned more about my Anabaptist roots reading "Not Regina" than I had all my years at church. I was awe struck by the zeal of our early fathers. What they believed was worth dying for. I was proud of my heritage and admired this kind of faith, although it made me more convinced something basic in my life and belief system was missing.

We finished the job in Elliot Lake at the end of February and began working in Sudbury again, which meant I was home every night. I began reading "Not Regina" to Benjie at bedtime. He liked the book and said he was so excited because God lives in him. That was so rewarding for me. He is smart too and seems to excel at whatever he does. He won the "Squire of the Year" award at Crusaders and received a trophy and a book. Caroleen seemed content to participate in most of the activities but actually preferred to be alone, especially outside in the bush.

I got laid off from Laamanen's near the end of March 1981. I was determined not to spend another winter working outside and started sending out resumes. On March the 30th I spent 3 hours on a job application for "Youth For Christ" and before I could finish, I had to run an errand. While out I picked up the mail and opened a letter from Helen Lindhorst who wrote me on a regular basis. The letter was her usual encouraging words reassuring me that God loved me and would meet all our needs and specifically find me a job. The exciting thing about this letter, which I still have, was that it was written on the back of a newsletter she had received from "Youth For Christ". She wrote so many letters that she saved all her mail and scraps of paper to write on. Little did she know I was in the process of filling out a job application for a position with them. I wondered if this was a sign from God.

It took me another 3 hours to complete the application but now I was filling it out with great expectations. This was not the first time I was wrong and it wouldn't be the last. I was very disappointed when I opened their response letter thanking me for my interest but informing me they had chosen someone else for the position.

## A New Career

A new couple, Paul and Gwen Reid, began attending GTT and immediately fit into the small group Marja and I were involved with. Paul worked for ICG Liquid Gas the propane division of Inter-City Gas Corp, "ICG". He had recently been promoted to Branch Manager in Sudbury and was looking for a salesman. He knew about my Filter Queen sales success and that I was looking for a job. To him this seemed like a perfect fit, along with the fact I was a "Pentecostal". Paul was a "PK", a preacher's kid. His dad had been a career Pentecostal pastor. On May 5 1981 I started my career in the propane business.

ICG was a large company of over 5000 employees mainly in the natural gas sector. The propane division was one of the smaller divisions but employees still enjoyed the same benefits. I was given a propane powered, company vehicle and a desk in the corner of the showroom at the branch on Kelly Lake Road. Superior Propane, the largest propane company in Canada, was the only serious competitor with 80% of the market. Auto-propane was just taking off due to the substantial government incentives, a part of the "Off Oil Program". This was ICG's time to get a bigger piece of the pie and my opportunity to shine.

My task was to sign up Conversion Centers and Filling Stations. The big Car Dealerships were the best place to convert vehicles to auto- propane and the busiest gas stations were the prime locations to set up propane filling stations. We all knew profits were in selling fuel. Superior wanted to do conversions in their own garage, in an attempt to immediately get the fuel sale by directing vehicles to their plant to fill up. They were willing to sell conversion parts cheap in order to create the fuel load. This was made easy by the government rebates for business like school buses and taxis, who could virtually convert free.

So as the competition concentrated on giving away conversions I began establishing a network of prime location filling stations. There was much paperwork to be filled out for each installation; a fuel contract, an application with the Provincial Government, a building permit with the city to install the tank, to name a few. A concrete pad and bumper posts had to be installed. Drawings were required showing exact location of buildings, property lines, hydro wires, sources of combustion and any flammable objects etc. To my surprise my high school drafting training came to good use.

The most important document was a form called the R.O.I. The "Return on Investment" determined whether or not it was going to be profitable for the company to invest thousands of dollars on the installation. The costs were easily determined; the sales had to be projected and the selling price set. Everything had to be done right or "no approval". I was a detail person and enjoyed the challenge of opening every new filling station and was rewarded with commissions accordingly.

At the end of each month I received a report showing each customer's consumption. I took pride at the uniformity in the prices I offered; each one was based on the amount of fuel they sold. The more fuel they bought the better price they received. I could show this report to new customers as a tool to prove the fairness of the price they were paying. As far as I knew, this was unheard of in the "dog eat dog" gas business. Over the next several years I established a good network of filling stations across Northern Ontario. At the end of the first year, 7 months after I was hired, I had sold close to 700,000 liters of auto propane and increased Sudbury's total volume over a million liters. Paul Reid and head office were pleased but this was only the beginning. I managed to sell an average of more than a million new liters of auto propane each year for the next five.

With my new job came an expense account and I got in the habit of taking people out to eat and paying the bill. On one of our outings for dinner with Risto and Aino, I proudly announced that it was my turn to pay the bill. This was going to be a business expense and I therefore had to spend a little time promoting "auto propane". Risto had a fleet of at least a dozen trucks, which made him a good candidate. He was aware of the cheaper fuel but he needed to be educated on how much he could save and the other advantages of converting his trucks to propane. I soon realized this was not going to be an ideal time to discuss business because Risto's brother-in-law, Mauri and his fiancé Roxanne were along. It knew it would be primarily a social evening but I had to justify the expense, which would exceed $200. So I mentioned a few details about propane when I could get his attention. He just politely brushed off the topic a couple of times and then finally told me he really wasn't that interested. Even though his fuel bills were significant they were really not a major factor in the bottom line, of his successful construction business. The topic was a little awkward and I was not getting far but decided to try one last stab to generate some interest. So I brought up the topic again. He looked at me and sternly said "We are not going to talk about it anymore." That was that. I got the message. This was the last time I talked to him about auto-propane and I can't remember paying for dinner again either.

## Moose Hunting

Now that Johnny was back in Northern Ontario he couldn't resist the call of the wild. The summer of 1981 we put our names in the lottery for a moose tag and were awarded a bull tag. Plans were made and a trailer borrowed. The Friday before the season opened Johnny and I were in the bush back in his old stomping grounds behind Worthington. We set up in the parking area where most hunters left their trucks and mounted their off road vehicles. We had to walk the last few miles to what was to become our happy hunting ground.

There were two other hunting parties nearby. Johnny's brother Ken, and two brother-in-laws, Don Forbeck and Brian Horner along with Raymond St. Jean, was one group. They had hunted here since Johnny was a boy and had their camp near the famous lookout "Old Baldy". Johnny's cousin, Gary Moxam also had another group close. Johnny knew the area well and we would not infringe on their territories. For several days we hunted in cold wet weather walking through thick bush climbing up a high rock every once in awhile to get our bearings, make a fire, eat and dry off and enjoy the view of bush in all directions. Little else other than the super-stack was visible in the distance. I loved the bush, the quiet and the idea of being so cut off from all civilization; more than anything I wanted to shoot a moose.

I had been here once before, 8 years prior. Barry had loaned me his 44-Ruger, drove me into the same spot, pointed me in the right direction, said he would be back before dark and drove off. I remember I walked for a long time, calling for a bull, not sure if I was doing it right or not. To my surprise, after a couple hours, I got a response from a nearby bull. Quietly and slowly I began walking in his direction, down into a swamp. My heart was pounding. Suddenly he appeared amongst the bulrushes, about 40' away. For the first time in my life, on my first moose hunt and all alone, I was face to face with a huge bull with a monster rack. Without hesitation I lifted the gun and fired and down he went. A second later he was up and running. I tried to fire again at his rear-end, which was disappearing as quickly as he had appeared but I was shaking too bad and then he was gone. I checked for blood but found nothing.

Later I told Barry the story. He said I probably shot high and hit the antlers, which was common for inexperienced hunters. This would knock him down, unhurt. He assured me though, that it was a good thing I didn't kill him because I was so deep in the bush that we never would have got him out. That was my introduction to moose hunting.

Anyway, the longer Johnny and I walked the stronger the desire grew to redeem myself. Every sound or sign, that may announce the big game is near, set my heart pounding again. After 3 days we were tired, dirty and discouraged. Our last night, I went out side to be alone and prayed. It was a clear cold night and the stars shone bright. My heart cried out to God to please bless our last day of hunting. As I fixed my attention on the splendor of the Milky Way I pleaded for guidance. To my shock, almost instantly, a bright shooting star streaked across the sky in its final display of brilliance.

Although, this star probably burned out long before I was born, God had arranged for me to be here and looking up at exactly the right time and praying for direction. My heart instantly leaped for joy but there was one problem. If this was a sign from the Supreme Deity, He was telling us to go home. The star trail pointed straight towards the road, out of the bush, home. Any other direction would have sent us scurrying through the bush in the morning with renewed hope.

Although, Johnny respected my spirituality, the next morning we decided to scout around in all directions looking for any fresh signs from the night before. By early afternoon we packed up and headed down the long, lonely road back home. There was little conversation as I drove. We were exhausted and depressed. It would be another year before we could return.

Approaching the village of Worthington, as we rolled over a little hill I couldn't believe my eyes. There, 10 feet off the road a huge bull was standing statue still, proudly displaying his rack in all its splendor and glory. It took a minute to register; Johnny and I turned for a brief second to glance at each other. Was it true; was there really a bull-moose standing beside the road directly in front of us?

I gently pulled over onto the shoulder slowed to a stop. Johnny quietly opened the door, put a bullet into his rifle, and leaned on the hood of the truck. The bull stood there staring at us not sure what to make of this encounter. The silence was abruptly broken by the thundering sound of a high-powered rifle echoing to the hills and back. The bull slowly turned, took a few steps away from us and collapsed in the grass beside the driveway. He was still breathing when we got up to him so Johnny handed me his gun and I finished him off.

The old bachelor who lived there alone in the little house at the end of lane sauntered out to see what the shots were about. His name was John Hamilton and Johnny knew him and his family from way back. We chatted for a few minutes and he said we could gut it right there and then added the wolves would have a feast tonight. We promised to bring him some steaks in a few weeks and he was happy with that. He even had a tripod with a winch. The whole animal was easily lifted on the truck without cutting it into quarters.

This was our first moose-hunting excursion together but would be far from the last. For the next 15 years we would make the trek back to our happy hunting ground with our sons tagging along when they were old enough. The meat in the freezer would last for months and the tale of the shooting star pointing home and the of thrill of the kill would be rehearsed time and again for many years to come.

## Living with Eczema

Although I was supposed to grow out of my skin problem in my teens, at age 31 it was still a constant irritation, especially during the cold dry winters. Cortisone over the years, eventually became ineffective, so I learned to live without it. I continually experimented with a variety of ointments. Each morning I still use different creams for the various parts of my body. I use a rather expensive cream for the sensitive area around the eyes and another face cream for the rest of the face. For my beard, which, I have worn for over 20 years, I apply olive oil in the morning with a toothbrush and before bed 98% pure Aloe Vera gel. I have recently, 30 some years later, started using, very sparingly, mild cortisone for problem areas on my face and a stronger one for elsewhere. I literally apply some kind of moisturizing to almost every square inch of my body even soles of my feet. When sores on my scalp appear I spread the hair apart to dab suave on them. I mix the lotions with olive oil in the morning but with Aloe Vera in the evening to avoid oil stains on the bed sheets.

I realize this is extreme but in order to maintain an equilibrium and an ability to function without being preoccupied with itch I will try almost anything. Of course every evening the sweat and dirt of the day now mixed with the mornings creams had to be washed off and new cream applied. You can see why I didn't sleep over at a friend's house very often growing up. When I was in the bush at the moose camp, it was hassle and a little embarrassing to try to get cleaned properly with no shower but I did the best I could. Before bed everyone present would have the pleasure of observing me heat water on the propane stove and wash from a basin, dry myself and then apply my creams. Deep breathing and meditating on good thoughts like the scriptures seems to relax me and help somewhat.

## Life at ICG

Life was good at ICG. Paul hired two pleasant ladies from GTT, Anne Misenheimer, Harry Barc's sister and Angela Anderson. Anne's husband Kirk had died Christmas eve the previous year. Anne is a capable and confident secretary. She would later transfer to Woodbridge, where ICG's largest branch in Ontario was located. She eventually married Don Peppy, ICG's Administration manager. When I wasn't on the road I spent time at the office show room selling barbecues and propane appliances. I also got my license to fill vehicles and cylinders and helped out with "front end" duties, which gave Paul more flexibility to come and go, as he pleased. This allowed me to get familiar with all aspects of the business and to get know the other employees.

Marja and I continued our up and down relationship. We were busy and spent little quality time together, although I somehow found time to have a steady diet of sports. In September Marja started a full-time job for Laamanen Construction. Benjie also got his first job delivering the local newspaper. He pays Caroleen to help him. They are quite the sight; a fair-haired, half Finn boy and dark skinned, black haired Indian girl. Ben played hockey again that winter and Caroleen started figure skating.

In 1982 we got more involved at GTT. I can't remember how it started, but I was asked to be the Master of Ceremonies for several functions in the church. I remember a couple of wedding receptions, one for Doug and Wanda Crouse and the other for Anne Misenheimer and Brian Courville. I also did an anniversary or two. My notes from an anniversary of Helen Cretzman and her husband reminded me how much fun these occasions were. At these functions I was comfortable being silly, making people laugh, something I was apparently good at. At least I got a lot of laughs from this crowd. I think it was partially because we were in "God's house" and normally here we all tried to be holy and reverent. It was kind of like, a small kid or an old man, letting out a loud fart at an inopportune time during a church service. Why was the sound of passing gas so funny at these times? It must be for the same reason my jokes got so many laughs at these functions. Whatever the reason, I was a popular Master of Ceremonies for a short time.

## Grandma Gascho

My grandmother Annie Gascho died on October 14 1982, a month before her 60th anniversary. She was 80 years old. I was in the bush moose hunting and didn't make it to the funeral, which I regretted later. I wouldn't be surprised if I was one of the few 25 grandchildren and 24 great-grandchildren that didn't attend. She was loved by all of us and it would have been a special, although sad occasion, one I should have never missed. There are so many regrets in life. How can we count them all? Hopefully they serve as a reminder of often we miss the mark and make us more tolerant with others. Dad's Aunt Barbara Steinman died on December the 12th the same year. She was 92 years old. I do not remember being at her funeral, either.

## Creeds and Doctrines of Man

More and more conversations with our church friends and especially the pastors gravitated to the teachings of the Bible. Even though I was busy I never lost my hunger to learn more. I read some of the Pentecostal material, including the "teacher's manual" for the youth Sunday school class I was teaching. I didn't care for it much; it sounded corny so I took most of my class material from the Bible. Some of the church's doctrines I just couldn't agree with and found it disturbing almost everyone readily accepted what was handed down from headquarters as gospel. No one seemed interested in further study. In fact to question these sacred cows was frowned upon and viewed as insubordination. Things were settled and it was out of line to question them.

One day, I got in a discussion about a doctrinal issue with Pastor Cassidy, who had grown up in a Pentecostal Church. Things got a little heated and I asked him this question; "Can you not see, the reason you view these teachings the way you do is because this is the way your parents, your Sunday school teachers and your Bible school professors taught you to understand them?" I suggested that if he had grown up in, God forbid, a Baptist Church and went to their seminary he would have a different view. He was steadfast. He believed what he believed because it was the truth. There was no room for discussion. It was spelled out in the church creeds a long time ago and there was no need to revisit these teachings. This baffled me. We remained friends but things were never quite the same.

By now I had settled into my sales position with ICG and built an office in my basement where I could do a lot of work from home. Several days a week I was on the road because of the large territory I had to cover. At the end of 1982 the Sudbury Branch propane volume had increased by 2.9 million liters. We made a good profit, which meant a good bonus for myself and for Paul Reid. Bills and credit cards were getting paid on time, and my Dad's mortgage was being paid down.

I took the necessary training and received my diploma from the Propane Gas Association, as "Instructor Qualified". I then began training ICG's customers in fuelling propane vehicles, refilling and visual re-examination of cylinders. I held classes on a regular basis for our fleets and filling centers so they didn't have to wait for Cambrian College to hold a class. I enjoyed teaching a lot more than I did being taught in school. I found it especially rewarding because I had a room full of students who were sincerely interested in this practical information mainly because their job depended on it

During this period, almost every large, school bus fleet, in the area was converting as many buses as possible to propane because of the savings in fuel. Also the City of Sudbury and the City of North Bay converted many company vehicles including most of the police cars. I held private classes to train policemen and school bus drivers and eventually Cambrian College hired me to teach the government course as a night class.

## Todd

One Sunday evening at church we met Todd Petahtegoose, a young, Indian man, with a troubled past. He was first attracted to us because of Caroleen our Indian daughter. As we talked he shared a bit of his past and his desire to "go straight". We ended the conversation by giving him our phone number and telling him to call us if we could help him in any way. Sure enough not long after he did call and said he needed a place to stay. We opened our home to him not knowing what to expect or how long it would be. We set up a bedroom in the basement and he moved in along with his weights. "Pumping Iron" was one thing he did to keep out of trouble and it made him feel good not to mention the way it made him look. He was over 6 feet tall and had a huge, upper body with many tattoos and could bench press 350 pounds.

The kids liked Todd and Ben took an interest in lifting weights. Todd was eager to be his trainer. Weeks led to months and Todd was doing well. He had some experience cooking and now that Marja was working he often had most of the evening meal ready when we got home. This responsibility and someone to answer to had a good effect on him. Ben and Caroleen looked up to him as a big brother and he was careful not to be a bad influence on them, although he enjoyed telling stories of his time in jail etc. Whenever he went outside for a smoke and Ben or Caroleen asked him where he was going he would say, "Up north Alaska to hunt moose eggs". Everyone got a kick out of this. Or if one of the kids asked, "Do you know where Mom is?", his response would be, "She went for a walk and the bears got her". This also got a laugh.

I helped Todd get a job at Estaire Bus Lines, my largest propane customer. He particularly enjoyed driving the big buses around the yard to refuel them. The honest labor was good for him and he began saving money. To our surprise and delight after a couple months he had fully paid for a $900 stereo with huge speakers. He brought it home and announced it was a gift to our family. We played countless hours of music on this system for the next 22 years and then sold it with our house in 2005 because it was built into a wall unit and the speakers were mounted high on the wall in the large open living room.

Todd had a long criminal record and one charge in particular was still pending trial. When it came time to go to court he asked me if I would testify on his behalf. He hoped the judge would believe that he was keeping out of trouble and was staying clean as far as drinking and drugs go. Of course I agreed. The judge was Guy Mahaffey, the man who had been my lawyer 13 years prior. He had periodically come into ICG to purchase propane supplies and we had renewed our acquaintance. As soon as Todd's lawyer called me to the stand, Judge Mahaffey recognized me and he said he could not continue to hear the case because he knew me and we had some business dealings together. He called a recess and said he would have to locate another judge, which he did and the case proceeded.

Todd's lawyer once again called me to the stand and asked of my involvement with Todd and to tell the court about his life in our home. The judge seemed most interested and impressed with my testimony. He kept looking at Todd and then at me as I spoke, as if it was too good to be true. I am sure the fact Judge Mahaffey wouldn't hear the case because he had done business with me gave me some credibility. Todd received the lightest sentence his lawyer imagined possible. In any event, they were both delighted, although it was back to jail for Todd, albeit with a much shorter sentence than it could have been. His biggest fear had been getting "hard time", which meant at least 2 years in a penitentiary. Instead, he was allowed to work during the day and go to the District Jail each night after work. This ended his stay in our home but we kept in touch.

Todd later married Corrie Ethier the daughter of Leonard Ethier and Margie (nee Moxam), one of Johnny's 10 sisters. They had a daughter together and named her Rylee Rae. He tried to stay straight but it was a continual struggle. After the life he lived as a kid he was convinced, as he told me several times, "I just don't have the parts". His marriage eventually fell apart and we lost touch with him. I would like to think he never returned to his life of crime but we heard different. When we started having problems with Ben and Caroleen in their teen years, I couldn't help wonder about how wise it was to bring his influence into our home with two children at such an impressionable age. Ben celebrated his 11$^{th}$ birthday and Caroleen her 9th while Todd lived with us. Ben in particular spent a lot of time with him working out and they reconnected after Todd was married.

I have made so many mistakes in life that it seems so easy to second-guess many decisions. I am thankful I will be judged according to my motives and the intent of my heart not by the outcome or the apparent wisdom in the decisions I made. Like Todd and many others I was doing the best I could, at the time, with the parts I had been given.

## Fun in the Sun

In November 1983 we went to Florida for a two-week holiday with Kel and Mary-Lynn Honsinger. We had a great time and had a chance to renew our friendship and catch up on news. We read a lot and talked about our goals in life. As it turns out Kel was not satisfied being a career pastor of an affluent urban church. He knew God had more for him than organizing fellowship meetings and preaching weekly to the faithful in their *comfortable pews.* In 1991, he accepted the position of Executive Director of Mission Services of Hamilton and stayed there for almost 13 years. Their mission was to serve the less fortunate of society, the people who would most likely never darken the door of a fancy religious edifice. The 50+ employees ran a half way house for the homeless street people, a men's shelter, a soup kitchen, food bank etc. They also worked with abused women and those seeking addiction recovery.

My dad was still working with Indians in jail and invited Marja and I to accompany him and Mom to a Pow-wow inside the Kingston Penitentiary for women. We saw many sad faces there with sad stories to tell. Dad especially thrived in this setting and many were happy to see him. The only men they saw regularly were the tough guards who gave them little respect. They responded warmly to Dad's love and concern for them. He wanted to give them hope; to help them not give up on life or on white people and especially not to give up on their Creator. I knew Dad wasn't getting paid much for this job. He was making a lot more money driving truck long haul but he was visibly happy doing what he was doing.

1983 ended as another successful year at ICG. Auto – propane sales increased by 1.2 million liters. Now that our finances were back in order it was time to buy our own house. Marja's Dad offered us $5,000 for a down payment. The summer of 1984 we found a house in Walden, on Ronald Crescent, just off Black Lake Road. Mauno Kauppi the owner of Pinehill Lumber had built the house in 1957 for Charlie Jacobson, the long time owner of Water's General Store. His widow had been living there and was moving to an apartment. She was a heavy smoker and the walls needed a lot of scrubbing and many coats of paint, especially in the living room where she spent hours sitting, smoking and watching television. Other than that the house was solid and in good shape. Marja's dad also built a beautiful sauna for us in the basement, with a heated floor and all the Finish touches. It got used a lot.

I continued as the World Vision rep and working with the Glad Tidings youth group. Although Ben was only 12 he was allowed to attend and fit in immediately. He was interested in the things of God and got involved in the activities even prayer meetings. "Heaven's Gates and Hell's Flames" was a production we played in together. A team came and spent the weekend with our group holding auditions and rehearsals. Regular times were set to pray for the Sunday night production. I was chosen to play the devil and Ben one of my helpers. The play included several real life scenarios where someone was killed. If they were not "saved" I would laugh a long, hideous laugh and sent out my cohorts to go drag them off to hell as they screamed in fear. I have little regard this kind of evangelism anymore.

I also helped Youth With a Mission organize their Night of Missions in Sudbury. They were going from city to city sharing their strategy for reaching Asia and the Pacific, which they saw as the most desperate and un-reached region of the world. We arranged a night of fellowship at Glad Tidings with a media presentation and a guest speaker. Marja was involved in Women's Ministries at the church and established several close friendships. Although we had little quality time together we were too busy to think about it much. She was in the prime of life and beautiful. I was proud to have her as my wife and I'm sure some folks wondered what a good looking lady like her ever saw in a guy like me. Of course I wonder that about a lot of couples. A cliché that comes to mind seems to be applicable; "Beauty is in the eye of the beholder".

**Bruce Martin Comes to the Rescue**

As time went on I began to wonder what good all the programs at GTT were doing, especially the ones I was involved in. More and more I questioned the leaders about challenging folks to get out of their comfortable pews and do something. The same issues that bugged me about my home church and caused me to leave in 1972 were resurfacing. The thing that bothered me the most was that everyone seemed content to put on their Sunday best once or twice a week, go to church, sing a few songs, hear a positive sermon, pay their tithes and offerings, shake a few hands and go out the door and back to their easy life. I couldn't figure out why the many verses I had learned growing up about serving Jesus and loving God with your whole heart haunted me and no one else. Many scriptures, even though David Terrell used them for his own gain, still lingered in the back of my memory, refusing to go away, and needed to be dealt with. Teaching these biblical principals in a Sunday school class and throwing them in the face of the church leadership seemed to scratch my itch of condemnation and give partial relief. While pastor Cassidy and I were still friends he got a job offer in a bigger church that he couldn't refuse. For a career "Senior Pastor" this was the best promotion he could expect.

Bruce Martin's entrance on the scene was timely. He had the background and the skills to rescue me and keep me reasonably content for awhile longer. He had grown up in a Mennonite home and church as I did. His father who was also a preacher joined the charismatic renewal of the 50's and from there ended up in the Pentecostal denomination. We hit it off almost immediately, partially, because of our backgrounds. He also had great respect for the Honsinger family and was impressed that I had worked with Kel and more so that we were good friends. Besides, this big man had a big heart and was a genuine people person. I couldn't help myself; I liked him as many others did; he was very likeable. He had long heard about GTT because David Mainse, the host of 100 Huntley Street had been the pastor here when Bruce was growing up. He had made up his mind years ago this would be a good place to come and when he got the opportunity he welcomed it and us with open arms.

To my surprise and delight the better we got to know each other the closer we became. He quickly recognized my bold, out-spoken concern as "a prophetic gift" from God. He said men like me were welcome in the church and necessary to keep the church growing and in balance. He wanted me to be involved and help in a leadership role. Not long after he arrived he sent me a thank you card and in it wrote, "Be assured of your place in this body of believers." He continually made a point of reaffirming all those who were involved. I continued to teach Sunday school, usher and organize baseball and golf tournaments. He often asked me to pray from the pulpit Sunday mornings. We shared the same ideas about serving God with our whole heart. He did not come to Sudbury to play church, however he was a lot more patient and loving than I was with people. He brought in David Courey to be the youth pastor and I got less involved, with the youth. Interestingly, Johnny and Carol would soon get more involved.

**A Real Moose Camp**

The fall of 1984 we decided it was time to make our time in the bush, moose hunting, more comfortable. We went in a few weeks early and put up a 12′ x 16′ hunting camp. We built 4′ x 8′ wall sections at home and loaded them on a trailer to carry into the bush. It had been 3 years since we shot the bull on the road heading home and wanted to shoot another moose in the worst way. Johnny now had a "Terra-Jet", an all terrain vehicle, which easily pulled the trailer with our new camp parts. Permanent structures were not allowed on Crown Land so it was erected in a way that it could be easily dismantled if it was spotted and tagged by the ministry. It was located in the middle of a heavy evergreen grove hoping it would not be visible from the air.

A carpenter friend from church, Aki Tarvuud, joined the hunting crew, which made it easier to have a solid building up with a good tarp on the roof by the end of the first day. Bunks were then built and we furnished the camp with a heater, table, chairs, dishes etc. Luxury at last! This was our fourth year in this neck of the woods and we were getting to know it quite well. Although we had been skunked the last 2 years we continued to see many signs of moose in the area. We cut a trail down the slope to a long beaver pond where Johnny erected a tree stand where two could sit on a platform 20′ above the pond and see from one end to the other.

Less than a mile from camp was a larger swamp, which soon became my favorite spot and known as “Donnie’s Swamp”. I placed a platform about 12’ high in a tall spruce tree at the water’s edge. From my perch I could see 250 yards west and over 500 yards to the east. The swamp was about 130 yards wide. There was moose tracks all around but especially at the west end, close to my tree stand. Everyone knew this is where I would be and liked the idea and very quickly got into the same routine. All except me spent their mornings scouting the area and then slowly headed to my swamp from different directions around noon, with the hope of chasing the big game my way. Under the big tree we made a fire and ate lunch.

This fall as usual we were in camp the Friday afternoon before opening morning. Plans were made while we played cards and shared a few drinks, lots of laughs and big hopes. This was the time for serious male bonding. My son Ben, who would turn 12 in a few days was now allowed to join us for the first time. John-Jon, a couple years older was also along. The 5 of us tucked into bed early. Johnny was up at the crack of dawn making coffee and toast and warming the frying pan; we ate a hearty breakfast and rehearsed plans. Within the hour we were out the door, guns were loaded, packsacks put on and we headed off madly in all directions.

The four of them split into 2 pairs. I headed for my tree stand. It took me about an hour to get there. There was no direct route; I had to walk around the perimeter of the first swamp, which led into mine. It was slow going through a lot of heavy under brush and over logs and around fallen trees. Besides having an obstacle course to deal with I did serious hunting along the way. This meant stopping every few minutes to look and listen and wait. Every little sound told a story; it is amazing the amount of activity going on in the forest where man seldom goes. I am a creature of habit; every day I spent in the bush moose hunting for the next 10 years I would follow this same routine and once I arrived, I usually stayed in my tree stand until dusk. By the time I climbed to my perch and got settled I was warmed up but eventually cooled off just sitting. When I got too cold I climbed down, made a fire to warm up and then went back up again.

The odd time I brought a book along but seldom read much. I really didn't need anything for entertainment. The peace and quiet here was overwhelming; during these long periods of silence is when I could best hear the Lord's still small voice whispering to my heart. This sound of gentle stillness was beautiful music to my inner ear. Nothing soothed my soul like complete isolation and silence. It was always a happy / sad sight when I spotted a couple of orange hats bobbing up and down in the distance. I was glad to have company but I knew the close communion with my Creator would be temporarily broken.

This particular hunting trip was special because Ben was along for the first time. One moment in particular I remember well. Sitting around the campfire after lunch Ben fell asleep. It was hard work tromping through thick bush. Before the warmth and the glow of the fire knocked him out, he laid down, using my leg as a pillow for his weary head. This warmed my heart in a way few other moments in life have. Father and son knit together in one spirit and purpose is special. This would be the last time we got this close, physically, and maybe otherwise, for a long time.

By dusk we all headed back to camp, ate and drank and played cards and went to bed early but not before I had a sponge bath from my basin and then the tedious process of moisturizing my whole body before climbing between the cool sheets. Of course I was the only one who did this and I was the only one who had sheets. I envied these guys who could just plop into a sleeping bag, at the end of the day, and be snoring in a few minutes. If I didn't wash properly and put cream on I would be itchy all night. Even as it was I never knew if a good nights sleep lay ahead or not. This was the life I had become accustomed to.

Sunday morning we were up and out into the cool autumn air as soon as possible. I did a few stretches and breathed deep and headed for my swamp. By early afternoon we were all around the fire eating once again. To our complete surprise a bull and a cow sauntered out of the bush into the shallow water at the close end of the swamp. Bright, orange hats were thrown to the ground and guns were grabbed and the 3 men crawled to a spot where we could stay low, see down the swamp but stay unseen. I settled in a comfortable position and with safety off aimed my gun and waited. Moose have poor eyes, good ears and excellent noses. We were far enough away that they could not smell us or see us unless we moved suddenly. So we sat still and waited as they continued to walk closer. When they stopped, bent over and started drinking, Johnny fired the first shot. This was Aki's and my signal to open fire, also.

We only had a cow tag and were about 250 yards away. I had an old 303 Ross army rifle that my father-in-law had given me. It had sights that could be raised to fire up to 1000 yards. We had gone to the shooting range and sighted in our guns at 100 yards not 250. I noticed my bullets hitting the water in front of her a little closer each time. Before I could figure out the right range she was down. It took 17 shots but we did it. Well, I don't think I hit her unless I got a lucky ricochet off the water, which is highly unlikely. After the first shot they never moved. Their ears stood straight up and they lifted their noses trying to get a scent. They couldn't tell which direction the sound was coming from and they couldn't see anything so they stood still. Once she was down there was no sitting still. It was a time of celebration. Johnny led the dance parade, yelling as he went. We acted like a bunch of crazy kids for a few minutes heading for the beaver dam, the only way around the swamp, to the other side. The hunting rule of silence no longer applied; we had filled our tag.

Once the fun was over the work began. Johnny was the only one with any experience. He took off his vest and coat, rolled up his shirt sleeves as high as they would go, took out his knife and dug in. After slitting the throat he gutted her. Once the cavity was open he literally climbed inside as we held the legs open. He came out with the liver and heart. He was a bloody mess from head to toe and grinning from ear to ear. He was in his element and enjoying it to the full. The carcass was quartered and safely stored and the liver was taken back to camp. The night was cold and our precious meat did not deteriorate at all.

For supper we had a feast of fried liver with onions and potatoes and more liver. Every once in awhile someone would raise their glass and yell “to the moose”, the others echoed, “to the moose” and we took a drink of wine. We drank a little more than usual that night and definitely ate too much fresh, wild, liver. Not long after we were tucked in the air became saturated with an awful odor but we all slept quite well regardless.

In the morning the real work began. We had to carry the meat several miles on a narrow walking trail but we had all day. A hindquarter around 100 pounds was tied securely on my back and the two bigger men each carried a big front quarter. On level ground I managed all right but the trail was up and down around rocks and over the odd log. I was determined to carry my share of the load if I could. I walked carefully and slowly keeping my back straight but leaning slightly forward.

Near the end of the trail only 100 yards from the road was a beaver dam we had to cross. It was full to the brim and running over in spots. A thin layer of ice covered the pond. I probably should have rested before tackling this last most difficult stretch but Johnny kept leading and I followed. Half way across I lost my footing for a second; the weight on my back shifted; fortunately for me Aki was close behind, probably waiting for me to go, and he quickly grabbed my load and steadied me.

That was too close for comfort. I'm sure the water was over my head and it was cold. I never would have gotten the load off my back because it was tied securely. I realized I had made a serious mistake trying to carry the load across the dam and was so thankful for the Lord's mercy on me, again. He spared us all from disaster that day, although I didn't get off Scot- free. I discovered shortly after, the pain beside my groin that wouldn't go away was a hernia, which needed to be operated on. I guess this was one way to help me learn a valuable lesson.

## Enjoying the Life of a Salesman

By 1985, Off Oil incentives spurred a wide expansion of natural gas lines throughout the north. People in record numbers were converting to natural gas high efficiency furnaces. This created a problem for the Gas Company; they couldn't get the lines connected to the houses fast enough. This was a convenient problem for ICG and me. With a few minor alterations a new natural gas furnace could easily run on propane. There was another problem, though. Few Gas Fitters had propane tickets.

To rectify the problem, Paul Reid held classes in our back shop, training natural gas service men to get their propane fitters license. I decided to take the class and received my service license, also. We set up a program with the Gas Company to install tanks temporarily until the lines were hooked up. It was a hectic time but good for business. Besides the new "Base Load" volume I recorded 900,000 new liters of Auto-Propane and once again showed record profits.

Now that I had my territory well established I needed a greater challenge and had my sites on moving up the corporate ladder. The next step would be to become a Branch Manager and I made sure my boss knew I was interested in the position. During the year of 1985 ICG held two nation-wide sales contests for one month each. The first one was selling an ICG created product called the "Latch-it". It was device that could hold the trunk of a car securely opened about 10" in order to transport a propane bar-b-cue cylinder safely and legally. There were some minor prizes and recognition for the top salesman but nothing significant. However the reason I never took it too serious was because my focus was on Auto-Propane where volumes and profits were.

When the dust settled at the end of the contest month I was last in Ontario. There was also a prize for this dubious distinction as well. It was lunch with the Vice-President. Here the big loser had to explain to him "Where is the Beef?" or "Where are the sales?" Or could be translated "What is your problem?" The only good answer I could think of was that I was concentrating on selling fuel not giving away a gadget. He said he would buy my story, for now, but informed me another contest was soon coming and he would be watching me close.

Sure enough the second contest was shortly announced. Each salesman was given a quota of auto-Propane conversions to sell. The quota was based on past conversions, propane sales and the size of each area. The winning sales representative from each province would win a trip to Las Vegas to be wined and dined, first class. Branch Managers and both wives were also invited to come along.

My lunch meeting with the VP gave me some extra incentive and I was determined to do well in this competition. I pulled out all the stops and did what I could to get deals before the end of the contest month. I had a good rapport with most of my customers and when I shared my story about the contest, they agreed to put their orders in early to help me out. At the end of the competition I was the big winner and when the VP saw me next he had a big grin and offered his congratulations.

On May 10th it was off to Vegas, the city that never sleeps. Approaching the city from the air was quite a sight. After many miles of desert I spotted a little green patch in the distance. No grass grows there without pumping  water in and running the sprinklers day in and day out. As evening approached I found why they say the city never sleeps. There is around the clock entertainment and gambling; there are literally millions of lights on the main streets that are so bright it was impossible to block the light out of our Hotel room.

We were booked into the Las Vegas Hilton. In their brochure they bragged about being the largest Hotel in the Free World with 3200 rooms and 10 acres of lush lawn, including a small golf course, beautiful trees and flowers, all on the Hotel roof. Several business meetings were scheduled in order to be able to call it a business trip. As it turned out, at the end of the year, when I received my T4, I learned the trip was a $1700 taxable benefit. If I would have know that ahead of time I may have stayed home however, my boss and the VP would not have been impressed.

Every night was a different show; big name entertainers and singers. The first night a herd of pink flamingo dancers came out strutting their stuff. I thought to myself, "how boring is this" but as they got closer I noticed the ladies were topless. Now, I hadn't bargained on that. Some of the wives were a little embarrassed but the men didn't seem to mind. One night the famous magicians Sigmund and Roy, with much fan fare, made a live tiger disappear. Not sure how that works but I didn't care.

I looked into golfing but green fees were $100. I couldn't justify the expense, besides none of the others were golfers. If my boss had been a golfer I would have bugged him about taking me but he was not. Some of the guys had the time of their life. As for me; I can now say, "I went to Vegas, been there done that".

## More Changes at GTT

Only 16 months after coming to Sudbury, the totally unexpected happened for Pastor Martin. He received a call from Kennedy Road Tabernacle in Brampton. This was not only one of the largest churches, in the fastest growing denomination, in Canada, it was also the church Bruce's father had been pastor from 1953 to 1960. When the call came he was torn but could not refuse the opportunity, of a lifetime, to pastor the same, now huge, church as his father did. On November 27th, 1985 Bruce distributed his resignation letter; he would be moving to Brampton at the end of the year.

The only bigger church in Ontario and maybe even Canada, was Queensway Cathedral in Toronto. Ralph Rutledge, the brother-in-law of David Mainse, was the senior pastor and had a staff of a dozen or so young pastors in charge of different ministries. We had attended Queensway once, for a David Wilkerson conference. Mr. Wilkerson gained renown in the 60's with his book "The Cross and the Switchblade", which documented his ministry to street gangs in New York and the dramatic conversion of Nickie Cruise. Like David Terrell, Wilkerson also preached prophetic warnings to wake up lukewarm Christians.

I liked Wilkerson's, face like flint, boldness. Actually he was a lot like Terrell but Wilkerson was accepted in the denominational churches. I had heard about "Put the Trumpet to Thy Lips". Terrell had mentioned the book a few times from the pulpit, accusing Wilkerson of stealing his vision and writing about it as if it was his own. After one service I took the opportunity to talk to Mr. Wilkerson and mentioned David Terrell's name. He immediately said, "I know him; He stole my vision pretending it was his own". It didn't matter to me who was telling the truth, although I leaned towards Wilkerson as being the truthful one.

A few minutes after he took the pulpit for the first time he turned around and looked directly at all the young men sitting on the platform behind him and said, "I can't believe all you guys actually work here". He went on and said, "Don't you have something to do; why are you just sitting around?" The next night when he took the microphone he turned around again and just scowled "Are you still here?" He shook his head and started preaching. He spoke with the same kind of boldness as Jesus had, not like the scribes. I interpreted this as a sign of God's anointing on his life.

**Theodore Batten**

Even though our lives were crazy busy we always felt there was more we should be doing, so we decided to take in a foster child. His name was Theodore Batten, the only child born to a mentally challenged couple. By the time he was 11 years old, he had outgrown his parents mentally and was a handful for them, to say the least. Shortly after Theo moved in with us my friend and moose-hunting partner Aki told us he knew him; he had recently done a job at the school he attended. He said the 3 weeks he worked at the school he saw Theo sitting in the hall every day. Apparently, he was so disruptive, the teacher could not keep him in the classroom. We were up to the challenge and cheerfully accepted him into our family, well all of us except Ben, who was now 13. It is not that Ben didn't accept him but he saw nothing cheerful about sharing his room with this obnoxious brat. We didn't make the connection at the time but Ben started hanging around with his friends more and staying out later in the evenings. Even in the winter he would often stay at the playground rink as close to bedtime as he could.

Theo needed a lot of attention and made a career out of getting it anyway he could. It wasn't that he was bad but more that he was hyper, loud and always in you're face, demanding to be noticed and attended to. He literally could not sit still for one minute. At the dinner table when his hands were busy feeding himself his legs would shake or his feet would tap. He had no awareness of how he affected people around him. He seemed oblivious to the fact that anyone else was even there. He acted the same in public as he did at home. He would speak out loud in the middle of the church service or stand up and throw his coat never realizing he was making a scene. He didn't seem to notice people were looking at him.

Until Theo came into our home I didn't realize I had a temper. I do remember, as a preteen, once getting angry with Gerry and yelling at him and striking him. Other than that, I had no recollection of ever losing my temper previously. So, it took me by complete surprise when I frequently started losing it with Theo. He knew how to push me over the edge like no one I had ever met. I knew corporal punishment was out of the question. My concern was that I would strangle him in a fit of rage. I did shake him pretty good a few times but managed to control myself before I shook his teeth loose. Caroleen seemed to understand Theo better than any of us. She actually enjoyed his silly antics. Like many Indians she had a healthy sense of humor and they carried on together quite well, most of the time.

As Bruce Martin's time to leave drew near I got more involved with his assistant, soon to be senior pastor, David Courey. We had many discussions about the lukewarm state of the church. I was more of a bother to him than anything else. He was young and was more concerned with filling the big shoes he was about to wear than finding fault in the system or the people he was to shepherd. He was not about to start making waves or ruffling any feathers.

As the days went on his messages from the pulpit seemed more plastic, the special music reminded me of professional singers looking for applause. The whole church routine, the programs and all activities became a chore. I vented my frustration to David Courey in a couple of letters. We had lunch together periodically and he tried to reason with me to no avail. I slowly gave up all my duties at GTT, one by one.

## My Son, My Son, My Only Son

Now that I look back, two church related events stand out that may have been the final straws that broke the camel's back. During a District Youth Rally held at GTT Ben was centered out and humiliated during an evening meeting. The visiting evangelist gave a typical enthusiastic message about serving the Lord. Near the end he had the lights dimmed and told the hundreds of youths present to close their eyes and started asking them a series of questions. First he had them raise their hands and then stand up and then eventually, with several sincere youths, including our son Ben, still standing the lights came on. The way Ben was tricked into being made a spectacle humiliated him and broke my heart. It also made me angry. I didn't mind bold preachers who told it like it was but this was different and this was not right. Even if this fast talking Scottish Evangelist was sincere his means did not justify the end.

The other occurrence took place when our youth group was invited by Calvary Baptist Church to join their small group for a weekend. The pastor, Charles Quail, hoped the influence from our large enthusiastic group would rub off on his lonely few. Some of the older boys from our church had no interest in spiritual things and were there for a weekend away from their parents. I didn't enjoy babysitting rebellious youths and didn't like my son hanging out with them either so I kept a close eye on them. A few in particular caused me great concern. Saturday afternoon I became suspicious when several of them felt the need to congregate in the men's washroom. I quickly walked in on them to realize my suspicions were well founded and to top it off there was my son, literally "holding the bag". I stretched out my open hand out and looked Ben in the eye. He could tell I was upset and slowly set the bag in my hand. I was not just upset. I was shocked and hurt. Ben was 13 years old. He had been so excited about serving the Lord not many months before and now he had lost whatever it was he had.

Here I was sacrificing my whole weekend to help these kids find their way in life. My reward was the bad influence they had on my son. My immediate inclination was to escort my son, with his little sack of illegal substance, to the City Police Station a few blocks away. So that is exactly what I did. What a joke that was. I told the clerk I needed to talk to an officer in the Narcotics Department and we were led to a small office. I told the young officer the story and handed the bag of weed to him. He looked at Ben and in his gentle soft voice told him he really shouldn't smoke this stuff because it wasn't good for him and then looked back at me. I stared at him in unbelief. "Is that it?", I thought. I was hoping he could show him the inside of a cold, lonely cell and put some healthy fear in him by warning him that this is where he was headed if he didn't smarten up. I guess things had changed in the last 25 years. Had smoking up actually become a normal and accepted habit in today's society, like smoking cigarettes did in my time? Poor Canada!

I don't know what good the whole experience accomplished. Ben seemed to become more distant and aloof, spending more time with his friends and hanging around the house less and less. He was gone for hours some evenings and weekends. When I questioned where he had been or what he had been doing we got the standard, universal, teen answers "out" and "nothing". At the time we never thought that Theo coming into our family was a factor and today I am still not sure. It seems we operate in this life so much of the time looking through a veil of ignorance and uncertainty as we stumble along.

In spite of his apparent drifting away he continued to get good grades at school. Not unlike his dad school came easy to him all through the elementary grades. My fear was his grades and his life would fall apart, like mine did in high school, especially now that our suspicions were confirmed about him experimenting with pot and no doubt drinking also. The kind of boys he was hanging out with in the neighborhood concerned me the most. I well knew the influence friends can have.

In June, 1986 the night of Ben's grade 8 graduation things came to a head. After the ceremony we invited him to go out with us to fancy restaurant to celebrate, since we were all dressed up. We wanted to do something with him on his special evening but he was totally uninterested. He had his own plans; partying with his classmates. I was against it and made up my mind, as long as

I could, I would do all in my power to protect my only son. I was 18 when I started smoking pot and look what it did to me. I was terrified of the consequences of a 13 year old getting addicted.

He hated us and if looks could kill I would have died on the spot. He reluctantly got in the car sulking and fuming. We tried to brighten him up in the restaurant but he would have nothing to do with it. It was a terrible atmosphere. I wonder if this is God's way of sharing the burden He has for His wayward children. I could now better relate to what I put my parents through. There was a deep ache in my gut as I observed the contempt in the eyes of my only son for his father.

Once home from the restaurant he was still determined to go find his friends. I said, "Ben, I'm sorry, but you are not going." I started walking towards the house. He said, "I'm going" and started walking. I grabbed him and we tussled for awhile on the lawn and I literally dragged him into the house. I felt terrible. I was still strong enough to handle him physically but when it came to helping him I was totally useless. I was a little apprehensive, to say the least, of the fast approaching day, when I would lose total control of him. In the meantime I had to get up tomorrow morning and go on with my life as a father of two other needy children, and a husband to a wife that doesn't see enough of me; not to mention the responsibility of earning a living and doing the Lord's work, all at the same time.

**Alpha Coffee House**

As life at church became more strained, I gravitated to other means of ministry. I had been involved for some time with Alpha Coffee House, a street ministry for young people and when I was nominated to become the director, I accepted and was voted in. The first venue, as director of Alpha, was a concert with Gene McClellan. I knew he was a great musician, singer-songwriter. He won the Juno Award for songwriter of the year in 1971 and became well known for his songs "Put Your Hand in the Hand" and "Snowbird" that Anne Murray made famous.

That night the place was packed and it was a good performance but all was not well with Gene. He had a rough life and eventually committed suicide by hanging himself in 1995. I read a bit about his life after he died. Apparently he had grown up in a Baptist church and was haunted by God's high standard of holiness and his own inability to live up to it; I could relate.

The Alpha board members decided we should find our own building and make it available every weekend. We rented an old building close to downtown that had been used by a service club for their meetings and other functions. Every Friday and Saturday evenings we set up tables, had a live band or played music and sold soft drinks and junk food making ourselves available to be there for young people who wanted to talk. I became friends with several of the board members; Kelly Keen, John Austin, Michel Sharky and Jeff Trudell. Other than that I don't think we accomplished much. I probably should have been at home Friday evenings and did something with my 3 kids. I knew Caroleen and Theo would have been all for it; Ben would have not wanted anything to do with it.

**The Big Promotion**

While many aspects of life appeared to falling apart things at ICG were going well. I had been there over 5 years, longer than any other job. By the fall of 1986 we were on target to earn $250,000 in profit, another record for Sudbury. Things were going so well that before the year ended Paul Reid was promoted to manager of a big new Branch in Ottawa and I was promoted to Sudbury Branch Manager. Besides the main Branch ICG owned and operated a Satellite Branch in Kapuskasing, and operated a retail gas station on the Kingsway in Sudbury, which was also my responsibility.

The opportunity to oversee the whole operation is what I had been working for and praying for. This had been my goal from day one. I had enjoyed the sales job, that lasted 5½ years but knew all along it was only a steppingstone. Management is where I wanted to be. I hoped this job would lead to even bigger and better things someday. I had observed Paul Reid on the job and thought to myself "He is not any smarter than me, I could learn to do his job." There was a lot more to it than I realized as I would soon find out.

A smile came to my face as I admired the big ad in the Sudbury Star, with my picture, announcing my promotion as Branch Manager responsible for all the companies activities in Northern Ontario. I was 36 years old and in my prime and pleased I was doing a good job at something. Along with the promotion came a brand new GMC ½ ton truck with a built in cell phone. Along with the prestige came a bag full of headaches for which I was not prepared but for the moment I enjoyed my time of glory.

**Ye Good Old Lo-Ellen Park**

In September Ben was off to the same high school I attended, Lo-Ellen Park Secondary. Early into the school year one of the older teachers said to him, "So you are a Bast?" When Ben replied in the affirmative he asked him, "Who's your daddy?" When he said Don they said "Oh no!" and laughed.

I went into the school office one day to drop off something for Ben. To my surprise Miss Perry was still sitting at her familiar spot, 17 years after I had graduated. Another familiar face was visible over the counter; it was that of Mr. Dewar. I said to them, "Wow, Miss Perry and Mr. Dewar, You guys are still here?" He replied with a grin, "Some things never change".

**Free to Leave**

As 1986 wound down I was to the point of totally giving up on GTT. It was then I was informed that I had been nominated to serve as a deacon. I wondered if in this capacity I would be in a better position to effect some worthwhile change. At least being on the management side of the fence would surely help, somewhat, if I did get voted in, that is. I had been so active for the last 7 years that almost everyone knew me. It would be somewhat of an honor to be on the board of such a successful church. It was the fastest growing church and already had the largest congregation in Sudbury and the biggest, newest and most impressive edifice in the city. As far as a business goes, it was well supported and well run. It was a profitable enterprise. The pastors were eloquent speakers and respected men. Everything was ideal. I knew this was a model, modern church but what was missing was what haunted me.

I longed for the reality I had experienced the first time I walked under David Terrell's revival tent and heard him preach his simple message "Behold the Lamb of God". There was something about the powerful message of Christ and Him crucified that I wanted more than all the glitter and prestige here. In any event, I didn't have long to reconsider staying and the possibility of being a deacon. At the end of January 1987, I received a letter from the Board of Glad Tidings stating they couldn't allow my name to stand for election because I didn't fit all the criteria to be a candidate.

It was news to me, but made it sense (cents), one had to have given at least $1,000 in offerings in the last year to be eligible. The few years prior I would have easily qualified but some time ago, I had decided to support organizations that represented more worthy causes. After this Marja and I both became totally restless and found services almost intolerable.

One Sunday evening while sitting in the balcony, watching a professional visitor entertaining in song, our ever-increasing burden of grieving turned to a gentle but definite release. It was as if the Lord whispered into each of our hearts at the same time, "You are free to go". We told a few close friends we were leaving and after 7½ years of being part of the Glad Tidings family, we just stopped going to services.

A few weeks later the board members of Alpha Coffee House paid me a surprise visit to find out why I stopped going to GTT. I told them my story and I guess they understood to some degree. They went away pleased to know that at least I had not turned my back on God. No one from Glad Tidings contacted us to see why we stopped attending. This was the third time I left the church system and I sensed it would be the last. This would also mark the end of another chapter in my life.

To Be Continued